PERSPECTA 31 **READING STRUCTURES**

EDITORS CAROLYN ANN FOUG AND SHARON L. JOYCE

THE MIT PRESS   CAMBRIDGE, MASSACHUSETTS

CONTENTS

CONTRIBUTORS

Thomas H. Beeby is Professor (Adjunct) of Architectural Design at the Yale School of Architecture. He was Dean of the school from 1985 to 1991 and Director of the School of Architecture at the University of Illinois at Chicago from 1979 to 1985. As principal in charge of design with his firm, Hammond Beeby Rupert Ainge, he has overseen the planning and design of a variety of projects including Chicago's Harold Washington Library, the Hole-in-the-Wall-Gang Camp in Connecticut and the more recent Baker Institute at Rice University. He has written and lectured on the work of Mies van der Rohe and the relationship of ornament to structure including "The Grammar of Ornament/ Ornament as Grammar" published in *Via 3* in 1976. He received his B.Arch. from Cornell University and his M.Arch. from Yale University.

Gregory K. Dreicer is a historian, museum curator, and exhibition developer. He is currently a fellow at the New York Public Library's Center for Scholars and Writers and is a faculty member at the Center for New Design, Parsons School of Design, New School University. Mr. Dreicer is a recent Loeb Fellow at the Harvard University Graduate School of Design and received his Ph.D. in science and technology studies from Cornell University.

Hugh Dutton is a principal of HDA, consultants for glass and structural design in architecture. Previously he worked for fourteen years with RFR, the Paris based team of engineers and designers founded by Peter Rice. He co-authored *Structural Glass*, a review of work at RFR in glass, and collaborated in the design of a patented glass support system. Projects by HDA include the glass wall and ramps at Columbia University's Lerner Hall with Bernard Tschumi, the Osaka Maritime Museum with Paul Andreu, Seoul's new Inchon Airport with KACI as well as diverse consulting work in Europe and Asia. He has taught at Columbia University and lectured at Ohio State University and the University of Pennsylvania. Mr. Dutton received his B.E. from the University of Waterloo and his Diploma from the Architectural Association. He is a member of the Royal Institute of British Architects and the Ordre des Architectes, Ile de France.

Lucie Fontein is an assistant professor at the Carleton University School of Architecture in Ottowa, where she teaches design studio and architectural technology and is also a thesis advisor. She has held teaching positions at Cornell University and McGill University and has written papers on the relationship of technology and design. Her research interests include pedagogical issues regarding architectural technology and experimental approaches to lighting. Ms. Fontein received her B.Arch. from the University of Toronto and her M. Arch. from McGill University.

Antonio Juarez is Associate Professor of Design at the Madrid Polytechnic University School of Architecture. He is also a visiting professor at the Barcelona Escola Superior d'Arquitectura in the Universitat Internacional de Catalonia. He practices architecture in Madrid. His contribution to *Perspecta* is a selection from his dissertation on Louis I. Kahn. He was a visiting Fulbright Scholar at Columbia University and the University of Pennsylvania from 1995 to 1997, where he completed his dissertation, "Continuity and Discontinuity in Louis I. Kahn: Material, Structure and Space." Mr. Juarez graduated from the Madrid School of Architecture in 1992.

Guy Nordenson is a structural engineer and an associate professor at the Princeton University School of Architecture. He established his structural engineering office, Guy Nordenson and Associates, in New York City in 1997. Prior to that, he was director of Ove Arup & Partners in New York, which he started in 1987. Recent projects include Steven Holl's Kiasma Museum in Helsinki and Richard Meier's Church of the Year 2000 in Rome, now in construction. His office is currently working on The Museum of Modern Art expansion with Yoshio Taniguchi and Associates and a new dormitory at MIT with Steven Holl Architects. Mr Nordenson received his B.S. from MIT and his M.S. from the University of California, Berkeley.

Alan Organschi is a principal of Gray Organschi Architecture, a rapidly growing and acclaimed young firm. His partner is Elizabeth Gray. He has taught at Wesleyan University and Yale University. He received a Bundeskanzler Fellowship from the Alexander Von Humboldt Foundation for research on Berlin's urban renewal and inner city self-help housing movement. He was also the co-editor of *Perspecta* 27. Mr. Organschi received his B.A. from Brown University in 1983 and his M.Arch. from Yale Univeristy in 1988.

Tom F. Peters is Professor of Architecture and History and Director of the Building and Architectural Technology Institute at Lehigh University. He is currently Chair Professor and head of the Architecture Department at the Chinese University of Hong Kong. He has worked and lectured in Canada, Germany, Switzerland, Hong Kong, China, Denmark, and the United States. He founded the ACSA Technology Conference in 1986. Mr. Peters has written numerous books and articles including, *Building the Nineteenth Century* (MIT Press, 1996) and an article published in *Perspecta* 25. He was trained as an architect at the ETH Zurich where he received his doctorate.

Herman D. J. Spiegel is Professor Emeritus of Architectural Engineering at the Yale School of Architecture where he taught structures for thirty years. He was also Dean of the school and Director of Studies in Architecture from 1972 to 1976. He founded his office, now Spiegal Zamecnik & Shah, in the mid-fifties while teaching at Yale. His firm has served as consultants on a wide array of projects including the interior conveyance system for Saarinen's St. Louis Gateway Arch, Roche & Dinkeloo's University of Michigan's Powers Theater, and Frank O. Gehry and Allan Dehar's Yale Psychiatric Institute. His notable contributions to the profession of architecture were recognized by the American Institute of Architects with an honorary membership and the Rhode Island School of Design with its Alumni Award. Mr. Spiegel has lectured around the country on the work of Gaudí and Le Corbusier. He holds degrees in both architecture and engineering from the Rhode Island School of Design.

Carles Vallhonrat has been a professor of architecture and lecturer at the Princeton University School of Architecture since 1972 and has also taught at the University of Pennsylvania and Yale University. He was principal assistant to Louis I. Kahn from 1960 to 1971. Since 1977 he has been principal of C. E. Vallhonrat, Architect. His article "Tectonics Considered: Between the Presence and Absence of Artifice" was published in *Perspecta* 24. A native of Barcelona, Mr. Vallhonrat received his Diploma Arquitecto from the Universidad Nacional del Litoral, Argentina, and his M.Arch. from the University of Pennsylvania.

Peter D. Waldman is a professor at the University of Virginia School of Architecture. He was chair of the Department of Architecture there from 1995 to 1998. He has taught for nearly three decades at various schools including Princeton, Harvard, and Rice. He is the recent recipient of the Rome Prize and is currently a fellow of the American Academy in Rome for Spring 2000. As an architect, his work has been widely published in *Global Architecture* and *Architecture*. Mr. Waldman received his B.A. and his M. Arch. from Princeton University.

READING STRUCTURES

This issue of *Perspecta* grew out of a search for connections between the architecture studio and the structures classroom. As students at the Yale School of Architecture in the mid-1990s, my co-editor and I encountered two discussions of structural engineering, both taking place in the Art and Architecture Building, which had little to do with one another; in studios were images and romance, and in classrooms were numbers and toil. *Reading Structures* was borne out of the apparent impossibility of linking these two discussions. It later developed into a body of evidence suggesting that architects can acquire technical knowledge without being consumed by it and that structural objects are as worthy of analysis as any text.

In my experience, structural systems were referred to but not analyzed in studio discourse. The tendency to encourage students to look first for inspiration from broader culture before making architecture fostered a dreamy treatment of structure in school projects. Pinning up pretty xeroxes of dirigibles had become an acceptable way to understand structural shells. I came to see that the passion for ideas that makes studio so valuable can also blind – it is easy to overlook the merits of examining structural systems and behavior as design elements when so many non-quantitative, sexy theories beckon. But if the images in the xeroxes are researched and the design and construction behind them are understood, then the seduction may be overcome; structural concepts can enter into design. When structure is admitted into the realm of ideas, one finds that there is something meaningful about gravity and wind, something poetic about post tensioning and bending stresses. When these discoveries are followed up with a thorough understanding of precisely how structure works, then an image of a building that is bending, straining, and alive comes into focus in exquisite detail.

It is instructive to speculate on why it is necessary today to make an argument for the consideration of structure in the design studio. It may be that in the rush toward other fields to find inspirational concepts, the physical behavior of structure is the first part of architecture to be left behind. The randomness with which architects borrow ideas is telling: deconstruction, chaos theory, structuralism, virtual reality. That such diverse approaches have been used so interchangably suggests that they are only temporary vehicles for design, with few intrinsic links to the architecture that appears to develop from them. It is difficult to predict the final success of a building based on which acquired theory is said to have generated it or how clearly the theory is understood. If the architecture itself is strong, then the architect's shallow reading or misinterpretation of an appropriated idea is often forgiven. But an unformed or un-integrated idea based in structural design draws criticism, because the flaws in reasoning are visible in the drawings, models, and, eventually, the building. Structure can indeed be limiting, but to turn away from it is to miss opportunities. When carefully considered in the context of architectural design, structure can be manipulated, expressed, or hidden with fluency; it can contribute to conceptual thought.

In the spirit of engagement between disciplines, this *Reading Structures* issue of *Perspecta* examines structure that has been processed by architecture. To varying degrees, the articles that follow share an object-oriented approach: buildings and structures are scrutinized as artifacts and read carefully. An important caveat to this exercise is that structures must not be considered as isolated products of human ingenuity but, rather, as heterogeneous products of their cultural context, embedded in the history of architecture and the built environment and, in turn, intimately connected to the surrounding economy, legal system, and political climate.

As editor, I learned that the analysis and design of structure can be the subject of heated debate as well as measured conversation. We include a written response to each article to show that there is much to discuss about structure once the topic is broached, and that the engineer's world is not to be taken for granted. My hope is that readers of this issue of *Perspecta* will gain a sense that the decisions behind structures are not only ripe for reexamination but also well worth arguing about.

Carolyn Ann Foug

PAST POLEMICS

Most important [to the integrity of architecture], probably, is structure. Not only the way in which a building is put together, or the simplicity of its structural idea, but how this is expressed without striving to make the bones be the whole answer. Structure that has been hidden, twisted, or polluted as an idea, will seldom produce good architecture. Pietro Belluschi

Structural honesty seems to me one of the bugaboos that we should free ourselves from very quickly. The Greeks with their marble columns imitating wood, and covering up the wood roofs inside! The Gothic designers with their wooden roofs above to protect their delicate vaulting. And Michelangelo, the greatest architect in history, with his Mannerist column! Philip Johnson

To us clarity means the definite expression of the purpose of a building and a sincere expression of its structure. One can regard this sincerity as a sort of moral duty, but I feel that for the designer it is above all a trial of strength that sets the seal of success on his achievement; and the sense of achievement is a very basic instinct. Marcel Breuer

The principle of structure has moved in a curious way over this century from being 'structural honesty' to 'expression of structure' and finally to 'structural expressionism.' Structural integrity is a potent and lasting principle and I would never want to get far away from it. To express structure, however, is not an end in itself. It is only when structure can contribute to the total and to the other principles that it is important. Eero Saarinen, *Eero Saarinen on His Work*

I am embarrassed when architects talk about beauty; like happiness it is only a by-product. A building should be handsome, elegant, strong, lean – beauty is too vague an attribute. A building comes from the inside out and has to be gutty, though if it becomes too gutty it becomes forced. To turn a building inside out to show its entrails is a short-lived fashion. Mechanical systems aren't that basic. Structure is the thing. Harry Weese

One becomes conscious that there are many ways to organize a building; that structure is not an end, nor a beginning, but a means to an end – and that end is to create space that is an appropriate psychological environment. Perhaps the greatest chapel of this century, Ronchamp, has a most impure structure – sprayed concrete covers everything. It does not resort to the crutches of geometry and pattern-making, but creates breathing, dynamic spaces appropriate to human use. Paul Rudolph

Only through structure can we create new architecture. In nature, form and structure are one, and this should also be true in architecture. Nature is simple, but unfortunately it does not simplify. It is up to us to search for this simplicity, to express logic and clarity, and to understand structure. Form is structure, no matter what other names are given to it, and therefore structure is architecture. Craig Ellwood

We had a period...where we felt that if a structure was sound it must be beautiful. This is a fallacy. Structure is the nature of the universe, and as such lacks the human quality which we are trying to build into the universe. Architecture is not structure per se, but is based on structural elements and goes beyond any structural achievements. A structural achievement is a poor reproduction or copy of more sophisticated structural systems which nature offers in the micro and macro cosmos. Paulo Soleri

Our time has made us aware that forces and strains flow in patterns which have little relationship to the rectilinear concepts of the Victorian engineers. We have become aware of the almost alive quality which our structures achieve, and we seek the forms which give the most life to our structures. Bertrand Goldberg

I haven't been called upon to experiment too much with structure and it wasn't my tendency. The elements of most buildings are small and the simplest way to accomplish the structure is by a flat slab, free of beams, with columns placed on practical centers. Structural tricks are expensive and do not prove too much. Edward Durrell Stone

The profession of architecture, as practiced today, is a slave function, exercising good taste in purchasing and assembling industrially-available components, a superficial veil to cover the steel or concrete frames which are completely conventionalized and organized by the engineers. Buckminster Fuller

These quotes, except the Saarinen, were taken from Paul Heyer's 1966 book *Architects on Architecture*.

Thomas H. Beeby

TOWARD A TECHNOLOGICAL ARCHITECTURE?

CASE STUDY OF THE ILLINOIS INSTITUTE OF TECHNOLOGY COMMONS BUILDING

The campus at the Illinois Institute of Technology in Chicago is one of the few existing complexes in this country that demonstrates how the dictates of High Modernism were executed by a major architect. Mies van der Rohe began the planning for the new campus immediately upon his arrival in Chicago in 1939. This commission represents his first large scale attempt to apply his European design experience to an American building situation. As the Director of the School of Architecture at IIT he drew upon the curriculum of the school and its student body to explore the conventions and possibilities of architecture at that moment.

In 1950, the inclusion of the Institute of Design, the school of Moholy–Nagy, into the body of IIT as an independent design school posed the question of the fate of the Bauhaus legacy in Chicago. At a dinner held that year in the Blackstone Hotel to celebrate this union, three speakers rose to deal with the potential of the moment. Serge Chermeyeff, the successor to Moholy, spoke at length about the possibility of the industrial strength of Chicago being directed toward the development of a truly technological architecture made of prefabricated assemblies that would change the nature of building. Walter

Gropius, the founder of the Bauhaus, urged the architectural profession to abandon the antiquated notions surrounding the idea of the architect as the lonely creative genius isolated in his studio and turn to group decision-making practices. Mies in a characteristic manner spoke the least and insisted on the significance of architecture as a cultural and spiritual force in a world that had apparently lost its bearing.[1]

The three talks taken together could be interpreted as the advanced intellectual thrust of European Modernism about to be released on the architectural profession in America. For that reason the buildings being erected twenty blocks south of this event at the IIT campus can be evaluated in terms of the critical positions put forth that day, for they not only represent the intention of the architect but reflect the significant critical forces from Europe that surrounded the creation of this work.

The discursive writing that most directly relates to the work of Mies van der Rohe at this period of his career is the monograph by Ludwig Hilberseimer, another former Master at the Bauhaus, who provides an apologia for Mies and his architecture. The book, *Mies van der Rohe,* appears in 1956 just prior to the completion of Crown Hall, the culmination of Mies's work at IIT.[2] However, to understand Crown Hall the work completed earlier at the campus must be understood, particularly those buildings that immediately preceded Crown Hall's design.

I have chosen to focus on one building, the Commons Building, with the intention of examining its detailed physical properties closely enough to ascertain the success of the building in terms of its original design intent as outlined by Gropius, Chermeyeff, and Mies. The research

on the building was done at the Yale School of Architecture by graduate students in the context of an elective course that I have offered for the past twelve years entitled 'Architecture As Building.' The course analyzes the major buildings of this century through detailed dissection of their methods of construction. Graphic display of the major systems of the buildings allows for a reconstruction of the design process and in doing so recaptures the thought patterns that formed the design priorities. Emphasis is on the relation of systems of structure and enclosure with their related assemblies. The possible loss of the Commons Building at the Illinois Institute

of Technology prompted me to embark on this paper before the built artifact is altered dramatically or eradicated completely.[3]

Hilberseimer traces the evolution of the campus buildings from structures based on square bays, to structures based on oblong bays, and finally, to structures which are entirely free from any interior supporting elements, where roofs are carried by trusses, which in turn are supported by outside columns. He also notes that the skeleton frame discards walls as support elements whereby the enclosure system is free to be placed between the columns, behind the

columns, or in front of them.[4] Mies experiments with these structural and enclosure typologies from 1939 until 1956. The critical assumption has always been that the evolution of building types improved both technically and aesthetically with time.

Following the approval of the master plan in 1940, Mies initially investigated the square bay typology with the skin placed in front of the structural support (Figure 1). This category includes Alumni Memorial Hall (1945–46), the Chemical Engineering and Metallurgy Building (1946), and, finally, the Electrical Engineering

and Physics Building (1957). This particular approach offers a high degree of standardization. Eventually, he used it on multistory buildings where the problem of structural expression with fireproofing was critical.

The second approach, pursued by Mies and described by Hilberseimer, is seen in the studies for the unrealized Library and Administration Building (1944–46) that combine a one story oblong bay arrangement with a hybrid system of enclosure (Figure 2). This enclosure expresses the long span situation with an infill of brick and

glass on the north and south sides while differentiating these from the short span by placing a skin in front of the structure on the east and west façades. The Library Project was proclaimed by Hilberseimer as Mies's finest project thus far. However, the scheme introduced problems of spatial directionality that disrupted the neutral presence of the frame. This characteristic was first mentioned by Colin Rowe. In any case, Mies never approached this exact typological possibility again.[5] Another aspect of this approach that was troublesome from Chermeyeff's point of view was that it conceptually moved away from a prefabricated repetitive skin.

A variation of this typology appears in unrealized projects for the Student Union (1946) and Architecture School (1952). It was finally realized in the Commons Building (1959) (Figure 3). After the Commons, Mies never returned to this particular typology in any of his later realized work. The singularity of this is worth analyzing in order to understand Mies's complete body of work constructed in this country. As a direct result of this experiment, he abandoned the strategy of all his earlier studies for the Architecture School and formulated his third and final typology for IIT, Crown Hall (1956),

where the structure is pressed to the perimeter of the building, clearing the singular room of internal support while the enclosure follows the back leg of the engaged I-beam columns (Figure 4). Visually the glass supports the enclosed volume like an air bubble trapped in a liquid environment by a metal cage. The virtuosity of this final structure relies on the previous sixteen years of experimentation by Mies. He was a methodical designer and it is my contention that the successes and primarily the failures in detail observed at the Commons informed him in a profound way how to continue in his patient

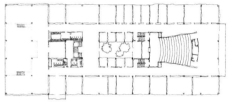

1 IIT Chemical Engineering and Metallurgy Building

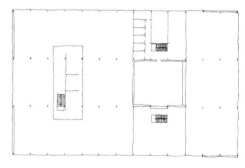

2 IIT Library and Administration Building

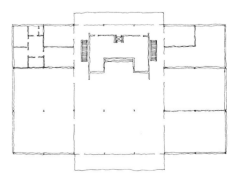

3 IIT Commons Building

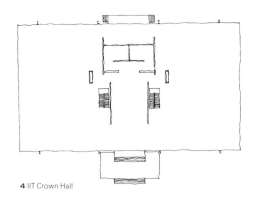

4 IIT Crown Hall

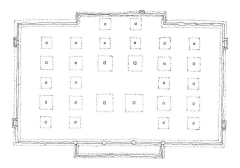

5 IIT Commons Building basement structure

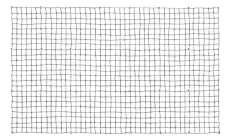

6 IIT Commons Building 4' modular grid

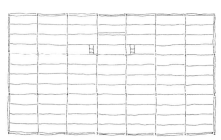

7 IIT Commons Building roof framing plan

search for a personal architectural expression. The failure of the Commons, for Mies, as a building that succeeded formally while remaining intellectually rational and spiritually moving, will become clear on closer examination. Mies also demanded that it reflect the American condition of building in contrast to earlier European preoccupations of process and intent, a difficult agenda for such a small and highly programmed structure.

The particular climate of American construction, particularly the climate of Chicago, provides an empirical background for this direct analysis of the Commons building. The method of analysis is simple and straightforward based on the building in question within the context of the way buildings are realized in this country, particularly in Chicago over the past sixty years. Construction can be thought of as a complex process that coordinates known manufactured materials, elements, assemblies, and systems into coherent and ordered environments made for human habitation. There are certain empirical rules of thumb that evolve. For example, smaller structures cannot economically absorb the cost of custom designed pieces because of the lack of repetition involved. Handwork and

elaborate finishes are prohibitive in small institutional work due to the scale of compensation demanded by union rates. Chicago is a 'union town' which means that the political structure of the city has always taken advantage of the building trade unions as a rallying force that can deliver large blocks of votes in an organized manner. Where else in the world would the municipal bandshell be named after the head of the musicians' union (James C. Petrillo) rather than a significant composer or musician? The union system is opposed to technical innovation unless it can be delivered by an existing trade.

For example, the plasterers' union blocked drywall for decades only to see it being taken over by the carpenters, a fact which led quickly to the demise of the plastering trade in Chicago. The electricians and plumbers resisted prefabricated assemblies, such as laboratory components, then insisted on disassembling these components and then reassembling them on the site, thereby more than doubling the assembly cost of a prefabricated unit of construction. In recent memory, one can point to electrical inspectors who insisted on enclosing low voltage wiring for computers in conduit, to insure union control of

electrical work, while simultaneously prolonging the introduction of major electronic technological advances.

What could be interpreted as anecdotal material, I think in this case has a valid purpose, for it suggests that design decisions that are often interpreted by architectural critics and historians as having an artistic or intellectual basis are often direct responses to the relentless realities of the marketplace. In Mies's case, he had clearly formulated artistic and often philosophical ideas about architecture that were put to the ultimate test by the pragmatic and often philistine attitudes of a city that pursues architecture with a passion seldom seen in this country while focusing its eye on the bottom line.

Analysis of the Commons Building began with the close examination of the 'construction documents' or 'working drawings' as they are commonly called. No effort of the investigation was spent on relating these drawings to earlier design studies of the building. Instead, careful examination of the completed structure is undertaken in order to understand the qualitative losses or gains that occurred between the stated intention of the architect represented by the construction documents and the completed,

occupied building. Access to shop drawings could further clarify the path from drawn detail to built artifact, for the manufacturers of building components often alter the detail to fit their standard product or lower its cost of manufacture through change of material or method. The architect's response of red-lining the shop drawing and his ensuing negotiations with the contractor and subcontractor can alter the final appearance and performance of the building – an incremental change which can be dramatic in Mies's minimal buildings of this period. Unfortunately, shop drawings for this building

are not available, for historically they were destroyed at the end of designated periods of professional liability called for by the statute of limitations of the State of Illinois. The design drawings of Mies at this time were executed by his office in great abundance, however the construction documents were prepared by an associate architect, Friedman, Alschuler and Sincere, in the case of the Commons Building.[6] Lack of communication and conflicting intentions were always a possibility. Problems in the buildings of this period also occurred due to differences in the training received by draftsmen in the office of the associate architect and those in the office of Mies.

A building can be imagined as it will be realized in the field by the contractor. The various subcontractors price and eventually supply their piece of the work at the appropriate time in the construction process. Coincidentally, the architect provides a detailed breakdown of material and activity in his specifications (the written component of the contract documents), describing each of the myriad pieces, assemblies, and finishes that go into the completed structure. An analysis that graphically isolates these

components and processes as described in the specifications allows an objective view of each category of work in juxtaposition to the others. The logic and performance of the structural system necessary to support the enclosure can be compared to the mechanical system necessary to insure human comfort. Design priorities can be proven by tracing the distribution of construction funds throughout the building. Prejudices can be gleaned by identifying the departures from normative construction, unusual techniques, exotic materials, and unproven systems. Finally, the decision-making patterns of the architect become visible through the evidence displayed in minute

detail at the smallest scale in contrast to large schematic patterns at the other end of the scale of graphic representation.

The Commons Building faces Wabash Street, which is currently discontinuous from the Chicago Street grid, now serving as a private road for IIT. The building backs against the State Street elevated track structure, which was intended to be abandoned at the time the building was designed because of the high level of noise and vibration. The building has no acoustical deadening provisions in its constructional makeup. The structure is a 168'8" x 96'8" rectangle. It has a full basement supported by concrete walls and a concrete column and slab framing system (Figure 5). On top of this buried concrete volume rests an exposed steel frame with a prefabricated, precast concrete deck. The building has a continuous perimeter footing that supports the concrete basement walls. The reinforced concrete structural floor slab of the basement is 8" deep with a waterproof membrane above, topped by a 3" finish slab. 14" x 14" internal columns on spread footings are arranged in a 16' x 24' structural grid except for the central space that is supported by 24" x 24"

columns on a 24' x 32' grid. Engaged piers occur on the column grid along the perimeter wall to support the slab and to resist lateral loads. A 10" one-way slab supports the ground floor with the exception of the central area that requires an 11" slab and shear heads on the columns because of the increased span below. A separate footing supports the 6" entrance slab at the front of the building and there is a mechanical vault under the rear loading dock. There are two areaways at each of the shorter ends of the building with security grating allowing light and possibly air to enter the space. The basement was designed to

accommodate public toilets for the entire building and staff lockers as well as mechanical areas. Atypical openings appear in the end walls to accommodate special equipment located on the ground level. Although approximately 85 percent of the floor area is called out as inactive storage on the plans, it is clear that the expenses incurred by providing larger bays in the center section anticipates another use of the space as do the windows on the ends of the building. The stairs leading up to the ground level are detailed in the manner and cost of the other public stairs on campus. The architect's decision to place half of the habitable space underground has pro-

duced a disproportionate amount of sub-standard environment that is paying for better above grade space and finish elsewhere within the structure. It should also be remembered that for the most part the concrete structural grid found in the basement in comparison to the steel framing above is divided in half to a 16' x 24' grid that would allow for an economical flat slab with an attributable area of under 400 square feet per bay, thereby avoiding excessive reinforcement, costly shear heads, drop panels, or structural capitals. This decision produces another spatial penalty placed on the basement

to support the economics of the main floor.

The ground floor is framed with standard hot-rolled wide-flange sections (WF). These sections have squared flanges and were used for columns and beams alike. The edge beam condition was framed with built-up boxes assembled from welded steel channels. As would be expected from Mies's office at this period, the structural grid is a perfect 24' x 32' oblong bay (Figure 6). The centroids of the columns fall exactly on this gridline. This structural grid is subdivided into a 4' square planning module that determines placement of all the manufactured

elements and assemblies that make up the completed building. The 4' planning module is a departure from the 6' vertical and horizontal module proposed in the master plan and used in all previous realized buildings on campus. This change in module to a 4' dimension that already was an American standard suggests that Mies was abandoning his initial concept of custom prefabricated parts and is accepting the realities of the American market.

The steel columns above ground level are 8 WF 31 sections. Thus they are 8" long in the direction of the web and, in this case, chosen for

the fact that they have 8" wide flanges. 31 is the weight per linear foot, a critical factor in the economics of the building, for steel is priced by the ton when using standard rolled sections. Since not all the columns are loaded similarly it is obvious this particular section was chosen for its dimensional characteristics that allow for consistent details and modular stability in relation to other building parts and systems. The columns are consistently arranged with their flanges aligned in an implied plane parallel to the front and rear of the building (Figure 7). Their webs are aligned in an implied plane that parallels the sides of the building. This arrange-

ment presupposes a different wall expression for the front and rear in relation to the sides since all construction is exposed. Normally the superior strength of the web of the column is aligned with the long span while the flanges align with the short span. This would help equalize lateral loading characteristics of the long face of the building in relation to the shorter sides, although there are only four welded moment connections from front to back while there are eight from side to side. In any case, the specific structural characteristics of a square column this small makes choice of column direction mathe-

matically unclear. It is clear that in this building the expression of the exposed frame has more to do with the formal idea of the structure than the actual demands of wind and gravity.

At this point in Mies's practice, he insisted on dead flat roofs, a condition that normally demanded the horizontal alignment of the tops of all steel structural beams. The major beams are 14 WF 53 rolled steel sections that run from front to back on 24' centers. They are actually 13.92" deep and are structurally welded to the vertical flanges of the columns (Figure 8). The bottom of the beam is set at an elevation of approximately 16' off the finished floor. The minor beams are 12 WF 27 rolled sections that span between the main beams at 8' centers. These beams are also welded horizontally to either the major beams or to the vertical face of the column every fourth beam (Figure 9). The bottom edge of these beams is also set at approximately 16' off the floor to coincide with the position of the bottoms of the major beams. Usually the tops of all structural members align to simplify the transferal of gravity loads onto the beams. Instead of aligning the tops of the beams, the physical presence of the column at their junction avoids the problem of the dimensional dis-

crepancies between major and minor beams at their intersection, which is visible from the space below. The top of the larger beam projects up approximately 2" above the smaller beam, disrupting the implied plane of the exposed decking surface. Mies's office, anticipating this problem, chose precast channel decking with formed edge beams allowing for a raised center span that exceeds 2" (Figure 10). Since the concrete decking bears on the minor beams it was possible to center the void of the concrete decking on the parallel major beams allowing the tops of the 14" WF beams to pass through the raised hollow formed into each precast piece. This space would

eventually allow horizontal distribution of other technical systems at roof level in a position that is barely visible from the floor below, although the construction documents clearly imply that electrical, plumbing and mechanical systems were meant to be totally invisible.

The steel edge beams of the roof structure display properties that are even more removed from normative structural practices. As with the vertical displacement of the major beams to resolve an architectural detailing dilemma from a visual standpoint, the perimeter structural beams required further detailed architectural

invention to overcome the dimensional discrepancy between major and minor beams. Despite the much touted exterior expression of the Library and Administration Building (1944–46), which dramatized the differences between the major and minor structural members as the major theme of the building, in the Commons (ten years later), Mies carefully suppresses those earlier expressive tendencies found in the Library project with a neutralizing abstraction that reduces the structure to lineal trabeation framing the exterior enclosure assembly.[7]

The external face of the edge beam (now lit-

erally a fascia) is formed by a structural channel 15 | 33.9 that perceptibly covers the ends of the 14" major beams (Figure 11). This fascia runs continuously around the building, being field welded flush to the exterior plane of the column flanges on the front and backside and flush welded to the ends of the column flanges on the sides. Facing the interior of the building on the front and rear sides another channel 12 | 20.7 is welded to the interior flanges of the column in a similar manner. This channel bears the load of the precast concrete deck panels. Because of the fixed dimensions of the standard rolled sections

available it was necessary to insert a flat bar between the bottom flanges of the channels and continuously weld each joint to form an unbroken surface when ground smooth. This curious and expensive detail also removed the forbidden visible curved flange edge that all steel channels have. A less aesthetic condition occurs at the top of the newly formed box beam where the junctions are not visible. A similar technique is used on the sides of the building where equal 15" channels could be employed (Figure 12). An idiosyncratic procedural detail occurs at this point where a small section of concrete decking had to be poured out of sequence to fill the gap between

the last 2' concrete plank and the edge steel box beam. Finally, it is clearly apparent that the combined weights of these edge beams at the sides of the building which are carrying only half of the loads of a normal bay (at 67.8 pounds per lineal foot), far exceed the structural demands of the load when the normative condition demanded only 55 pounds per lineal foot. The front and back edge beams also display similar characteristics in loading with a doubling in the poundage of steel to realize the detailed architectural solution. Clearly the modifications to the structure for artistic reasons has changed

this assembly from a prefabricated rational system to a hand-crafted façade expression.

Moving from the structural system to the enclosure assembly it is apparent that the structure which is visually so clear and almost impossibly slender has a hidden component that also is manufactured by the structural fabricator and actually supports and reinforces the enclosure of the building. Set at door height and running horizontally whenever there is masonry infill is a structural tee ST 6 WF 20 which has an 8" flange forming the sill ledge for upper window sections. It is welded in the field at both ends to the

columns. Below this line extending to floor level are structural tees 6 I 15.5 that are cut from I beam sections and have rounded edges to their flanges making them forbidden in Mies's office except in concealed positions. These members, because they are hidden, are also stitch welded, another practice normally forbidden in Mies's office in exposed situations. This system of horizontal and vertical steel tee sections projects 6" into the brick walls with the bricks cut and fitted to receive them. These members add steel poundage and further stiffen the columns as well as allowing some lateral load to be trans-

ferred from the steel frame to the brick infill panels (Figures 13, 14, 15).

The difference between the coefficient of expansion for steel and brick has subsequently wreaked havoc in the Commons as it has on most of the IIT campus, particularly where the frame is exposed to external thermal changes. Black paint further exaggerated the problem with surface temperatures of metal hot to the touch in mid-winter, while the light buff brick assumes outside temperature.

As noted previously the formal 'idea' of the frame visually appears in an absolutely ideal manner. However, this effect could only be

achieved through the use of concealed structure that would hardly be thought of as truthful by either Gropius or Chermeyeff, nor efficient by an engineer. Although assembled from ready-made industrial products, it requires highly skilled hand craftsman to assemble and was therefore not economical.

The standard brick size when the Commons Building was built was 2 $\frac{1}{4}$" x 3 $\frac{3}{4}$" x 8" long. The brick infill wall panels are of two lengths depending on bay size. The front and rear are 23'3" long and the side panels are 31'3" long. Two impeccably drawn elevations appear next to

each other on the fifth page of the architectural construction drawings showing each course and all the necessary bricks to illustrate the English bond arrangement of the bricks including the necessary $\frac{3}{4}$ bricks to conclude the pattern at its ends. Cut bricks were normally forbidden in Mies's office except in structural bonding. The 32' bay has called out 43 stretchers + 2-$\frac{3}{4}$ bricks + 44 joints = 31'3". Similarly the 24' bay has called out 32 stretchers + 2 $\frac{3}{4}$ bricks + 33 joints = 23'3". The choice of the 8" square column courses in perfectly to the brick system with a minimal $\frac{1}{2}$" on each side for a soft caulk joint between steel and brick. This dimension proved inadequate to deal with the actual movement of the steel members.

The glass portions of the enclosure system are developed in as systematic a manner as possible following the methods developed in Mies's office to generalize the details whenever possible, opening the possibility for repetitive pieces and procedures while satisfying the demands of a minimal aesthetic. In the Commons Building inexpensive bar stock in standard sizes was combined and assembled in an ornamental iron shop and either welded in place on the job site or

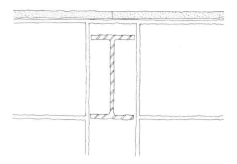

9 Minor beam detail at column

bolted in place where possible. The cost of ornamental iron rose continuously during the period of the construction of the IIT campus, eventually becoming a budget concern of some consequence. Prefabricated steel pieces are used throughout. The standard mullion is made up of a central vertical bar that measured 1" x 2 $^1/_2$", with the 1" face turned out on each side of this central bar (Figure 16). Two 1" x 1 $^1/_2$" fixed steel glass stops were plug welded on the interior side of the mullion, forming a $^1/_2$" deep reveal when in place. The exterior configuration is symmetrical in plan, with the glass placed on the centerline of the mullion. The exterior stops are

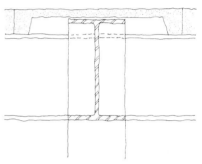

10 Major beam intersection with column detail

attached with screws to allow for glass installation. The building was glazed from the exterior for it is only one story high with extremely large glass pieces. The horizontal mullions are in the same configuration as the vertical muntins, forming a reveal that is continuous with the mullions and muntins on both interior and exterior faces of the skin. The corner of the fixed glass stops on the interior are mitered, welded, and ground smooth. The base of the window wall where it extends to floor level at the front and back of the building is supported by an adjustable angle support that is raised 1" above both interior

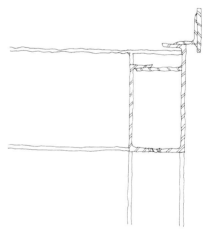

11 Perimeter beam connection at front and rear of building

and exterior ground level. The finish surface elevation is the same from outside to inside, maintaining the same reveal dimension at the base of the window wall. In the areas of full glazing at the front and back where greater lateral loading occur the central 1" x 2 $^1/_2$" steel bar is lengthened by 2 $^1/_2$" to become a 5" member on the interior of the building and is thus transformed from a negative reveal to a positive projecting major mullion without widening the mullion dimension or altering the slenderness of the exterior expression (Figure 17). This condition only occurs at the center of the bay in fully glazed

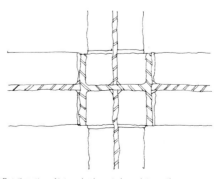

8 Detail section of internal column to beam intersection

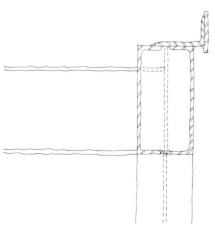

12 Perimeter beam connection at sides of building

16

areas where the loads demand it. The atypical mullion configuration illustrates Mies's attitude concerning the relationship between craft and industrial product. The window details are made up from ready-made pieces of steel just as the structural frame is assembled. Uniformity of formal expression for each system is maintained through the use of assemblies that disguise or betray their constructional origins in order to appear visually consistent. The appearance of an apparent industrialized system that also coincidentally follows the formal tendencies of a minimal constructivist aesthetic has replaced the

prefabricated, genuinely technologically superior system found in the earlier buildings at IIT.

The overall effect of the exterior expression of the front of the building is one of incredible tautness of surface relieved by the shallow modeling of the reveals, setting off the extraordinary slenderness of the framing and glazing members which merge into a continuous linear filigree (Figure 18). A line provided by the horizontal tee mentioned earlier is introduced at standard door height of 7' and encircles the entire building. The exterior is continuously glazed above that line. The sides of the building (figure 19) have solid brick infill below that line that extends in two

bays on the front and back facades bracketing the central three bays that are fully glazed. This expression exactly defines the central public social space from the secondary programmatic areas that abut it. A minor system of fenestration comprised of a continuous band of hoppers is located above the brick infill wherever it occurs. The lower glass sizes are immense, the largest piece being 6' 6" high and almost 16' 1" long. When viewed from the front, the glazed upper portion of the entire volume of the building reads as one space contradicting the realities of the internal compartmentalization. The rear eleva-

tion of the building, (which is never represented in any publication of the building), faces onto the loading dock (Figure 20). The central section of that façade is opaque and bracketed by entry doors with glazed surrounds identical to the front façade. The solid sections are accomplished through custom hollow metal panels constructed so as to be identical with the pair of hollow metal doors that make up the centered primary service elevator to the building. A singular and atypical horizontal support member made up from a 7" channel is a jarring intervention necessary to support the typical upper level windows that encircle

the building above door level. Curious $1/2$" x $1/2$" astragals are welded to the door leafs to form a draft closure and a 12 gauge bent metal sheet forms a drip over the door. All of the atypical custom metal work in this part of the skin has corroded badly and is rusted through in some places.

The only applied finish material in the building other than paint is the terrazzo floor. The aggregate and matrix of the terrazzo has been carefully chosen to create as black a surface as possible. This surface is polished to a mirror finish that dematerializes its presence. Stainless steel divider strips occur on the planning

module making visible what one immediately feels on entering the building, the incredible mathematic clarity that ties all the component pieces and assemblies visually together. The shining lines run through the space centering or bracketing structure, enclosure, and technical systems. The internal spatial reading is more complex than expected when viewed from outside. The volume of the center social space is screened at eye level by frosted glass from the clutter of the commercial programmatic space that lies on the other side of the screens. However, the ceiling is high enough to sustain the notion that the building is one grand space

because of the expansive views to the exterior through the transparent clerestory glazing. The promise of Crown Hall is introduced here in a modest but compromised manner, for this building has too complex a program to be an entirely open glass volume (Figures 21, 22).

The internal partition system in the Commons differs in relation to the earlier type of campus buildings in several ways. The material is changed from an autonomous detailing system based on material expression, such as the wood entry and surrounds in Alumni Memorial Hall (1945–46), to a system that attempts to

relate in a direct way to the exterior expression of the fully glazed entry façades. This change is another indication of Mies's inclination to move to an architecture where inside and outside converge into a spatial singularity through increased transparency.

In the back corners of the building are suites of offices which require internal partitioning. Self-supporting concrete block walls with hollow metal frames similar to the partitioning found in basement areas of the campus are found here and the working drawings call for glass ceilings in some areas, a detail that was never realized.

13 Exterior column condition at sides of building

14 Exterior column condition at front and rear of building

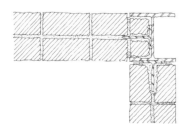

15 Exterior column condition at corner of building

Because of the complexity of the program as well as changes of proposed use during the design of the building, 'hidden core' elements have crept up onto the ground level where it was impossible for Mies's office to contain them within the conceptual detailing schema.

The most enigmatic element in the design still remains to be explained. The kitchen and service counter of the central dining hall is a cubic volume that 'floats' in the center of the space. Its position was carefully studied to retain its visual autonomy from the primary structure of the building, and its presence was meant to control the various spatial components that make up the building without destroying the reading of one primary central spatial volume. The wall planes that enclose the volume on each side extend as planes in detail from the central kitchen volume, giving a directional character to the primary circulation paths that glide along the surface of these planes. Their presence insinuates an isolated service area at the rear of the building. The cafeteria counter is simultaneously protected from primary circulation. The working drawings show lower screen walls further protecting the central dining area from pedestrian circulation. As in the later plan for Crown Hall, these loose spatial enclosures are placed within the central space forming an implied square public seating area, the hierarchical center of the building.

In the working drawings, the kitchen volume and its planar extensions are carefully detailed in a wood paneling system with revealed joints and edges. Facing the dining area is located an oversized wood grill, dissimilar to any other on campus, screening the actual sheet metal grill provided by the mechanical contractor. This was a method used by Mies's office to avoid reliance on the mechanical engineers for dimensions and co-ordination. The joints of the wood enclosure system were based on a 3-foot module so that it did not exactly correspond to the constructional grid of the building itself. This strategy was meant to be a subtlety to ensure that the entire self-supporting core would be interpreted as a potentially demountable assembly that conceptually did not compromise the clarity or geometric perfection of the actual structural system. Sometime between the issuance of the construction documents and the beginning of construction the wood wall assembly was removed (no doubt for economic reasons) and a plaster system replaced its articulated surfaces of oak paneling with unbroken surfaces of paint – a major blow to the architectural conceptualization being put forth by Mies with this building.

The apparent volume and presence of the kitchen core increased with the loss of the wood panels. Also, the almost hidden presence of a mechanical fan room pressed between the ceiling of the kitchen and the exposed underside of the precast concrete roof decking became more apparent. Although the walls of the fan room are set back from 1 to 3 feet from the planar surround of the kitchen it is clearly visible from the front entrance doors, and the fact that everything is now one material that is painted white, in high contrast to the rest of the building, makes the entire construct visually more problematic. The unfortunate engagement of two black supporting columns coplanar with the front wall of the fan room volume further destroys the illusion of the body of the kitchen floating freely within the vast and singular spatial volume of the entire building. The first embryonic indication of a floating core element such as this appeared in the lobby of the Chemical Engineering and Metallurgy Building (1946) with its curved figural end to the auditorium that visually combined with the detailed treatment of its flanking stairs and reached its culmination in Crown Hall (1956). The desire for one rational structure to form a grand open room countered by the necessity of furnishing this room with a miniature edifice that houses the programmatic anomalies of use remains an enigmatic aspect to Mies's work. Pretending always to be made up of temporary screen walls that could disappear at any time but usually grew ever larger to eventually truly satisfy the needs of the user, it became a conceit that remains a strange strategy unique to Mies and his following.

A pair of stairs descend on each side of the kitchen into a well that leads to the basement where the public toilets are located. They follow the pattern of the detailing found in the earlier campus building with stringers made up of 12" channels on the stairs and 15" channels forming the edge of the opening through the floor. This geometry allows the stair stringer to join the edging at the same common dimension. All the joints are welded and ground smooth in the field and the rounded flanges on the channels are ground square for appearance. 1" bar stock

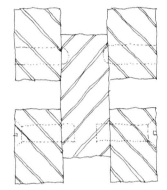

16 Typical glazing mullion

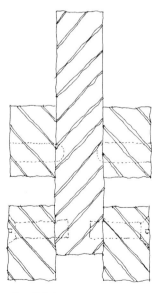

17 Glazing mullion at full glass

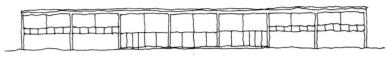

18 Front elevation

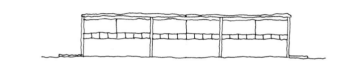

19 Side elevation

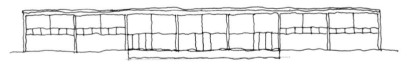

20 Rear elevation

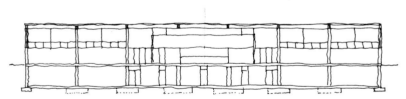

21 Longitudinal section

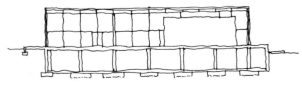

22 Transverse section

railings are shop fabricated and screwed into place in the field. The vertical supports of both the stair enclosure and the stairs line up in plan. The position between the stair support verticals and the nosing of the stair varies – not the ideal solution for Mies, who always pursued absolute consistency. Isometric drawings illustrate the approved design for the terminal support of the stair where the horizontal plane of the post top is expressed as well as the symmetry of post position and horizontal turn of the railings at the head of the stair (Figures 23, 24). The channels, while serving as stringers, are the forms for

the structural concrete slab that supports the stair. A $3/4"$ reveal separates the concrete from the steel continuously all around. The finish surface is identical to earlier stairs on campus with hand applied terrazzo troweled onto the treads and risers and the cavity of the steel channel stringer hand packed with terrazzo. The grinding of the terrazzo was accomplished with a hand-held grinding wheel in order to realize the tight radii of the polished surface. The elevator is a standard design service elevator that opens off the service area at the back of the building. It has no significance in the public use of the facility although the loading doors, elevator, and the

loading dock are hierarchically centered with the back façade of the building.

The mechanical, electrical, and plumbing systems that serve a modern university structure are a substantial part of the cost of the building. The co-ordination of these systems with the structural system and architectural details consumes a considerable amount of an architect's time and energy and therefore affects his financial situation. An examination of the technical systems in the Commons is revealing in the consistency of approach that Mies's office deals with this aspect of design. A glance at the construc-

tion documents of any of Mies's IIT buildings reveals immediately a sense of graphic clarity not always associated with mechanical, electrical, and plumbing layouts. Absolute symmetry, even when concealed, organizes horizontal runs, and dense accumulations of vertical runs are pressed into a minimal number of chases. This characteristic is particularly apparent in the Commons where the entire structural system is exposed, the wall assembly is either a single pane of glass or 8" solid brick, and the secondary framing systems for exterior glazing are assembled from solid bar stock. There are no cavities within any of the wall and ceiling assemblies that would allow concealed passage of electrical, plumbing, or mechanical systems. Hilberseimer suggests that the Greeks would have recognized the purity of this building as would the Goths. Even Alberti would have approved of the exact equivalence of inside to outside. Gone is the false differentiation of outside finish from inside elevation. Gone is poché that separated room finish from structural enclosure.[8]

Unfortunately, also missing is the capability of dealing with the emerging technology of the day. The mechanical, electrical, and plumbing

systems in the Commons Building are minimal conventional systems. There is no attempt to invent new methods or search for creative technical applications. If anything, the ordinary technical systems are asked to perform in applications that no engineer would suggest if left to his own devices. Engineers were asked by Mies's office to accommodate inventive structural and architectural designs. Significant visible and even invisible signs of the presence of technical systems were always symmetrically displayed. In the Commons Building, the area drain in the loading area, the elevator, the air risers to the basement, and the service ejection pump all lie

on the center line of the building. In this building, by thinking of technical systems as either unfortunate additions to architecture or hierarchical anomalies, Mies indicates that his true interest lies in minimal formalism and not emerging technological development.

The site utilities are gathered into the building through a mechanical room beneath the loading dock, outside of the envelope of the ground floor enclosure. The electrical transformers and the steam converter are located here. Sewage is ejected out of the basement by a pump that is located centrally between the two toilet rooms in

the basement. The mechanical system, once inside the building, is comprised of hot water pipes looping the perimeter of the basement ceiling and connecting to standard convector units placed against the outside walls on both floors. Supply and return pipes are ganged along the ceiling of the basement feeding up and down. There was no attempt in the construction documents to architecturally deal with them in any way as this was considered sub-standard space. An air system located in the fan room over the kitchen delivers air on both floors through grills located centrally on the face of the kitchen wall upstairs and simi-

larly on the face of the wall enclosing the toilets in the basement. This air system provides fresh air to meet code as well as make-up air for the toilet and exhaust fans in the kitchen. There is a central return opening directly into the fan room on the upper level, a noisy proposition. The complete lack of any horizontal duct runs would have been extremely economical, however air quality in enclosed spaces with no make-up air was problematic. Apparently the line of hoppers on the ends of the building was meant to provide fresh air. They actually had insect screens, not always found on Mies's buildings at this time. Some time

within the first ten years of use, the clear glass located above the frosted glass screen that contained the programmatic areas at the sides of the building was cut down by one half in some areas to allow for circulation of air, destroying the delicate luminous division of internal compartmentation as well as the acoustic isolation between functional units.

A second fan system is located in an enclosed plenum space built along the front wall of the basement beneath the primary entrances. At each end of the space directly under the doors are located small fan-coil units not dissimilar to house furnaces in size and operation. Custom floor-

mounted stainless steel punched grills directly inside of the doors are air returns that are meant to draw the cold air down to be reheated and then ducted into the central plenum space where it is introduced up through lineal stainless steel grills that parallel the large glass areas of the front elevation. These grills are raised for sanitary code reasons onto terrazzo plinths with continuous curved sidewalls that make the transition from floor to grill. This method of dealing with down drafts in cold weather proved immediately inadequate. In busy times, the front and rear doors opened and closed simultaneously, resulting in

strong drafts of cold air making occupation of much of the dining area uncomfortable. The removal of the low wood screen walls for cost reasons exacerbated the problem.

As earlier mentioned, the electrical main is brought into the below-grade mechanical room located under the loading dock. From there electricity is distributed through the floor fill in conduit to the convenience outlets spaced intermittently to meet code along the interior face of the exterior walls. Because of the 8" solid brick wall, raceways had to be cut into the brick and the outlets themselves were placed carefully in a

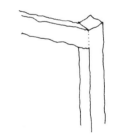

23 End stair railing detail

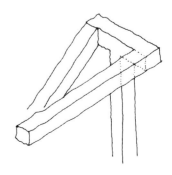

24 Stair railing detail at landing

generalized way to conform to the modular brick pattern. Interior demising walls in the suites of the programmatic area had conduit stubbed up into the walls where necessary. To save money, the lights throughout the building are switched off at the circuit breakers that are ganged in banks in the service area on the rear wall of the kitchen core. The construction documents show two alternate lighting patterns: one comprised of a regular pattern of banks of 16 foot fluorescent fixtures running the length of the building from side to side. An adjustment in pattern to the generalized plan had to be made

to fit around the kitchen. The alternate plan had 24 foot fluorescent fixtures running from front to back. A handwritten note on the working drawings calls for alternate prices for each scheme. The more expensive scheme, that ran from side to side and had 50 percent more lights, was chosen because it balanced the lights perpendicularly to the route of entry, a positioning normally favored by Mies. The exit signs are individually drawn and detailed at a large scale showing the attachment of the fixtures to structural steel framing members. A whole sheet of working drawings is given over to the steam press for the dry cleaner's operation that

requires a unique vent through the brick wall. Either unforeseen or ignored, this grill does considerable damage to the pristine elevation. Most of the drawing related to the detailing on the electrical sheets is crossed out. An elaborate and expensive method of mounting the fluorescent lights had been illustrated that cut two holes through the precast concrete decking for each fixture, allowing the wiring to run freely through the insulation that lay on top of the concrete decking. A handwritten note is scribbled on the drawing calling for the conduit to run exposed between the ribs of the precast slabs.

This is another instance of an unforeseen economic intervention that compromised the absolute visual control desired by Mies's office.

The plumbing for the building has similar characteristics to the electrical system. Primary access to the building is through the space under the loading dock. Supply piping is distributed through the concrete fill located above the structural slab except in the toilet and kitchen areas that are stacked to allow hidden horizontal runs and vertical runs through the walls. Specialized water supply and drains in the side programmatic areas were stubbed up in anticipation of

present and some future positions, since equipment changes made to the building after construction would have to be completed with extreme difficulty due to the exposed nature of structure and enclosure. The roof drains proved a particularly difficult problem due to the requirements of Mies's office at that time for dead flat roofs that require more drains than sloped roofs. The risers for roof drains were located next to columns so that the vertical drain pipe could be partially concealed in the space against the column, hidden between the flanges. Unfortunately, the deflection of the

beams pooled water on the roof mid-span between columns, creating premature roof failure. Within ten years the drains were relocated to the center of the bays and sloped horizontal runs of drain pipe appeared within the primary space, running diagonally from the drains to the vertical risers in their original locations.

The campus at IIT, which was once an ambitious, bold, and experimental building program has become a candidate for a historical preservation plan. It has been forty-five years since construction of the Commons Building. I would suggest that this building should at all cost be preserved, for it best illustrates not only the brilliance of Mies as an architect but the limitation of any singular way of thinking about architecture. Mies, as any architect is, was limited by his own talents and weaknesses. The prejudices he had gained from a lifetime of practice that began in the nineteenth century appear consistently blind to some characteristics of twentieth century technology related to architecture. The rising significance that technical systems other than structure would play in the conceptualization of building was not appreciated by Mies or his office. The amount of funds that had to be designated for these systems was resisted by

Mies. The expansion characteristics of steel, the problems of flat roofs, the amount of energy required to heat buildings with no insulation did not interest him. Nor did the fact that ice formed on the interior surfaces of steel enclosure systems force his office to alter their methods or materials. When they were obliged to deal with mechanical, electrical, and plumbing systems it was not in a positive way to encourage new technology to inform their design process.

Emanating from the Bauhaus and Gropius was the idea of the significance of prefabrication spurred by technical production. This was a pri-

mary ideal behind all of Mies's early work in America. The conviction in a rational architecture produced by groups of dedicated collaborators was a primary thrust of the early years of the Architecture Department at IIT and was supported by all those affiliated with the Bauhaus and their descendents, such as Chermeyeff. These ideas were slowly abandoned by Mies at the IIT campus as he realized the magnitude of production necessary to produce well designed components for fabrication. There is a sense also that he must have realized that the earlier campus buildings at IIT lacked the spatial invention and

artistry of assembly that characterized his earlier European work. The Commons Building represents the moment when Mies chose to abandon his own cubic spatial system in order to pursue architectural notions other than systematic generalization of detail and uniformity of dimension for manufactured components.

With this building, the emerging theme of one grand space was attempted and, in the end, failed due to program complexity. However, the poignancy of that failure lies in the fact that Crown Hall was tested here and many of the architectural problems not totally resolved in the Commons were fully realized in the artistic virtuosity of

Mies's performance at Crown Hall. Conversely, the technical failures that resulted as a direct outcome of Mies's particular personal biases in the Commons were in many ways magnified in Crown Hall. His aesthetic ran counter to the realities of the emerging technology of the day, forcing him to diminish the performance of his buildings as places for human habitation in order to realize the artistic and spiritual qualities necessary to sustain his interest as a creator of individual genius.

1 Program notes privately published by the school of architecture at IIT containing the speeches by Chermeyeff, Gropius, and Mies van der Rohe, Chicago, 1950.

2 Ludwig Hilberseimer, *Mies van der Rohe*, (Chicago: 1956).

3 The Commons Building is currently a component part of the proposed new student center by Rem Koolhaas.

4 Hilberseimer, *op. cit.*, 49.

5 Colin Rowe, "The Chicago Frame," in *The Architectural Review*, November 1956, 285.

6 Construction Documents for the New Commons Building for The Illinois Institute of Technology, 3202-3218 South Wabash Ave. Mies van der Rohe, Architect, Chicago, Ill., Friedman, Alschuler and Sincere, Associate Architects and Engineers. Commission number 2557, 4/27/53.

7 Hilberseimer, *op. cit.* 51.

8 Hilberseimer, *op. cit.* 40

25 Front view

26 Front and side view

27 Interior view front to back

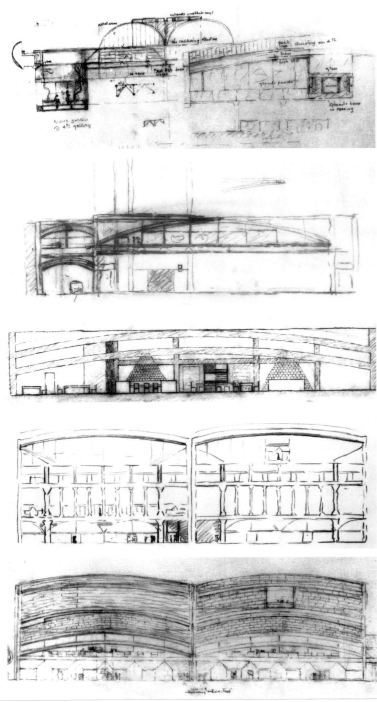

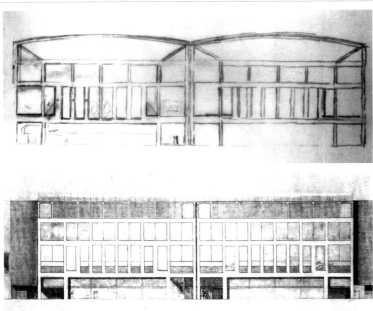

1 Chapel street elevation studies, British Art Center, Yale University.
New Haven, Louis I. Kahn (1969-74)

LIBER TERTIVSDECIMVS. 447

primi. Ex tribus igitur angulis talis superficialis figuræ, possibile est solidum angulum cõstitui, ex quatuor autem aut ex pluribus impossibile est: propterea quòd ex talibus figuris superficialibus (quæ cum quadrilateræ sint ipsæ æquilateræ atquo æquiangulæ) unicum solidum quod cubum dicimus, fabricatum est. Triangulorũ autẽ æquilaterorum sex anguli, sunt æquales quatuor rectis ex 32 primi, pauciores ergo minores, & plures, maiores, igitur ex sex angulis talium trigonorum aut ex pluribus, impossibile est angulum solidum fieri, ex quinque & quatuor & ex tribus possibile. Cum itaq; tres anguli trigoni æquilateri efficiunt angulum solidum, perficitur ex triangulis æquilateris corpus quatuor basium triangularium atque æquilaterarum. Cum uerò quatuor consurgunt: corpus octo basium, quod octoedron diximus. At uerò si quinque triangulorum æquilaterorum anguli, solidum angulum contineant, fiet corpus icosedron uiginti basium triangularium & æquilaterarum. Quare ergo tot & talia sunt solida regularia. & quare plura his non sint, dictum est.

Euclid. ex Zamb. Problema 5. Propositio 17.

17 Dodecahedrum construere & data sphera comprehendere, qua & prædictas figuras, ostendereq; quòd dodecahedri latus irrationalis est ea quæ appellatur apotome.

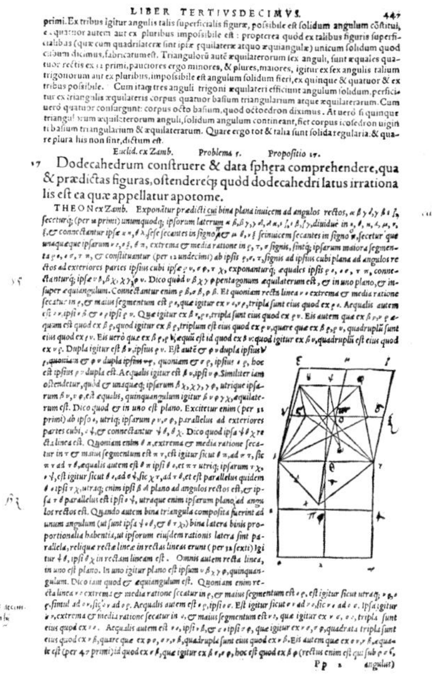

2 Page 447 from Book Thirteen of the 1533 edition of Euclid's Elements (from the Department of Rare Books and Special Collections of Princeton University Library)

Carles Vallhonrat

THE IN-VISIBILITY OF TECTONICS

GRAVITY AND THE TECTONIC COMPACTS

'You are lucky....You know that....If we didn't have the computers, every time you ask me to reconsider the position of one element it would take us four months to go through the multiple equations. By hand, I mean. You know that!' Abba Tor[1] looked at me, his facial countenance between exhausted and resigned, as if saying: again? The work of the then Mellon Center for British Art and British Studies[2] had architect Louis Kahn, from the beginning, exploring the possibilities of layering the four floors so that the structure of each level would define different sizes and sequences of spaces and different conditions of light, to accommodate different aspects of the collection (Figure 1). So, that vertical plane of the elevation was in fact a four-storied multiple frame that had, for each version, a different number of vertical struts for each floor.

In retrospect, that aspect of the project, i.e.; the geometry of the structure of the façade, that plane, contained at least two pervasive ambiguities as represented in it. One, inherent in all concrete, that of allowing us to read the travel and nature of the stresses. The other, of course, also inherent in all concrete linear systems, appears when the linear structural elements we see get fat (Figure 3). The thick lines that make the frames' configuration are sized for moments of deflection and do not imply elementary vectors. That the lower horizontal layer of the frame had fewer vertical elements, in the early designs, than at least the two layers above it, was perhaps the worst condition. Traces of Mr. Vierendeel's work, five times over. That vertical grid of irregular cells was not just columns and beams, but a closed multiple frame of some complexity and, of course, cost. The politics of the job, which had to represent and be handled by too many constituencies at a very politically difficult time for Yale, killed it. That is, killed that original scheme.

1 Abba Tor had inherited the Pfisterer and Tor firm after Henry Pfisterer's death. Henry Pfisterer had been the engineer of the Yale Art Gallery. Abba Tor, as a younger engineer with Amman and Whitney, had been the engineer for Saarinen's TWA pavilion at Kennedy Airport.

2 Today's British Art Center at Yale.

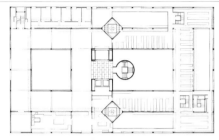

3 Plan and model of Chapel Street elevation, British Art Center. Final scheme using single module throughout.

(I've told that story elsewhere.) The plan of this project, which originally made a considerable number of distinctions for sizes and character of rooms for a very varied collection, became a plan done with a single module. That vertical plane now is the edge of the plan grid (Figure 3), and the thicker line, at the top of the first floor, is just a beam, carrying a point load of a second floor column every other bay.

Those ambiguities make for the lack of direct correspondence between the appearance of the frame and the trajectory of the stresses. It is then to the inner nature of concrete that we have to return, to speculate on what degree of visibility concrete gives us to understand its behavior. Much of this we know. When it is a big 'plane,' a wall, or a deck, we understand quickly that some sort of cage or cages in the form of a matrix of steel rods at whatever increments, will do. That is, will do while we keep unreinforced concrete out of mind and in its current lack of use and lack of prestige. (We should remember that a lot of Wright's Unity Temple is unreinforced concrete.) As soon as we move to structurally more ambitious shapes, as in frames, cantilevered elements, girders, plain beams, or hinges (as in some bridges!), (Figures 7 & 8), the concrete's ability to demonstrate the trajectory of stresses to the points of support decreases to the point of obscurity.

We learn internal rules of material behavior by analysis, professional practice, and by that substitute called codes. At the risk of appearing too exacting, I feel it is worth-while to review some detailed points which are of consequence, such as: (1) The depth of concrete cover of any bar to the surface of the finished element. (2) The distance between bars, as a ratio of the diameter of the bars. (3) The texture of the bar surface, so that some engagement is assured between the concrete and the steel. And each of these has a history. First, we know that depth of cover alone is an issue that has practically proscribed shell construction in this country. Our code require-

ments make them so heavy that they cease to be shells. Tor told me once that the 'shells' at the TWA pavilion are, near the supports, fourteen inches thick, a shell theory impossibility.[3] One should remember that depth of cover is, roughly speaking, useless concrete in all edges with tension stresses. (There is a stealthy theme coming in here, which is that that concrete is preventing the steel from rusting…steel galvanizing not withstanding).

The next issue, the distance between bars as a ratio of their diameter, becomes crucial when heavy, concentrated stresses within the mass of concrete call for more steel and less concrete, progressively, until the amount of concrete left is so small that only the minimum distance allowed by code remains. When the number of bars reaches its maximum, one wonders if we can still talk about concrete in the accepted sense of the word. That density of steel is a not an uncommon condition near points of support in large structural elements. Swiss engineer Robert Maillart, certainly the most gifted and insightful designer of the known concrete engineers of this century, pushed that condition to its most daring limit in his miraculous(?) solution for a hinge on the Arve bridge near Vessy-Geneve (Figures 7–9).

The importance of the texture of reinforcing bars, particularly how it governs the 'adherence' of steel and concrete, stems from the need to avoid slippage of the rods within the concrete mass. Over time, the increasingly coarser texture of the reinforcing bars, demanded and obtained from the bar-extruding plants, changed the geometry of the cage diagrams. In the longitudinal section of a single span beam, for example, the cage was first built with curled bar ends and diagonal bends at shear points (Figure 10), then with straight bars, with the consequent reduction in cage manufacturing labor costs. It also went from extensive use of relatively thin bars to fewer thicker bars, as the cost of a pound of steel became less, relative to the cubic yard cost of

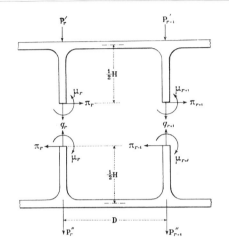

Abb. 4.

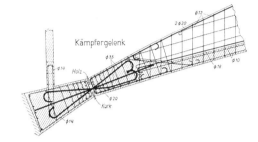

top to bottom:

4 Vierendeel's original stress diagram

5 Vierendeel's analytical stress diagram for one bay

6 Vierendeel's bridge over the Escaut at Avelghem. Built in 1904. One of Vierendeel's first bridges using his truss system. It is hard to understand why he used that application when traffic is parallel to the plane of the trusses.

top to bottom:

7 The Arve bridge at Vessy-Genf, Robert Maillart (1936). Section showing the reinforcing of the abutment 'miraculous' hinge. Notice: Holz (hardwood) and Kork (cork).

8 The Arve bridge – Reinforcing of the 'miraculous' hinge

9 The Arve bridge – Full view

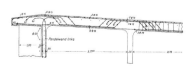
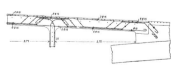

10 The Aare bridge in Aarburg, Robert Maillart (1912). Sections through beams.

11 Kimbell Art Museum, Fort Worth, Louis I. Kahn (1966–72)
Model showing the 'vault' end 'beam' with the even profile.
12 Kimbell Art Museum, Fort Worth, Louis I. Kahn (1966–72)
Side elevation showing curvature of end panels.

finished concrete. Yet no exposure of these changes was ever thought worth presenting, or worth being perceived. This matter of the 'adherence,' incidentally, got perhaps its most precarious theory from Nervi in his experiments with what he called 'ferro-cemento.' He manufactured a very thin plate of concrete with wire mesh, placing wires one millimeter thick at one centimeter intervals. He presumed that some modification occurred at the surface of contact, an alteration that changed the chemistry of the materials at and around the contact surface.

One can't avoid reflecting here that the desired coalescence between concrete mass and linear steel seems to obscure that first conventional understanding of the nature of reinforced concrete, which is that steel takes care of tensile stresses and concrete takes care of the compression. Under analysis, neither the separation of the two elementary stresses of compression and tension, nor the rendition of (1) tensile stresses as vectors, thus linear, along with (2) some other kind of representation of compression give us a clear visual clue. Perhaps ever since S. Timoshenko represented (in his classic *Theory of Structures,* of 1926) all internal forces, external forces, and reactions (of a rigid body constrained and loaded in one plane) as vectors, we think of readability as having to do with linearity. We seem to *need* the use of linearity to understand structural behavior – linearity of the two-dimensional and three-dimensional variety. It seems to be all vectors. That's how we understand.

Looking in more detail at that example of Tor's work on the multiple closed frames for the Yale British Art Center brings out the complexities of the mechanics of a piece. Each intersection between a horizontal 'cord/beam' and a vertical 'strut/column' is a crossing of flexural stresses that we cannot easily read as linear. In the elementary case of a simply supported concrete beam, what we ordinarily do not do is compare it with a truss of equal total outline. Its geometry and complexity aside, that truss would have considerably less weight. The most significant point here being that we would be eliminating *useless* weight. One is reminded here of that ideal apho-

rism, of his invention we thought then, that that wonderful teacher Robert LeRicolais brought up at every opportune time in his classes: 'Infinite span, zero weight.' By that paradigm, of course, the truss would be better. We don't use the truss because the labor involved in producing it would make it, overtly, more expensive.

Thus, we come to the issue of the legitimacy of the choice at any size. If the span was rather large we would probably use the truss because of the lesser quantity and the lesser weight of the materials in use, and read a lot (of the trajectory of the stresses). If it was a small span we would just chop a two by four, cutting out most of the labor cost, and read nothing. So, the description, the linearity, the legibility, has a matter of scale.

But now, having dealt with some very detailed aspects of structural specificity we can get into tectonics in its fullest scope. We know that concrete can be made to represent the full operational characteristics of tectonics. That is, beyond the limited scope of the separable structural requirements, concrete can (1) shelter of its own accord, solving what mass materials, masonry, and the like, have always solved (closure and structure at once). It can (2) solve the appearance (not the looks, but the coming out or about) of compound stresses within its mass. And (3) it can absorb innumerable directional forces by the incorporation of a rich repertoire of reinforcing techniques. Column and lintel, or wall and deck, can be said to be at the beginning of tectonics thinking. It is represented in Kahn's dictum: 'The walls parted and the columns became.' For him it would also be the beginning of light. That lintel though, the beam, requires a leap of faith.

I suggest then that concrete can of its own be what I propose to call a 'tectonic compact.' Meaning that it can be made into enough of a system to give us the defining criteria to build well. The degree to which the 'tectonic compact' can choose what set of tasks it can accomplish and represent, means that it can be precise, separable, and sufficiently descriptive to serve the art, making the case for the character of the compact. We'll come back to that later.

'I will not do it! I...will not do it.' That was August Komendant's answer to my request that he stay with the original profile that Kahn wanted for the end 'beam' of the 'vaults' of the Kimbell Museum. It had seemed to become an understanding in the office that Komendant liked me a bit better than others in the staff because I knew a little more engineering (perhaps). Kahn, who knew of my work for LeRicolais at the University of Pennsylvania, thought I could persuade Komendant. Komendant had brought a large drawing with four (plus two variations) different fully designed and fully calculated profiles for that end 'beam.'[4] None with the equal-width outline that had already been drawn in a number of sections and elevations in the office (Figure 11), and that Kahn wanted. Maybe Komendant wanted to have his engineering knowledge show, that time. It seemed rather improbable to me then (and now) since, in the same project, a number of high-wire-act structural elements (at which Komendant was a master) went unexploited, or unexpressed, or were not made readable. That couldn't be the reason for Komendant's obstinacy. Nothing was being expressed about: the horizontal vierendeels, the postentioning strands, the horizontal beam restraints, the several kinds of 'vaults,' etc. So, why was that end piece chosen to demonstrate engineering skill? (There were other things that made him cantankerous and strained his relationship with Kahn. Komendant had not liked the contract with then-East Pakistan, now Bangladesh – he resigned from that job – and the finances of Kahn's office were very difficult at that time...financial matters that brought grow-

ing friction and the eventual break up.) It seemed that he was saying, 'You are not listening to me.' That end beam had to remain as a choice of one of the four (six) options that Komendant brought with him. Also, how could several options represent a rigorous result of the forces converging at that edge? It was unclear to me, everything else having been already locked in and decided. The profile read with some sort of specificity as if the curved 'beam' was responding to a larger moment in the middle of the span and to a smaller one at the supports. This was the kind of literal specificity that Kahn disliked. (We have so many more things to do in a building, he might have said). Only Kahn's extraordinary skills, which would allow him to redeem other people's (sometimes the client's) impositions on a design, allowed him this time also to restore the *elementary* profile of that end 'beam.' He did it by maintaining the profile of the parallel edges he started with, using the edge of the infill travertine panel of the end wall, and by making it fall congruently with the width of the column (Figures 11 & 12). The issue of Komendant's contribution to Kahn's work between 1959 and 1964 is a subset of the issue of structure's contribution to tectonics and deserves a separate article. Another contributor who also deserves special attention is that immensely able and wonderful man, the late Richard Kelly, a master lighting consultant (a graduate of Yale's school of architecture, by the way), who contributed so much to the quality of the light in those vaults. He helped make the light, and the readability of that vaulted space, the miracle that it is.

4 For this article, I spent several hours at the Kahn Archive at the University of Pennsylvania, looking for that sheet amongst Komendant's drawings without success. Although disappointed, it didn't surprise me that that very efficient man would have discarded those unused solutions.

13 Rietveld-Schroder House, Gerrit Rietveld (1924). Interior view of top floor, showing Red-Blue Chair, background left
14 The lesser-known High Chair, Gerrit Rietveld (1919). Friedman Gallery, New York

Thinking of miracles, it is inevitable to go back to reflect on how and where did modern architecture consider the issue of tectonics, as generally understood. I always find it useful to go back to the painter Kandinsky and his request to the observer to think of himself as being in the space of the painting. A painting is no longer a representation, but a space of which you, the observer, are an inhabiting part. The architectural parallel is also a new conception of space, and as such it has some aspects new to the then conventional thinking. The newly conceived space is (1) boundless, open ended, continuous (as per inside-outside). It (2) is up there, and ignores gravity. As in painting, it (3) doesn't represent, thus it has no 'character' (as in representing function). It (4) isn't the result of composing, since there are no parts to assemble (since there are no boundaries). And it (5), very importantly, draws on the abstract. Since it doesn't represent it draws on things which are elements of the realm of the abstract, e.g., numbers, science, the psyche, math, elements of the arts themselves, color, light, sound, the physicist's space itself.

A very effective example of that conception of the new space was Rietveld's Schroeder house in Utrecht (Figure 13). Just as clear, were his chairs (Figure 14). Everyone used the Red-Blue Chair as a paradigm of the new thinking, including El Lissitsky, who at about the same time (c. 1922) is assumed to have been responsible for the acceptance of the use of the term 'constructivist' to describe the Soviet '-ism' of those years – a rather unclear choice of name if one thinks that constructing would have something to do with tectonics. They liked Rietveld's chair because it was made with sticks of the same thickness (like abstract lines, elements) bypassing each other, tangentially and open-endedly. The shape of the sticks was not affected (except for the arms, which have a double width) by joints or by the character of their function (as legs, cross bracing, back support, etc.). The rectangles of the seat and back were also unbound and unaffected by construction intersections. Even the colors in which the pieces were painted were used to somewhat dematerialize the pieces by having some adjacent faces painted in different colors.

Parallel in calendar time was of course the explosion of new knowledge in science. Its revelations unsettled forever our understanding and our perception of the physical world. (We were now seventy percent water!) What we could see seemed to be so much less than what was there, so much less than ever before. It was all happening at the beginning of the century. It is useful to remember here that Roentgen's discovery of X-rays was in 1895.

Yet, was it that absence of the notion of gravity as understood in the nineteenth century or the emerging gravitational theories brought out by the progress of contemporary physics that provoked gravity's apparent disappearance from art? And, more importantly, would those new conceptions or scientists' knowledge alter or fix our understanding of gravity today? (Whether gravity should be dealt with conceptually, or made legible, or not made legible, is an artistic decision of which we will talk later). Gravity, like abstraction, or physical reality, or perception, is a concept that, inarguably, we must not just understand but take a position on. It seems then that it is the physicist's view, the scientist's truth, rather than the artist's or the philosopher's, or someone else's, that we should review.

Of course, the understanding of gravity was, at the turn of the century, Newtonian. In his most extraordinary (and wild perhaps) book *The Fabric of Reality*, David Deutsch, the British physicist, says, in some of the most reassuring parts of his text: 'Newton gave us the first universal theories of gravity and a unification of, among other things, celestial and terrestrial mechanics...In the nineteenth century, few things would have been regarded more confidently as real than the force of gravity. Not only did it figure in Newton's then unrivaled system of laws, but everyone could feel it, all the time, even with their eyes shut...or so they thought.' And then: 'Today we understand gravity through Einstein's theory rather than Newton's, and we know that no such force exists. We do not feel it! What we feel is the resistance that prevents us from penetrating the solid ground beneath our feet.' And then, as if we could have expected the very reassuring statement: 'The list of acceptable modes of explanation will always be open-ended, and consequently the list of acceptable criteria for reality must be open-ended, too.'

Roger Penrose in his *The Emperor's New Mind* is more detailed in going through the evolution of the understanding of gravity. He begins recalling Galileo's great insight that all bodies fall equally fast in a gravitational field. (This is Galileo dropping two rocks from the leaning tower of Pisa). Then, Penrose recalls Newton's distinction between a body's mass and a body's acceleration, referring to the conditions of 'free fall' in space (no air, no air friction), which means 'following the appropriate orbit under gravity. There is no need for this 'falling' to be straight downwards,' toward the center of the earth. Then Penrose describes how 'the viewpoint of general relativity is to regard the freely falling motions as natural motions.' We can 'call world-lines of freely falling particles geodesics in space-time. Of course, we are already on the physics of the universe,' and, '...a concept of 'curvature' for space-time can be used to describe the action of gravitational fields....New physics does come in when we try to combine this picture with what we have learnt...of special relativity – the geometry of space-time that we now know applies in the absence of gravity.' One can't avoid thinking that these speculations on the space of the physicist might have fed the early modernists' conception of space, with its unmentioned 'absence of gravity.' Penrose continues, 'But when gravity is present...a flat surface gives an approximate description to the geometry of a curved surface.' If we take a 'more powerful microscope to examine a curved surface...then the surface appears to be flatter and flatter.' Significantly, Penrose concludes, 'We say that a curved surface (as in gravitational fields) is *locally* like a Euclidean plane. In the same way, we can say that, in the presence of gravity, space-time is *locally* like...*flat* space-time, but we allow some 'curviness' on a larger scale.'

It is comforting to be back in Euclidean space and to have Penrose describe Euclidean geometry as a 'sublime and superbly accurate theory of physical space – and of the geometry of rigid bodies' while saying that, 'We now know that Euclidean geometry is *not entirely accurate* as a description of the physical space that we actually inhabit!...Over a meter's range, deviations from Euclidean flatness are tiny indeed, errors in treating the geometry as Euclidean amounting to less than the diameter of an atom of hydrogen!' (The exclamation point is his.) Not bad for Euclid, whose 'sublime' *Elements* was written around 310 B.C. (Figures 15 & 16).

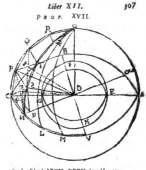

15 Cover sheet from a 1533 edition of Euclid's *Elements* (from the Department of Rare Books and Special Collections of Princeton University Library)
16 Page 307 of Book Twelve of *Euclidis Elementorum* (from the Department of Rare Books and Special Collections of Princeton University Library)

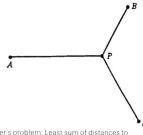

17 Steiner's problem: Least sum of distances to points A, B and C.

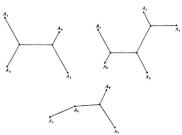

18 Shortest networks joining more than three points. As per Courant.

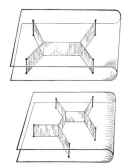

19 Soap bubbles demonstration of the shortest connection between four and five points. As per Courant.

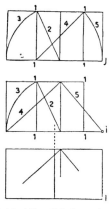

20 From Modulor 1. The middle diagram is a geometrical impossibility: If 4 and 5 are at 90 degrees, point 'i' cannot determine two contiguous squares.

$$P - E + C + 1$$
$$35 - 86 + 52 + 1$$

21 From Cyril S. Smith. Euler's formula for two-dimensional networks, applied to a diagram of a Picasso painting.

It is useful here to remember that the Greeks expressed geometric magnitudes as numbers in order that they could be studied according to the laws of arithmetic. Again Penrose: 'The ancient Greeks thought of real numbers as things *given*...as properties of 'actual' space....'Real' numbers were things to be extracted from geometry of physical space.' Physical space was there first, understood through geometry, so, the geometry of physical space was also there first. 'Now we prefer to think of the real numbers as logically more primitive than geometry. This allows us to construct all sort of different types of geometry, each *starting* from the concept of number.'

That lead toward the abstract anticipates in one of the clearest ways that frontier point where we can sense the separation between physical reality and the abstract, which I have argued is the dramatic break that makes the modernists new. We can get there via mathematics. 'Mathematical objects are just concepts; they are the mental idealizations that mathematicians make, often stimulated by the appearance and seeming order of aspects of the world about us, but mental idealizations nevertheless. At the same time, there often does appear to be some profound reality about these mathematical concepts, going quite beyond the mental deliberations of any particular mathematician. It is as though human thought is, instead, being guided toward some external truth – a truth which has a reality of its own, and which is revealed only partially to any one of us.'

The mathematician Richard Courant, in his book *What is Mathematics* in the chapter on maxima and minima, presents what is known as Steiner's problem. Three villages on a map, or three points on paper, are given in a roughly triangular pattern, and a fourth must be found that will make the sum of the distances between each point (A, B and C) and the fourth (P) the minimum. The resultant three lines will represent the smallest amount of path needed to connect the three points A, B and C to each other through point P. Then he goes on to demonstrate mathematically that the angle between any pair of lines at the central point is the same, 120 degrees (Figure 17). (And, obviously, the total length of path will be less than the sum of the length of the triangle formed by A, B and C.) Then he demonstrates the same recurrent 120-degree angle for four points, five, and so on (Figure 18). He then turns to soap solution (soap bubbles or 'films' being a favorite of mathematicians). We are in the realm of nature now. He takes two parallel acrylic plates and connects them with three, and four, and five perpendicular bars and immerses the object into soap solution. He withdraws it to see the soap film

form a system of vertical planes between the bars that connect, at angles of exactly 120 degrees! (Figure 19). Is it nature (the film) imitating math? Of course, it isn't the mathematician's idealization needing a natural observation for its inception, or for its confirmation, either.

(It is because math makes as feel so close to the structure of physical nature that one finds it difficult to see why mathematics is not part of most of the curricula for architectural programs in this country. Corbusier had his doubts, of course, when in 1907, paying his respects to the elder grand master, he was told by August Perret, 'I would study mathematics, if I had time.... They form the character.' Which made Corbu say shortly afterwards, somewhat cynically: 'I studied mathematics and in practice they were never of any use to me afterwards. But they *may* have formed my character.' If anyone has doubts, he should read *Modulor 1*, carefully.) (Figure 21)

That break between the physical, natural world, and our ability to recognize, devise, and use elements of the abstract, I have argued, makes abstraction a break-away world that feeds this century's art, and thus architecture, with a non-physical 'substance' legitimate enough to exist with total independence. We no longer abstract the natural reality to find its skeletal structure. Instead we recognize that abstract elements are real, however immaterial. Of course, it isn't that these ideations belong to the twentieth century alone, but now more than before we do not use them to confirm our understanding of the physical. They seemed before devised to solidify our perception of the physical world. Now they network, let's say, with the physical, with its own structure, independently of our *perception* of the physical world.

Perception, in this sense, not understood as consciousness but, as *Webster's* offers, 'a sensation interpreted in the light of experience.' And that physical sensation interpreted in the light of experience still, and complicated by the macro and micro offerings of science, is what we have that allows us to read art.

Recognizing the impact of science's offerings of the macro and micro scales seems imperative every time someone resorts, not knowing very well, to the refrain: 'gravity is not what it used to be.' Our comfort is in reading in Penrose that relativity's correction on the straightness of a Euclidean line a meter long is on the order of the diameter of an atom of hydrogen. That is, within our piece of the gravitational fields.

As we reexamine our understanding of gravity and of geometry, we can better pursue a legitimate understanding of the material structure of what we can perceive. And here our knowledge of structure owes much to the irresistible lessons of microstructures, somewhere between 'molecular structure,' as in molecular structure of steel or crystal lattices, and 'subdivision of space,' as in soap froth as the archetype of cellular systems. Geometry, in its new (mid-nineteenth century) branch as 'analysis situs' or topology, gives its organization and rigor to graphic and numerical aspects. Although its object has been hard to define, it is given by Courant as 'the study of the properties of geometrical figures that persist even when the figures are subjected to deformations so drastic that all their metric and projective properties are lost.' Topology has proven fundamental to the manipulation of planer and three dimensional form. Its Euler formulas are considered basic for problems of subdivision of space in two and three dimensions. The wonders of Euler's law made Cyril S. Smith, the author of that wonderful book *A Search for Structure,* say, 'Even more than Euclid, hath Euler gazed on beauty bare.'

Euler's law, (Figure 21) observed first by Descartes in the mid-seventeenth century and consolidated by Euler in 1752, was incorporated into topology as it developed in the middle of the nineteenth century, and has presided over most of the theories of reticulated structures ever since.

Perhaps more than anyone else working within the panorama of architecture this century, Robert LeRicolais, drawing on his formidable instincts, formulations, and much of these authors' revealing work (including Hibert's *Geometry and the Imagination*) did bridge the scale of micro structures to our own. In his course Experiments in Structures (at the University of Pennsylvania between 1957 and 1974), he produced an extraordinarily varied set of configurations that challenged the geometries and computational methods of the conventional repertoire of structural solutions used up to his day (Figure 22). He chose model building (he insisted that his students touch the models with their hands) while (as if following Euler) he worked on graph theory for computational control. And, of course, he used loading and strain gauges as the mechanisms to test the theoretical hypothesis of configuration. He used steel almost exclusively. The linearity resulting from its fabrication, as rolled, extruded, or in cable form, paralleled the linearity of configuration and analysis in spite of steel's isotropic character. That linearity meant mostly the manipulation of the directional axial stresses of compression and tension, with rare concerns about buckling and torque. Bending, of course, was decomposed into compression and tension for the obvious reason of conceptual clarity. Many of the geometries he seemed to prefer appeared to sort compression and tension into clearly distinguishable elements, such as a single large solid tube for compression, and cables for tension. (Conventional structural pieces carrying compression and tension are, more often that not, indistinguishable in ordinary trussing or space frames.) Yet, he would be mischievously excited studying the potential of 'prestressed' cables to find that they could *absorb* or *release* compression.

One aspect that was never brought to light (during my tenure as LeRicolais assistant) was the fact that the lattice structure of bone, often a paradigm of three dimensional structures, is not only a network of vectors, since the thickening of the 'struts' at every intersection does not form a hinge – this thickening implies the ability of these joints to take bending as well (Figure 23). A complex composite there. It was the same network of flexural nodes we referred to in Tor's multiple frame at Yale, except that those were on a rectangular network, while in bone they are on a roughly triangular one. They are, of course, the same flexural stresses that we find in any ordinary concrete beam of even section, which we calculate principally for maximum bending

top to bottom:
22 From LeRicolais' Experiments in Structures laboratory. Preliminary model, 158" long; 1/2" steel tube diaphragm rings, 6 – 12" diam., and 1/16" aircraft stainless steel cable tension network, under load (1962-63)
23 Photomicrograph of bone. LeRicolais started to think one should devise a mathematical model to count holes, instead of polygons, edges, and corners, as per Euler.
24 Robert LeRicolais at left, with students class of 1960, during the construction of the 15' diameter 'monkey saddle' at Penn.

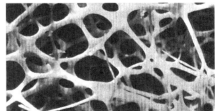

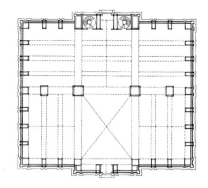

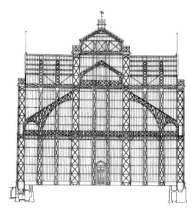

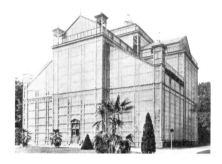

top to bottom:
25 Palm House, Park Herrenhousen, near Hanover (1879)
Plan and Section.
26 Palm House, Park Herrenhousen, near Hanover (1879)
1916 photograph.
27 Great Palm House, Botanical Garden,
Berlin-Dahlem (1907)

moment. And here is where, because that section has large portions of it in tension, concrete is disregarded, and one ends up talking about portions of dead weight. An aspect which is also intrinsically true of steel I beams – those much idolized icons of early believers in industry. But it would be too long here to expand on that. Let us simply state that bending in solid beams, frames, and cantilevers, seldom represents a very refined or very scientific structural display.

So, we have different stresses to be represented and we have subclasses of the same material (for steel, rolled steel, extruded metals, cables, etc.), all made harder to recognize by the fact that fabrication techniques avail the designer with a growing number of type options. It takes, for instance, a very trained eye to distinguish between the thirteen different kinds of steel in the Verazzano Narrows Bridge.

Perhaps because LeRicolais's structures were more structural elements than buildings, and he never built one (unless one counts a 15' span monkey saddle roof structure we built at the school, which later adorned a small courtyard of the campus for some time), (Figure 24), there were never ancillary building elements to obscure the structure itself. 'It' was 'it,' just as, in a different panorama of things, structure never was an issue of readability in the wonderful greenhouses of the nineteenth century, glass being what it is.

LeRicolais' aphorism 'zero weight, infinite span,' inspiring as it was and is, obscures the fact that structural systems must of necessity be closed or bound, and that weight or gravity in the realm of our Euclidean space is the reason for that. The notion of minimum weight is particularly significant because it points toward the ideal position of available material within the structural network for the demand of known loads. That is why *dead weight* can't but be seen as negative. That old statement of Nervi's that 'dead weight increases stability' rings false, or too coarse to offer a clarifying guideline. Excessive weight should be seen as a potential element to extend safety factors, or as material able to absorb improbable loads, or material to absorb decay (by fire, for instance) or weathering. The fact that any weight would get labeled dead was the reason why bending was always considered a stress equation to be minimized in LeRicolais' structures. He did, of course, go way beyond elementary equations, using pulleys to equalize tension in cable networks, or the pre-stressing and rotation of cables, to experiment with the 'travel' of stresses from areas of tension to areas of compression, within the same structural form.

left to right:
28 Great Subtropical House, Botanical Garden, Berlis-Dahlem (1909)
29 Great Subtropical House, Botanical Garden, Berlin-Dahlem (1909). Bracing detail

The fascination with nineteenth-century conservatories has to do with the fact that, unlike bridges or other emerging structures of what Corbusier called first 'the age of metal,' then 'the steel age,' and then 'the machine age' (writing around 1925), they were, first, transparent about telling (all)! and then clear about the inherent separation between structure and 'the rest' (what later we will call 'closure'), since there seemed to be no 'the rest' there, as another of the principle ingredients of tectonics. They also were the buildings which seemed to, very comforting that, avoid the querulous contention of architects and engineers being creators of different ilk. (Or equally as querulous if I said: the same ilk!).

The nationalistic French have made much about the fact that, although the nationalistic English with Paxton and others claim themselves pioneers of the emerging steel age, it was the French engineers/mathematicians Coulomb, Navier, Cauchy, Poisson, who laid out the basis for the establishment of statics early in the nineteenth century. Paxton to them was simply an empiricist, working by trial and error, doing greenhouses for the landed English. It is true that there isn't much structurally or mathematically innovative in the Crystal Palace (1851), or its immediate precedent the Great Conservatory at the Duke of Devonshire's estate (Bicton Palm House). We today admire it mostly as a devilishly remarkable precedent of prefabrication and assembly. It is the middle and second half of the nineteenth century that saw the basic criteria that were to spark the development of fabrication techniques for steel and steel structures later. Those greenhouses are a very satisfying display of building intuition, technique, economy, and craft. They knew much less than we do, and did much more.

Of the many conservatories throughout Europe, the Palm House in Park Herrenhausen, in Hanover (1879) (Figures 25 & 26), is a perfect example of a fully reticulated structure within the restraint of conventional orthogonal and planar geometry of walls, decks, and roofs. It was praised in its time for having resisted hurricane force winds (in October 1882) without causing any perceivable vibration,[5] a critical issue in many of the single curvature roofs. The Great Subtropical House at the Botanical Garden, Berlin-Dahlem (Figures 27, 28 & 29), shows a more refined resolution of the lateral stresses of racking, within the plane, due to wind pressure.

Other examples, such as the People's Palace, at Glasgow Green, or the Palm Houses at the Botanical Garden in St. Petersburg, or the Great Palm House at Schonbrunn, Vienna, show an audacity practically unparalleled for decades. They represent the introduction of single and double curvature roof structures barely behind the theoretical knowledge necessary at the time to make them feasible.

5 As noted by Georg Kohlmaier & B. von Sartory, *Houses of Glass*

30 Maison Jaoul, Neuilly-sur-Seine, Le Corbusier (1957)

31 Exeter Academy Library, Exeter, NH., Louis I. Kahn (1965–72). Exterior wrapper of the Tectonic Compact.

32 Indian Institute of Management, University of Gujarat, Ahmedabad, Louis I. Kahn (1962–74). Study Model. The arches' thrust makes the concrete restraints thinner.

It is easy, as I have done, to go from materiality to science to find the rigor that can make us believe we can choose good rules to control our urges to build. It is some of Perret's 'They [mathematics] form the character.' And tempting as it is, it does seduce us and makes us revert again to the expedient separation of 'structure,' where science reigns, and 'closure,' which is fully in the realm of art. The moderns with their invented theoretical space (not the physicists' as we've seen) nearly got it right. They almost avoided that separation...by denying gravity. Closure was chosen as if its parts and pieces could sustain themselves by the rigors of art. The mechanisms of holding and bearing and keeping themselves together intact didn't need to define what was left to be perceived. After planes of concrete cracked, and cambers flattened and sagged, steel rusted, plaster peeled off, and paint wasn't enough, 'building well' started to come back. Corbusier did it well, not with the Domino house, or its idea rather, but with the Jaoul and Sarabai houses. Kahn did it well because buildings had to, just like nature, 'show the way they were made.' What we like is that they did it as if with a 'compact' – few materials very well understood. *Webster's* defines compact as 'having parts or units closely packed or joined...being a metric space with the property that for any collection of open sets which contains it, there is a subset of the collection, with a finite number of elements which also contains it.' At the Jaoul and Sarabai houses, a barrel vault with ceramic tile (centering left to be seen) and simple walls do it (Figure 30). Kahn did it at Exeter, building with brick, things of brick scale, by the bricks' rules, wrapping around the large scale of concrete, built by the rules of concrete, with big heights, big spans, and big holes (Figure 31). In Ahmedabad (at the School of Management of the University of Gujarat) he built by the brick rules and when the arches of the openings were too big to avoid lateral thrusts, he brought in concrete so that the act of restraining the horizontal forces generated by the arches' thrust would prestress the concrete and make it thinner (Figure 32). They did not demonstrate structural behavior here and closure there. They built at once and with the enormous clarity that comes from the conception of what I here have thought to call 'tectonic compacts.'

'In-Visibility,' as in the title of this article might deserve some comment as a word. I did think that 'In-Visibility' put the theme where it belonged, that is internalizing the issue of visibility into that of tectonics, whether you see things or not. Tectonics, of course, is less than clearly defined anywhere, because of all that has been done to the word. We all vaguely think of the Greek origin in its etymology and satisfy ourselves with its generally accepted meaning of 'building well' (I like that) or 'art of construction.' *Funk & Wagnall* says for the adjective 'pertaining to building,' or 'relating to construction,' and reminds us that in Greek *tekton* means carpenter (and *tekhne* skill, of course). *Webster's* (Ninth New Collegiate) doesn't even have the term other than as a branch of geology concerned with structure, especially with folding and faulting. Maybe the word doesn't belong to us, after all.

Speculating on tectonics has kept people busy, as if 'disassembling' the full scope of our art should let us gain in clarity...as if subsets of meaning will keep us clear of ambiguities. This all made more complex on account of the so-called *expressive intent* (empathy, to some), which was being forcibly injected into *tectonics* in its relatively young life – I have covered only very partial aspects on a sort of epistemological track to understand its substance. Much more of this has to be done. The variations of that ambitious theme of *expressive intent* have occupied many theoreticians, historians, and architects since Semper and Boetticher in the middle of the nineteenth century. In one of the last issues of one of the most respected European architectural magazines, I recently read an article, not very long, in which the author, trying to pursue that evasive(?) exactitude, cites more than forty authors, from the middle of the nineteenth century until today, on the subject. I found myself reflecting on: What if tectonics had in its meaning the *full* latitude of 'expressive intent'? What then...would *architecture* be?

COLLABORATION

Guy Nordenson

GUY NORDENSON SPOKE WITH THE EDITORS ON SEVERAL OCCASIONS ABOUT THE CHANGING ROLE OF STRUCTURAL ENGINEERING IN ARCHITECTURAL DESIGN. WHAT FOLLOWS IS A SYNTHESIS OF HIS RESPONSES TO SEVERAL QUESTIONS ABOUT HOW ENGINEERS WORK AND THINK.

NORDENSON: It is sometimes useful to think of a structural engineer's practice as that of either technician, artist, or collaborator. Obviously these usually blend into a hybrid, but differences do exist.

The technicians solve the problem given by the architect. Sometimes that means the structure has a particular tectonic "look" about it as conceived by the architect. At other times it will mean that the structure disappears behind the scenes. I remember one engineer friend telling me he saw his task as making an exposed structural detail work as the architect imagined it did, executing a specific mechanical script. Often the result is a great project. But, in all these cases, if uncovered, the facts will show that the script was driven by an architectural idea, not necessity nor engineering.

The artists, like Maillart, Nervi, Candela, and Calatrava develop a distinct style out of the materials and methods of structure. Usually the form incorporates certain inventions: the deck-stiffened arch, ferrocement, the hyperbolic parabaloid shell. You might even say that the work is in some cases classical, or romantic, or even mannerist or baroque. The practice is clearly that of an artist working in the medium of structure.

The collaborators work as part of design, and sometimes construction teams, usually on-going. One thinks of groupings: August Kommendant and Louis Kahn, Paul Weidlinger and Marcel Breuer or Gordon Bunshaft, Fred Severud and Eero Saarinen, Peter Rice and Renzo Piano (and Tom Barker, the services engineer), Leslie Robertson and I.M. Pei. The collaborations evolve and deepen over a series of projects. The contributions are not always distinct or identifiable. Usually the only way to discern the engineer's contribution is by looking at the architect's work with or without them.

The hand of the collaborator engineer is elusive, but recognizable when projects are studied over time. It is manifested in a sensibility instead of a style. If two of Bunshaft's projects using Vierendeel trusses are compared, one with Weidlinger's involvement and one without, it is much easier to see the engineer's influence. In the Weidlinger projects, such as Beinecke Rare Book Library, the delicate connections between moment-resisting intersections are articulated with a precision that reflects the participation of someone who knows what is possible; they are pushed beyond the conventional.

Where there is no such evidence the conclusion would be that you are looking at more of a technician's practice. In fact, maybe the best way to think of these categories – technician, artist, collaborator – is as all interconnected in a circle, so that Rice is more artist/collaborator while Fazlur Kahn is maybe more collaborator/technician, and so on.

EDITORS: In describing how he and his colleagues* worked with Steven Holl on recent projects, Nordenson elaborates on the working method of the collaborators, emphasizing how fluid the structural design process is and how it can be woven into the architect's earliest conceptions. He lays out the process of embedding structure in architecture. His thinking reflects this conceptual experience and, in turn, embeds structural thought in an intellectual culture.

NORDENSON: In Steven Holl's work, the structure comes and goes in the space like an actor on the stage.

*Ove Arup & Partners were engineers for both Kiasma and Cranbrook, with Guy Nordenson as principal in charge and Mahadev Raman in charge of building services engineering. Guy Nordenson and Associates are the structural engineers for CALA and MIT, collaborating with Ellerbe Beckett and Simpson, Gumperz and Heger, respectively.

top left: KIASMA construction
above: KIASMA curved wall – view from the north

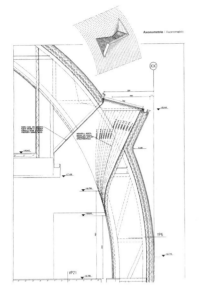

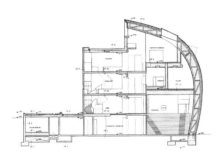

HELSINKI MUSEUM OF CONTEMPORARY ART: KIASMA

The large scale forms in the Helsinki Museum express Holl's idea of intertwining. A linear block intertwines with a curved shape. The torus geometry of the curve lent itself to a structural system comprised of trusses formed to the C-shaped section and spread along the curve every ten feet or so to delineate the shape of the building. The trusses rise from the ground and arch over to tall columns set inside the glass wall. The cavity in between trusses harbors the mechanical and electrical systems that feed the building.

Helsinki marked a new development in our collaboration with Holl's office. The formal moves – thick wall and glass wall – were tangled up with the technological requirements of the building from the very start of the design competition. The structure and mechanical and electrical systems are all closely integrated and become occupants of the form– there is an added meaning to this form, the curved wall, when you begin to understand that it has a significant, dramatic thickness, and that the thickness is occupied by supporting systems because the wall is designated as a chase. The thickness becomes part of the character of the space.

When Mies was given his architectural licensing exam in Chicago, he was asked what he thought about technology. He drew two lines on the blackboard. He pointed to the top line and said, 'this is the slab,' then pointed to the bottom line and said, 'this is the ceiling.' Pointing to the space in between he said, 'this is technology.' This zone, whether it is beneath the slab or above it in a raised floor, is the stuff of technology.

At Helsinki we turned that stuff in the middle, the poché, into an actor in the design. The thickness of the curved wall implies technology on some level, but it's not technological exhibitionism. Observers do not immediately become aware or may never become aware of the technological contents of the wall, except by inference. The cuts for skylights reveal the wall's thickness, and it is up to the viewer to sense that the building is supported by the wall – both structurally and mechanically.

top left : KIASMA section through light well
bottom left: KIASMA building section
right: KIASMA third floor gallery with light well

CRANBROOK INSTITUTE OF SCIENCE ADDITION

Again we were interested in housing mechanical and electrical systems in structural elements. The thick wall adjacent to the stairs contains these systems. The pre-cast planks, which support the floor of this gallery space are fabricated with hollows, to reduce dead load. We took advantage of these hollows and used them as ducts.

Within the thick central wall, flexiduct carries air from main runs to open ends of the pre-cast planks, where it is then forced into the voids and fed out into the space through openings in the underside of the planks. This had never been done before. We took this piece of structure – this ready-made, precast, hollow core plank – and ventilated it. It is in the tradition of hollowing out structure so it can act as a plenum, except the structure itself was not designed to perform that function, but was adapted to do so.

The building structure at Cranbrook is organized around a notion of base and super structure. There is concrete structure up to a certain datum, and above that is steel – in the form of trusses, two of which bridge between the two concrete ground forms. The exterior does not reflect this structural system (the masonry runs uninterrupted between the two levels) but instead reflects the circulation system – changes in material and texture show where interior ramps are. And inside the building, the idea of a steel frame popping out above masonry is expressed only locally in glimpses of the structure, a series of vignettes.

The glimpse of structure is part of the collaborator's repertoire – it is a rhetorical device, a synechdoche. At Beaubourg, you can walk right up to Peter Rice's enormous gerberette and inspect a piece of it. At Cranbrook we have a portion of a truss sitting quietly in the corner of a gallery. The idea is that in getting quite close to a piece of structure and trying to figure out why it's shaped the way it is, one enters into a local relationship with the piece instead of reading a

top: top floor KIASMA gallery construction
above right: KIASMA top floor gallery completed
at left: CRANBROOK view of entry

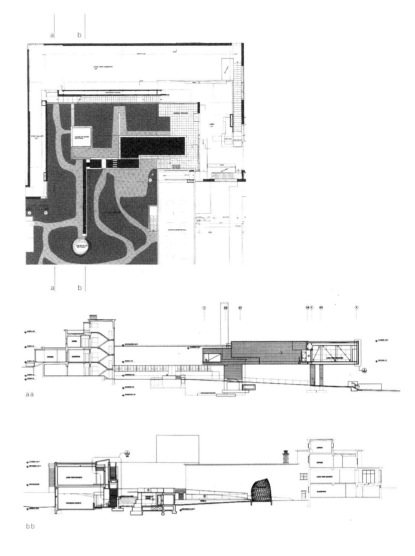

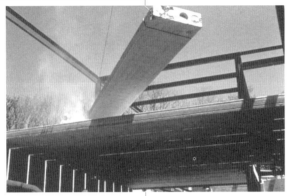

clockwise from top:

CRANBROOK – construction of stair supported by steel columns

CRANBROOK – upper level plan and sections

CRANBROOK – steel superstructure bridge

CRANBROOK – flexi-duct feeds into hollow cores

CRANBROOK – construction of steel structure atop concrete base

CRANBROOK – placement of pre-cast hollow core plank

41

diagram of the whole system. In a diagram building, with say, a giant truss like on the Hancock Building, one can see and understand the structure immediately from a distance. At Cranbrook there really is no evidence of technology at a distance. But at a smaller scale you get glimpses that add up to a knowledge of the systems figured out over time.

Since this is a place for science, the structure takes something of an archaeological character – you're shown a few bones of the dinosaur, and it's up to you to figure out the rest of the skeleton. The use of structure does not have to be blatant; it is not necessary to broadcast all of the components of the building at once. Much of the structure is hidden from view, or discovered by spending time in the building. Its organization – the concrete base and steel superstructure above, a full height truss that becomes the bridge – is very straightforward. Independently the structural vignettes have an order and clarity of organization, so that when observers want to understand what is going on through the evidence given, the exposed pieces, it is possible to assemble the system in their minds. Sometimes it's buried, sometimes it pops out, and where those things happen is chosen entirely by Holl's architectural aims in relation to one's movement through the building.

There is a tension between the episodic (slightly fetishistic) presentation of structure and the fact that it's not just a display of structure, it *is* the structure. This ambivalence is inherent in using the language of exhibits with structure, particularly when the glimpses occur in gallery space.

EDITORS: So you did not necessarily design a pure engineering structure to resist force, which would be selectively revealed by Steven Holl. You pay attention to where and how it is revealed and detail accordingly.

NORDENSON: There is no such thing as pure. There is only organized or disorganized. You either have an overall strategy for the structure, or you have to solve problems locally and independently. Most engineers have a strategy.

What you do is weave a collection of ideas together that work off each other, starting with form, then the organization of the structure, and then the resulting implications for structural expression. One of the examples of structure participating in circulation ideas at Cranbrook is the shearing column that occurs at the pivot point of the plan. It is not just a column, but an element of a larger truss running above. The column drops down to participate in circulation. This was Holl's expression of the circulation in the structure.

(clockwise from top)
CRANBROOK – exterior expression of interior stair
CRANBROOK – exposed truss in gallery
CRANBROOK – elevated galleries

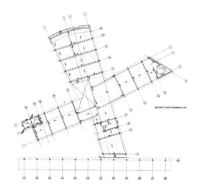

COLLEGE OF ARCHITECTURE AND LANDSCAPE ARCHITECTURE, CALA UNIVERSITY OF MINNESOTA
The idea of structure harboring technology that was developed in Cranbrook found its way into Minnesota. Again, there was an architectural idea of removing the clutter of systems from underneath the slab and placing it in a thickened wall. A good deal of effort was required here to design the concrete frame in a way that cleared a path for these mechanical, electrical, and plumbing systems. A series of independent frames marches along the two axes, braced by pre-cast concrete planks spanning between them. During construction, before the planks are in place, the frames will look like soldiers. In the finished building, no beams will connect the frames. The voids where perimeter beams would normally be allow for a clear reading of the zone of wall in between frames. Again, the airflow happens in the walls instead of in the floors.

MASSACHUSETTS INSTITUTE OF TECHNOLOGY
EDITORS: When do you begin to draw structural models that work with architectural ideas? When do the back-and-forth conversations become real structural schemes?

NORDENSON: The schemes as well as the ideas can happen very early on. At MIT, Holl is developing concepts for a dormitory, and we have been drawing the structure that goes with them. In one, the 'Folded Street,' the architectural idea of having public and private spaces ramp up around the core of the building clearly depends on a clean structural solution. Rooms are in blocks on both sides of building. Each room faces the exterior and on the other side opens up to the double height public space between the core elements. Both dorm rooms and public space wrap around cores and ascend. Our structure is a series of trusses cantilevered off the core, which allows for column-free space in the circulation areas.

In the second dorm project, the 'Sponge,' my colleague Christopher Diamond invented a new precast concrete 'perfcon' of which the exterior walls were made.

top left: CALA framing plan and section
top right: CALA study model

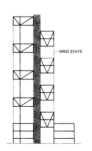

WIND STAYS

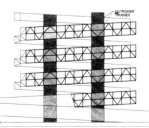

OUTRIGGER TRUSSES

top left: MIT sponge computer model
left: MIT folded street computer model
above: MIT folded street framing sections

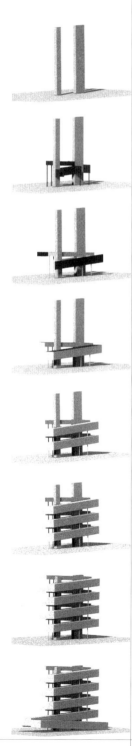

above: MIT folded street truss
erection sequence

EDITORS: You have described structure as being narrative, didactic, and rhetorical. What are the differences between these three treatments of structure?

NORDENSON: If you allow that there is a language of structure, architecture and technology, and assume it's a language that people are somewhat familiar with, it is possible to 'write' in that language in ways that are clear, elusive, or allusive. You could develop a rhetoric of structure.

The language that is employed in narrative structure – the conventions of trusses, arches, bridges, hi-tech– are used to tell a clear story. At Cranbrook the trusses were detailed in such a way that it was familiar enough that a part could speak for the whole.

Didactic structures give as direct an account of what's going on as possible, like those of Fazlur Kahn, or of Maillart. The goal is to be clear, straightforward, and complete – to show the whole of what's going on structurally.

Holl's work is more rhetorical. There is a hide-and-seek where a revealed part represents the concealed whole. It is similar with Mies. The exterior of Crown Hall tells a structural story that is incomplete, but clear – the series of frames is visible, but how they are stabilized across the grain remains hidden. Once inside that story is taken away – there is no way to tell what is column or mullion.

EDITORS: Can structure be subverted?

NORDENSON: Structure can be manipulated to express 'weightlessness' – not just by suspending it and making the supports invisible like a magic trick, but by manipulating structure so that the scale of the things still visible gives the appearance of weightlessness. Because observers can move around in buildings, it is possible to orchestrate these kinds of experiences. Looking at Crown Hall from a distance, one can perceive that roof trusses are being supported by columns. On the interior everything is de-materialized – you only see the ceiling plane. At Peter Rice's and RFR's La Villette project in Paris, the main stability for the structure is hidden from sight: a large concrete pillar sheathed in mirror finished metal. Some things are given, others hidden.

The critical analysis of structures, and their rhetoric, is impossible without a study of construction drawings and photographs, especially in collaborative work, for example Kahn's with Kommendant. There are always drawings; ultimately things get worked out, or they wouldn't stand up. Defiance of gravity is purely rhetorical. The challenge is in how to relate the reality, the deep structure of the construction documents, to the surface structure that is visible in the architecture, and how to work that language.

on TOWARD TECHNOLOGICAL ARCHITECTURE?
Edward R. Ford

Of the Mies buildings at IIT that are steel, built and unbuilt, there are three types, types that employ different, even opposite, methods of structural expression: 1) Utilitarian buildings, such as the boiler plant, one-story steel structures in which the method is literal – the steel is exposed. 2) Academic buildings – classroom and labs – that are two to three stories, steel-framed, and encased in layers of concrete, secondary steel framing, and brick. Here the method is symbolic- the visible steel is structurally representational, not unfunctional, but not structural in the true sense. 3) Institutional buildings – the Library and Student Union (both unbuilt) – that are long-span, one-story structures in which the method is also literal; the steel is exposed.

There are three explanations for this. The first, emphasized by Beeby, is that they reflect the development of Mies's architectural ideas. The second is that they are a reflection the building code – the multistory academic buildings required fireproofing; the frames of the one-story lab and library buildings could be exposed. The third, and the most convincing, is that they are typological, that these differences were designed to reflect each building's relative importance. This is an argument supported by the typological character of the non-steel buildings – the concrete framed-dormitories and load-bearing brick chapel.

Mies said that he wanted the Library and Student Union to be more 'monumental' and gave them longer spans and larger glazing sizes – requiring deeper mullions and thicker masonry walls. Unlike the square-bayed academic buildings they were framed with long and short bays on their front and sides respectively, giving each façade a different character. The difference in the corner details that Beeby points out is perhaps developmental, but it is also a reflection of the differences in the two building types.

The small Commons building of 1956 shares many characteristics with its predecessor, the 1946 Student Union. It is a one-story exposed frame symmetrical about its entry axis and has the same 'grain' of long and short bays. Thus while it is a design that looks forward to Crown Hall, with which it shares these characteristics, it looks as much backward to its predecessor.

While these buildings deserve preservation, it is with the understanding that they are poor models for literal imitation. The walls have no insulation, no waterproofing cavity, abound in thermal bridges, and use single-glazed, high-maintenance, steel-framed windows. The solid masonry wall required a header exposed inside and out, and Joseph Fujikawa recalls that in at least one building this could not be achieved without sacrificing a smooth surface on both sides due to variations in the lengths of the bricks. The headers were broken in half, smoothing out the wall but eliminating the function of the header in the process. It is true that many of IIT's shortcomings were common practices when built, but it is also true that Saarinen's GM Technical Center, built at the same time and often dismissed as derivative of IIT, contains none of these deficiencies.

1 quoted in, Fritz Neumeyer, *The Artless Word: Mies van der Rohe on the Building Art* (Cambridge, Mass.: MIT, 1991), pp.261, 270.
2 Joseph Fujikawa and Edward Duckett, *Impressions of Mies* (Knoxville: University of Tennessee), p. 8.

Edward R. Ford is a professor at the University of Virginia School of Architecture. He is the author of *The Details of Modern Architecture: Volumes 1 and 2.*

on COLLABORATION
William J. Mitchell

Guy Nordenson remarks that you could develop a 'rhetoric of structure.' I agree, and I'd add that cunningly constructed ambiguity— which opens up a space for multi-layered, cross-connected readings— is a particularly fundamental and effective rhetorical device. It's one of the things that distinguishes poetry from flat-footed declarative prose.

Take Steven Holl's 'sponge' dormitory project for MIT, for example. You might read the precast concrete exterior as a wall penetrated by a grid of punched openings, as in Aalto's nearby Baker Dormitory. Maybe (you can speculate) it functions as a stiff plate, thus allowing the conspicuous cantilevers in the plane of the exterior skin.

The ratio of solid to void subverts that reading, though, and suggests that you might think of it as a column and beam structure instead – more like some of the utilitarian industrial structures in the neighborhood. But why, then, do the verticals and horizontals have the same dimensions? And how do the cantilevers work if it's constructed that way?

Maybe it's not load-bearing at all, but a curtain wall hung from the floors? Then again, the frames of the square openings seem a bit too heavy to support that reading. In any case, where are the floors? Since the openings are uniform, perfect squares, and the floor lines are not expressed, it's almost impossible to tell. Maybe it's even in fill, a scaled-up version of the square glass blocks on the Necco factory up the road. No wonder the designers coined a neologism – 'perfcon'— to describe this baffling and provocative element!

It would be trivial to make some small adjustments which resolved its ambiguities — and that's precisely, of course, what most modernists would reflexively do. Create more solid and less void and you clearly have a wall with punched openings. Make the voids larger, while articulating the difference between columns and beams, and you end up with a pretty conventional trabeation. Lighten the structure, express the floors, and you're in curtain wall territory. But these are just the sorts of moves that Steven Holl and his structural collaborators have refused; they are playing a different game here.

It seems to me that this interplay of ambiguities offers a particularly compelling resolution to the problem of relating to an urban context that's a complex, diverse patchwork, and in the process of rapid transition. The limply historicist strategy of making new buildings look as much like their older neighbors as possible — much favored, unfortunately, by planning Pooh-Bahs in places such as Cambridge, Massachusetts — just doesn't work. There's no consistency to maintain. A strategy that picks up cues from the surroundings but internalizes multiplicity and contradiction, and sets up slippages and tensions that resist facile readings, has much more to offer.

William J. Mitchell is Dean of the MIT School of Architecture and Planning. He is the author of *City of Bits: Space, Place and the Infobahn,* and his most recent book is *E-topia: Urban Life, Jim – But Not As We Know It.*

IN RESPONSE

on THE IN-VISIBILITY OF TECTONICS
Ignasi de Solà-Morales i Rubió

It is stimulating that Carles Vallhonrat, with his long experience as an architect, as a professor at Princeton, and as a close collaborator with Louis Kahn at an important period in Kahn's life, presents the problem of tectonics from the perspectives of this experience.

His characteristic modesty and sensitivity bring him to use the term 'tectonic' with caution, relating it to the visible and the invisible.

Evidently, the manifestation and the intelligibility of the weight-bearing structure of a building is a typically modern way of making visible the invisible technical and weight-bearing complexity of an architecture.

When Vallhonrat refers to that laboratory of careful investigation, with Le Ricolais and Kahn reconsidering what were much more than a few technical problems of support, he is indicating a necessary direction. 'Tectonic' describes, it seems, the visible, and therefore synthetic, hierarchized manifestation of a central question of architecture: the Vitruvian *firmitas*; durability; the ingenuity to make support possible; defying force, gravity, and changes of climate.

There are, in my judgement, other possible architectures, other ways to narrate a building, beginning with other priorities – form, place, use, message.

If auto-referentiality is always a sure way for artistic narration, we also know in architecture how few referents, such as those of logic, reasons, decisions of stability in space and time, a building has at its disposal.

It is from this conviction that structure and its visibility put the architectonic appearance at the limit of visualizing simply the complexity of the invisible.

Ignasi de Solà-Morales i Rubió is a professor in the Department of Architectural Theory and History at the Architectural School of Barcelona. His article, 'The Origins of Modern Eclecticism: Theories of Architecture in Early nineteenth century France' was published in *Perspecta 23* and he has published several books on architectural history and criticism.

N PERSPECTIVE
ONCEPTUAL VS. ACTUAL STRUCTURE

IN ORDER TO LOOK LIKE A CONCEPTUAL STRUCTURE, A LOAD BEARING STRUCTURE MUST BRAZENLY DENY THE FACT OF ITS BURDEN

Robin Evans

Excerpt from *Mies van der Rohe's Paradoxical Symmetries*

Symmetry came and went in Mies's work, so it could be argued that neither symmetry nor asymmetry is central to an understanding of his development. His lifelong concern was with the logic of structure and its expression. Were we to look in this direction, we might find fewer paradoxes, and all those adjectives like universal, clear, rational, etc., might more easily fall into place.

Mies later recalled that he first realized the wall could be freed of the burden of the roof while designing the Barcelona Pavilion. The function of the column was to support the building; that of the wall was to divide space. Logic at last, of a sort.[1] The plan shows this clearly: eight columns, symmetrically arranged in two rows, support the roof slab, while the asymmetrically disposed walls slide away from the columns, away from each other, and out of alignment with the orthogonal matrix. A principle turns into a fact.

Well, this is not *actually* true, nor is it *apparently* true, except in the plan. Pass over the decided lack of candor in the construction, with its brick vaults beneath the podium and its armature of steel concealed in the roof slab and the marble walls – walls which give a tell-tale hollow ring when tapped. Ignore this, because, whenever such an observation is made about any of Mies's buildings, it always elicits the same response: Mies was not just interested in the truth of construction, he was interested in *expressing* the truth of construction. The most celebrated examples of this twice-stated truth are for the most part the later American buildings: the Lake Shore Drive apartments, Crown Hall, and so on. Should we say, then, that the Barcelona Pavilion was an early but none too successful attempt to get these two versions of structural truth to accord with each other, so that the building would express this newly discovered principle? I think not, for two reasons: first, because the principle is expressed very badly in the pavilion and, secondly, because the pavilion is so refined and so beautiful. . .

There are two reasons why we may think the Barcelona Pavilion is a rational structure: Mies said it was, and it looks as if it is. It looks rational because we know what rationality looks like: precise, flat, regular, abstract, bright, above all, rectilinear. This image of rationality is unreliable, however. The Guell Chapel has none of these attributes, yet it is consistent and logical in structure and construction. The entire chapel was to have been scaled up from a inverted funicular model made of wires draped with paper and fabric. Gaudí spent ten years, from 1898

to 1908, developing this model, which hung from the ceiling of a workshop. Each of the funicular wires represented an arch. As they intersected, these arches changed shape. The model grew into an elaborate, distended web of tensile force vectors, each modified by all the others. Gaudí tinkered with it until the whole thing was tantamount to a continuous surface. The model was wholly in tension. Turned upside down, it would produce a structure wholly in compression, thus avoiding persistent tension, against which masonry has little resistance.[2] This is a rational structure. By contrast, the structure and construction of the Barcelona Pavilion is piecemeal and inchoate.

We believe that Mies's buildings exhibit a sublime rationality because so many people have reported seeing it there. These sightings are only rumours. The whole matter resides in recognition. I recognize plant life when I see it, and I recognize rationality in architecture when I see it, because I begin to understand, after much practice, what the word is applied to. I am then tempted to think that all things bearing the same name, whether or not they are architecture, must share an essential property, but this is not necessary, nor, in this instance, is it likely. We may choose to believe that squarish, simple things are tokens of rationality in some wider sense, and that curvaceous, complicated things are tokens of irrationality, but our highly developed powers of visual recognition are exercising no more than a prejudice when we go out hunting for items to pin these terms onto. Yet, while prejudices may be without foundation, they are not without consequence. The belief that we can identify rational structure by these vital signs has rendered us insensitive to the two incomparable ideas of structure, both of which we think we see. Within the word structure is a latent oxymoron. In Mies's architecture this trivial confusion of thought is turned into an incredible apparition. The structure of a sentence is not the same sort of thing as the structure of a building. I have been treating the Barcelona Pavillion structure as a means of holding its own weight off the ground. This kind of structure is about gravitation, mass, and the transmission of loads through solids; it is concerned with concrete, physical things, even though our understanding of it is achieved by means of abstractions such as vectors and numbers. The other kind of structure is also present. We refer to the pavilion's gridded structure or its orthogonal structure, and yet these structures have nothing to do with material or weight. They refer to organizing formats which may be imposed upon, or discovered in, material objects, but which remain conceptual, like the structure of a sentence.

'The language of architects is notorious for its imprecision, pretentiousness, and addiction to cliché' admits Peter Gay, in a last ditch attempt to gain us some sympathy.[3] Architectural critics are just as guilty. I have some-

times wondered whether these failings conceal some advantages. 'Great things are never easy,' mutters the oracular Mies, quoting Spinoza.[4] Take the two distinct ideas in the word structure, and then make a building in which they appear to blend together as effortlessly as they do on the page. That is a way of taking advantage. It is not easy. Is it great?...

Since the mechanical structure of a building is nothing but a response to gravity, any architectural expression of mechanical structure would surely declare the transmission of load, not conceal it. Yet conceal it Mies does - always and in all ways. How, then, have his buildings maintained their reputation as expressions of structural truth and structural rationality? We need only return to the double meaning to find this out: as the buildings suppress all association with the stresses and strains of load-bearing structure, they begin to look more like conceptual structures. Conceptual structures are notable for their independence from material contingency. Think of a mathematical grid: it is not subject to gravity. Any substance, even the most adamantine, changes shape when a force passes through it. A mathematical grid, on the other hand, cannot change shape in any circumstances. The two kinds of structure could never be exactly identical. In order to look like a conceptual structure, a load-bearing structure must brazenly deny the fact of its burden. 'To me,' said Mies, 'structure is something like logic'[5]: a flaccidly ambiguous statement from a man whose buildings are taut with the same ambiguity.

If Mies adhered to any logic, it was the logic of appearance. His buildings aim at effect. Effect is paramount. In the period between its being dismantled and its resurrection, the Barcelona Pavilion was renowned for the transcendent logic of its determining grid.

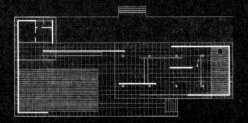

1 It is difficult to understand why this realization of 1929 should so often be cited, as if Mies had achieved some completely new insight. The principle had been announced some years earlier by Le Corbusier.

2 Isidre Puig Boada, *L'Esglesia de la Colonia Guell* (Editorial Lumen, 1976)

3 Peter Gay, *Weimar Culture* (New York, 1970) p. 101

4 Acceptance speech on receiving the AIA Gold Medal, 1960. See Peter Serenyi, abstract, JSAH, Vol. 30, no. 3 (October 1971) p. 240

4 Peter Blake, 'A Conversation with Mies,' *Four Great Makers*, p. 93.

IF MIES ADHERED TO ANY LOGIC, IT WAS THE LOGIC OF APPEARANCE

Basement, Seagram Building, New York City, Ludwig Mies van der Rohe
and Philip Johnson (1956–58)
(previous page) Entrance façade of Seagram Building

Lucie Fontein

READING STRUCTURE THROUGH THE FRAME

If we set out to read a building or structure, we could mean simply that we intend to have a closer look at the object, collect the numerous facts and weave an interpretation or explanation around them. Is this all it means to read an object, or can our reading go further than that? If an actor reads a part well, he or she not only delivers the lines with a particular interpretation, but also reads or speaks in a way that both reveals and creates a living character. To read a building as thoroughly would similarly require the reader to discern, to reveal, and perhaps even to recreate it.

In the case of architecture, we are all potential readers if we elect to exercise that role. Often, when we do choose to read a building, we reflect upon its layout, its symbolic expression, possibly upon the play of light, occasionally about the materiality. Our appreciation of the structure tends to be limited to the visual effects. Only in a clear tour de force of structural invention do we pay attention to the system of transferring forces. In most cases, the structural frame is taken for granted, a mere necessity.

We have also grown accustomed to seeing these two words, 'structure' and 'frame,' side by side, to the point where they are often used interchangeably. I would like to step back and consider the inflections of these terms more carefully. It is no accident that structure and frame are increasingly being considered synonymous. What kind of role does the idea of frame play in the interpretation of a building's structure? By reading structure 'through the frame,' one discovers how these terms differ and how they coincide, and how this pairing of ideas shapes our view of architectural structure.

In using the word 'through' in the phrase 'through the frame,' I intend a multi-dimensional interpretation: the sense of going through or beyond; the sense of being in the midst of; as well as its use in the sense of, by way of, or by agency of. All three meanings resonate here simultaneously.

Structure comes from the Latin 'struere,' which means to arrange, pile up or build, to set in order.[1] As Vico eloquently lays out for us in his master work, *The New Science*, we build upon the things that we already know and we know the things that we ourselves have made. 'The first people created things according to their own ideas...by virtue of a wholly corporeal imagination...for which they were called poets which is Greek for Creators.'[2] To build a structure is in its essence a creative act of interpretation. We put things together, and through the juxtaposition or arrangement of the constituent parts, we determine the particular nature of character of the whole.

In turn, we are able to read within the structure all the knowledge, dreams, and imaginations of the people who made them. In its ancient sense, all technological activity involved revealing, a bringing forth of things into appearance, the potential to liberate the manifold natures of things.[3]

Does technology still function in this revelatory capacity? Has the meaning of the word technology changed? Has the meaning of the word structure changed?

More often than not, we speak of a structural 'system' or 'framework.'

Frame, like structure, also means to fashion, construct, or make, but comes with the added connotation from the Anglo-Saxon 'framian' and from the word 'fram' (from), meaning to make progress, hence to prosper; to contrive; to manage; to determine or regulate the course of.[4]

Framing has the sense ordering but by means of enclosure, of removal from the context, of getting rid of extraneous material. The idea of economy and profit has been introduced.

Economy is achieved by means of repetition and pattern. Thus, we speak of a structural framework or grid, the delineation in three dimensions of 'neutral' space, which stands ready to be finished to suit a particular program. The grid is a skeleton waiting to be fleshed out. It is about hierarchy, the permanent frame is something upon which more mutable things are hung. This contrasts with the idea of arranging material in an additive way, building from the ground up, as the original idea of structure suggests.

Enframing (*Ge-stell*) is the word Heidegger uses to distinguish modern technology from the original sense of technology. Heidegger claims that the original sense of technology as the bringing forth of things into appearance has been subsumed by a single-minded type of revealing which he identifies with the modern instrumental way of thinking.[5] The things of the world are no longer 'brought forth' but rather they are 'brought about.' There is an emphasis on the issue of cause and effect which excludes other forms of revealing. The essence of modern technology resides in the fact that the things of the world are now ordered exclusively according to their ability to store energy (energy being the universal currency); they have been 'enframed.'[6]

I find myself in a building for lease, one very similar to a vacant parking garage. My horizon is trapped between two slabs of concrete held apart by row upon row of slender round columns which seem to be dispersed chaotically, until the vector of my movement through the space brings them into line. Order is never more than a few steps away. Occasionally, a hollow concrete shaft penetrates the space. These rectangular shafts keep the structure from shearing sideways and collapsing upon itself. Through the shafts, I am able to exit…

to another, identical floor.

The real estate agent points out the columns which will define the office space that I will be leasing. At $25 a square foot it's a bargain.

Is that gross or net area; does the square footage include the thickness of the curtain wall that encloses the building structure? It does, but the agent points out that one gains space vertically, since the flat planes of floor and ceiling are two way slabs, thickened to avoid beams. All the space can be used, right up to the slab's underside.

This is what my office area amounts to. I am leasing space, square footage, an enframed area defined by a structural grid.

I mention to the agent that it all looks rather bleak and anonymous. She tells me that I won't recognize it once the interior designers have done their parts. The structure will disappear. All this concrete will be covered over with drywall. I can have any style of decor I want.

How many such square feet are there in the world?

Enough to make us think of the rest of the world in similar terms.

How many blocks of urban slum to be redeveloped?

How many acres of suburban subdivisions to be carved out of agricultural land?

How many acres of tropical rainforest to be exploited?

How many barrels of oil to be found under the ocean floor?

How many gallons of water to be trapped for hydro-electric power?

Heidegger uses the following example to illustrate his point: the difference between modern technology and the original sense of technology is like the difference between a hydro-electric dam built into a river and a windmill built in a field. Both produce energy but the first traps the water and stores it as potential energy to be released when needed. In the case of the windmill, the power intrinsic to the wind is released as soon as it is captured in the rotation of the vanes and is converted directly to mechanical energy in the grinding of the grain. If the wind stops, the milling stops. The windmill does not unlock energy from the air currents in order to store it. The power of the wind has been revealed, yet it has not become the servant of technology as has the power of the water in the case of the dam.

In our enframed world, the danger is not only that everything revealed through the use of technology will be interpreted in terms of stored energy or profit, but in the face of such imperatives, it is possible that the concept of 'revealing as bringing forth' itself may be blocked or forgotten entirely.[7]

There is no doubt that the vast majority of decisions related to construction are made on the basis of cost. This is particularly true of the speculative project which by its very definition is being built to sell at a profit. Speculation implies an element of risk taking; as with any investment the challenge is to predict the market and turn that insight into a profit. The site is therefore chosen for its current land value in relation to its potential land value. Land is often bought and 'stored' until an appropriate moment when its stored energy, its dollar value, is released at a premium.

Decisions about construction materials and systems are made based on strategies regarding first cost versus life cycle costs. What is the value of the material now, and what will it be in the future? Will the building be difficult to dispose of or replace when it is no longer viable? In other words, what kind of energy does the material have stored in it?

This is the world that we have constructed. Vico suggests that there are aspects to our lives that are eternal (circular), and aspects that are historical (linear). The condition we face today is that the historical vector of technology, embodied in the idea of progress, has eclipsed those dimensions that provide critical balance. **We are caught in a tradition of progress (commonly known as the Western metaphysical tradition) yet we no longer have a larger view of where that vector is going.** It seems to have taken on a life of its own to the point where humans are also in the process of becoming enframed, stored energy to be released when needed.[8]

To deny this agenda would be to opt out of modern culture and dismiss the historical facts that have brought us to this point. Any decisions that I make about the space that I lease will inevitably have to take economic factors into account . The challenge is to remember that this is not the only way to interpret the world. I can choose to view these few square feet simply as an investment, or I can read into them other meanings. Depending on the extremity of the case, the extent to which it has been 'enframed,' I may have to resort to subversive or ironic tactics when it comes to adapting it for my own use. In whatever way I choose to inhabit the space, it is important to clearly demonstrate my intention with respect to the structural frame, one which acknowledges the role that it plays in my perception of space in general, and might allow me to think of this particular space differently. Imagining the possibility of other worlds is essential.

This is not a hopeless situation however. Heidegger makes a clear distinction between fate and what he calls 'destining.' He speaks of the open space of destining implying a freedom that derives from our ability to listen and hear, and not simply obey. **We need not push on blindly with technology, nor simply rebel helplessly against it.** We can, if we choose, imagine other worlds to coexist with the one we have created.

'It is precisely in this extreme danger that the innermost indestructible belongingness of man within granting may come to light, provided that we, for our part, begin to pay heed to the coming presence of technology....Everything then, depends upon this: that we ponder this arising and that, recollecting, we watch over it. How can this happen? Above all through our catching sight of what comes to presence in technology, instead of merely staring at the technological. So long as we represent technology as an instrument, we remain held fast in the will to master it.'[9]

The Saving Power What to do or think about these dangers? Heidegger suggests that the key may be found in two lines from the nineteenth century German poet Holderlin:

'But where the danger is, grows
The saving power also'

Intuitively, this is a reasonable way to deal with danger; accept it and confront it head on. Confront is probably not the right word, however. The metaphor of the balance of energy described in martial arts is perhaps more appropriate. You want to take the energy that

is coming at you and deflect it in such a way as to weaken or disable the power of the aggressor and through this deflection, open up the possibility of escape or exploration of other avenues.

Verwindung A similar sentiment is taken up by Gianni Vattimo in his book *The End of Modernity*. His aim is to perform an act of *Verwindung* on the metaphysical tradition; to remember and recollect the tradition, to traverse it once again but with a critical edge. 'The intent is to distort and dissolve the tradition from the inside, erasing the vestiges of metaphysical thought still present in it, while at the same time – inevitably, but with self conscious irony – prolonging it as well.'[10] The term '*Verwindung*' indicates, as Heidegger told his translators, a going beyond that is both an acceptance (or resignation) and a deepening, while also suggesting both a convalescence,

I now find myself in another concrete frame building. At first glance it appears to be not very different from the previous one. It is oppressively grey. A strict column grid runs throughout, while a concrete shear wall elevator shaft extrudes up through the slabs.

This building is the Carleton University School of Architecture in Ottowa, designed by Carmen Corneil and Jeff Stinson in 1973. Having worked in it for a number of years, and having seen the students inhabit it, attach to it, decorate and defile it, I have concluded that this is no ordinary building. Its structural configuration challenges us to rethink how we relate to our physical surroundings, and to each other; it points to larger questions about the frame itself. Unlike the earlier concrete frame building, the School reveals and twists the 'enframed logic' of technological imperatives at all levels of architectural design. The structural frame establishes the site wherein, or rather through which, the world may be understood anew.

This reading of the structural frame of the School uncovers the building's capacity to strike a delicate balance between accepting technological imperatives and offering a clearing, or alternative way to experience the architectural frame.

The School of Architecture is a three-story building structured on a regular grid of concrete piers spaced 16 feet from east to west and in a tartan pattern ranging from 8 to 32 feet from north to south. The ground floor, with its major east–west 'street' extending the full three-story height, is dedicated to public spaces, classrooms, and workshops. The design studios, computer labs, and faculty offices of the top floor are organized along another street, which runs perpendicular to the ground level. It becomes a bridge connection to the neighboring engineering building. The middle mezzanine floor contains the director's office and some faculty offices. Throughout the building the concrete structure is exposed; partitions of concrete block define the more irregular enclosed areas. There is not a square foot of drywall to be found.

The only exception to the standard 12-inch by 24-inch pier is a single 36-inch diameter round column which rises through a 30-foot unbraced height at the virtual heart of the building. It literally plays a pivotal role in the building, marking the intersection of the major north–south 'street' at the upper level and the east–west 'street' at the ground level. Paradoxically, it both shelters the intersection from but equally connects this intersection to, 'the pit,' the main collective space of the building. This robust column is at once part of the collective, as it takes its place along the regular column grid, yet it is revealed in its particularity. It oscillates between acting as a support to the activities in the pit and posing as an obstruction that must be acknowledged and respected. It establishes structure as a primary ordering device in the architecture of the School.

It would have been very easy to eliminate this column by means of a transfer beam. Nobody would have questioned such a move, which would have 'opened up' the pit to the major crossroads of the school. And yet, in so doing, structure would have been relegated to a more invisible role. Instead, the dominance of the structural frame has been accepted, but then twisted so as to make explicit its presence. It would be a mistake, however, to think of this column simply in terms of a linguistic anomaly or ironic comment on conventional building practice. Its presence has the palpable effect of anchoring the life of the school. It stands in a place where conventions are both accepted and respected for the knowledge with which they are imbued, but equally challenged to create opportunities for thought and imagination. The single-minded interpretation of structure as 'frame,' that which supplies and delineates usable space, has been weakened.

cure or healing and a distorting or twisting. As opposed to 'Uberwindung' (overcoming), which as a concept remains rooted in ideas of progress and utopian thinking, 'Verwindung' implies a sense of being with things in such a way as to **weaken the strength of the enframed world.**[11]

Returning to the martial arts metaphor, we can take the enframed energy of the structural frame and redirect it to a reading of structure that offers the possibility of interpretations other than that which 'puts to nature the unreasonable demand that it supply energy that can be extracted and stored as such.' Such a reading points us toward a world that exists in opposition to the enframed technological world, one that is set beside rather than overcomes the world that we have constructed.

'Human activity can never directly counter this danger. Human achievement alone can never banish it. But human reflection can ponder the fact that all saving power must be of a higher essence than what is endangered, though at the same time kindred to it.'[12]

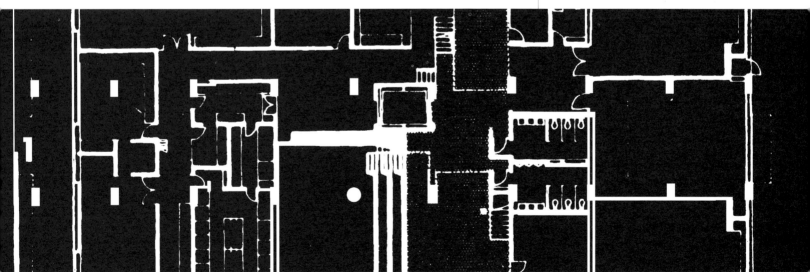

The presence of the round column sets into relief the other columns of the building. Whether consciously or subliminally, the students seem to recognize the extra layer of meaning attached to the structural grid of the School. Numerous installation projects have been done that attach themselves to the structure as if to take upon themselves some of its aura.

In attaching to the structural frame, one wonders whether the students aren't actually taking a clue from the other systems of the building. The mechanical systems are engaged in an elaborate dance with the structure: either bracketed by it, or bound to it, or woven around and through the frame. It is as if the strict rectilinear structural system finds its reciprocal in the more voluptuous aleatory wanderings of the air ducts. The system of electrical distribution acts as the sinew between the mechanical and electrical systems. At its extremities, it is a rectilinear conduit embedded into the bottom edge of the beams. These are tied back via round conduit and ultimately follow the duct risers back to the power source.

The partitions, all in concrete block, complement the poured-in-place concrete structure, juxtaposing the plastic quality of the concrete against the porous but rigid masonry unit of the same material. In a similar fashion to the mechanical systems, the structural and partition systems are in dialogue, the partitions sometimes framed by the concrete structure, at other times they slip right by as if seeking liberation from the frame's entrapment.

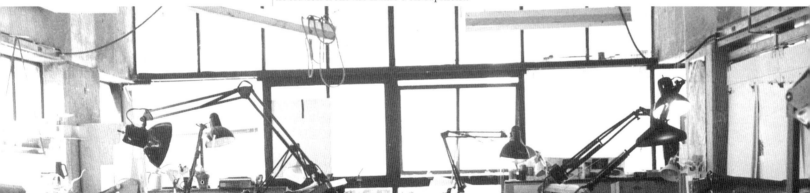

What does it mean for the occupants of the School to function within such an emphatic structural framework? How does it affect the life of the School?

Like most architecture schools, the building appears incomplete without the constant presence and ever-changing installations of its occupants. The overall impression is of a factory. The frame encloses an area that hums with activity and production all hours of the day. At the beginning of each year, the students intuitively respond to the inexorable concrete structure by engaging in a form of nesting activity, attaching to and personalizing their private spaces. Similarly, at the school-wide scale, the yearly student-organized Kosmic Party provides a pretext for the complete transformation of the familiar structure into an alien and wondrous landscape. During such times, a palpable connection to the building structure is established and endures well beyond graduation. Alumni constantly refer to the school building as the mnemonic device that structures their recollections of school life.

The structural frame also establishes places of politics within the school; it presents a series of stage sets that demand that we act, and take a stand. Evidently, the students are quite aware of the political dimension of the sites they choose for insertions into the School. The most provocative installation projects tend to be sited in the vertical public spaces adjacent to the pit, stair landings, and near the round column. Students intrigued with the idea of 'frame' are likely to explore the 'balcony' spaces on either side of the pit. These sites remain visually in the public realm but are physically less obtrusive. The more introspective installation projects involve insertions into the studio spaces, generally at the building perimeter, where the students are inspired by the gap between the piers, the cantilevered slabs, and the building envelope. In all cases, the location and means of attachment to the building structure are executed with extreme care, not because the students are admonished to do so, but rather out of a sincere respect for the integrity of the building.

At a more phenomenological level, the concrete structure stands as a mirror, 'the other,' against which life is set. At times, one may stand amid the concrete piers and feel empathy with the strength and stability of the material. Other days, the concrete frame appears inflexible and heavy. One feels confined until one recognizes this confinement as a way to act through the frame, to go beyond its limits while still in its midst.

In all its dimensions, the building defines and challenges us in our lives and our teaching. It situates itself as a pedagogical tool for the entire architectural curriculum, and shows how the system of framing may be used not passively, but in a way that reveals something to us about our own most ubiquitous structures.

'The irresistibility of ordering and the restraint of the saving power draw past each other like the paths of two stars in the course of the heavens. But precisely this, their passing by, is the hidden side of nearness.'[13]

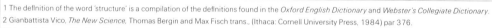

1 The definition of the word 'structure' is a compilation of the definitions found in the *Oxford English Dictionary* and *Webster's Collegiate Dictionary*.

2 Gianbattista Vico, *The New Science*, Thomas Bergin and Max Fisch trans., (Ithaca: Cornell University Press, 1984) par 376.

3 Martin Heidegger. *The Question Concerning Technology and Other Essays*, William Lovitt trans., (New York: Harper and Row, Publishers, 1977) p.13. 'From the earliest times until Plato the word *techne* is linked to the word *episteme*. Both words are names for knowing in the widest sense. They mean to be entirely at home in something, to understand and be expert in it. Such knowing provides an opening up. An opening up is a revealing.'

4 The definition of the word '*frame*' is a compilation of the definitions found in the *Oxford English Dictionary* and *Webster's Collegiate Dictionary*.

5 Heidegger, pp. 15–21.

6 Modern technology, Heidegger suggests, is incomparably different because it is based on modern physics as an exact science. 'Man's ordering attitude and behavior display themselves first in the rise of modern physics as an exact science. Modern science's way of representing pursues and entraps nature as a calculable coherence of forces. Modern physics is not experimental physics because it applies apparatus to the questioning of nature. Rather the reverse is true. Because physics, indeed already as pure theory, sets nature up to exhibit itself as a coherence of forces calculable in advance, it therefore orders its experiments precisely for the purpose of asking whether and how nature reports itself when set up in this way.'p.21

7 Heidegger, p. 27.

8 Heidegger, p. 27.

9 Heidegger, p. 32.

10 Gianni Vattimo. *The End of Modernity: Nihilism and Hermeneutics in Post Modern Culture*, John R. Snyder, trans., (Great Britain: Polity Press, 1988) p. xxvi.

11 Vattimo, p. 172–173.

12 Heidegger, p. 33.

13 Ibid, p. 33.

All the photos for "Reading Structure through the Frame" were taken in the Carleton University School of Architecture in Ottowa, Canada. The building was designed in 1973 by Carmen Corneil and Jeff Stinson

top: Bicton Palm House, Devonshire, Joseph Paxton (1838)
bottom: Le Grand Louvre, Paris, I.M. Pei (1983-89). Engineer: Nicoll

Hugh Dutton

AN INTEGRAL APPROACH
TO STRUCTURE
AND ARCHITECTURE

Glazing detail on Pyramid – a doubling up of 'structure'

PROFESSIONAL AND INDUSTRIAL TERRITORIES

Engineers design structure and architects design curtain walls. This professional definition is repeated on site, where structural trades (concrete, steel, etc.) and cladding trades
(glass, aluminum cladding, etc.) work in their discrete territories. The building industry
is organized around these distinctions between professions and trades to the extent that
everyone involved with a typical project assumes the standard procedure will hold: structure is employed for the single purpose of supporting the building, while cladding is an
envelope around the structure to keep rain out. But this assumption is not as ingrained
as it may seem to these builders – historically, structure and cladding were not distinct.
The façade of a brick or stone building was both a structural and waterproof skin. As the
construction industry developed and the building trades became more specialized, the
use of the weatherproof skin as structure became more and more rare.

This divisions exists for reasons of professional and industrial expediency. At the
design level, each profession concentrates on specific and distinct aspects of the building. To avoid risks of legal responsibility, one does not encroach on the field of the other,
a precaution that also simplifies the analytical process of understanding the different
parts of a building.

At the industry level, trades are defined by materials and often whether these materials are structural or non-structural. On site, the issue of construction tolerances and finish
quality again draws a line between visible cladding or finishes and non-visible structure.

Even some of the most sophisticated recent work, such as the Pyramid at the Louvre in
Paris by I.M. Pei, is characterized by this fundamental separation. An aluminum frame for
the silicone glazing system is fixed to an independent steel frame. This leads to a doubling
up of 'structure' – the main skeleton in steel and the cladding framing in aluminum –
despite the expressed minimalist architectural intention of maximum transparency.

Yet, it is possible to merge glass and steel into a single structural surface. An example of design before the modern tendency of 'layering' professions and trades is the
Bicton Palm house, where the hundreds of small glass panes form a daring shell structure with a delicate minimal steel frame and tiny glazing bars.

AUTOBIOGRAPHICAL NOTE My twelve years as an architect working in Peter Rice's Paris office, RFR, framed my own attitude toward design. RFR's work began in the early 1980s with the monumental green-houses at the La Villete Science Museum and developed with many other projects in and around Paris. An integral and holistic approach to design was the philosophy of the office. From the first days of the firm there was a culture of mixed disciplines; engineers, architects, a naval architect, and mechanical draftsmen worked in a closely knit 'laboratory' (to use Rice's own expression). The idea of distinct territories for these traditional 'professions' was a foreign concept in the office. Rice's work, either at RFR or at Ove Arup and Partners (OAP), continuously explored the architectural possibilities of an integral approach to design. My own design office in Paris, HDA, also believes in a hands-on approach to design and works as much with contractors and the industry as with architects and building owners. This crossover between different technical cultures is critical to the working method. This paper presents examples of design I have been involved with either by HDA or with Peter Rice and the RFR team.

Inchon Airport, Fentress Bradburn and KBHJW represented by KACI (2001)
Engineer: Sen Jaa
Consultants: HDA and OAP
Entrance Hall Roof Module – structural shell action

INTEGRATED APPROACH TO DESIGN

The construction industry's recent technical developments in engineering and material science and the building industry's new technical capacities provide new opportunities for architecture. These innovations can be used to integrate structure and the building envelope, or 'skin.'

For an integrated approach to design, borders between the distinct professional, industrial, and construction territories must be transgressed. The success of this exploration depends on architects understanding of the capacities and constraints of each separate field during the design process.

An extreme approach to integration lies in the use of structural skins. A lot of work was done in this area in the '50s, '60s and '70s by Buckminster Fuller, Frei Otto, Nervi, Isler and others, where the structural potential of curved surfaces was exploited through the use of shell or membrane analysis theory. In these cases, surfaces could be both structural and waterproof, and as such are perfect examples of integrated structure and skin. They are natural 3–D surface structures with very specific forms, which are the result of the optimal passage of loads in surfaces. The architectural images of these projects were total expressions of structure and its formal requirements. Today we can fully explore complex structural shapes because the description of surface geometric complexity has become more manageable and analyzable through the use of computers.

The following examples of integrated designs are presented in an order defined by scale, from airport to curtain wall.

INCHON INTERNATIONAL AIRPORT – ARCHITECTURAL DESIGN OF STRUCTURES

For this airport, ceiling structure was designed to work integrally with the ceiling surfaces. The design brief called for the architectural development of the roof and façade structures of the airport initially designed by Fentress and Bradburn of Denver in association with KACI, their Korean based partner for the competition. The design involved both a concave roof over the entrance hall spanning 95 meters and a repetitive module for the main roof measuring 60 x 70 meters, convex in shape with supporting masts and consciously reminiscent of a traditional Korean pagoda. HDA's work, done in collaboration with Ove Arup and Partners of London, concentrated on creating steel roof structures consistent with the architectural forms of the ceilings as well as making a clear expression of the structures themselves and how they function.

The configuration of steel truss members and the connection detailing intend to show how large scale wind and earthquake forces, which are as much a concern as gravity forces in this case, are resolved. The geometry of the architectural curves of the entrance hall vaults is exploited for structural shell action. The roof surface is entirely cross-braced with diagonal members, which makes it stiff in plane. As such, it is able to span on its own between stiffening edge trusses. The ceiling plane is then as free as possible of vertical structure, thus leaving a smooth surface. The ceiling panels are fabricated in triangles to express the bracing, allowing the viewers a clear view of all of the primary structure.

Critical to the success of a shell structure is the buckling analysis of the surface. Arup's work on the roof included non-linear 'snap-through' simulation for the diagonal members that was necessary to show that they remained in the shell plane in high compression loading configurations.

On the 'Pagoda' roof modules, a series of crescent shaped trusses are suspended from a central vierendeel spine truss and tall masts. The mast and spine truss configuration is designed for ductility to absorb seismic forces such that the suspended trusses are given a degree of protection from the seismic energy. The spine truss is open and clearly visible, with skylights above to highlight it. The crescent trusses are curved on their lower surfaces following the convex shape of the ceiling as designed by the architects. At each truss, the ceiling surface is cut open giving a full view of the trusses.

Electronic computer modeling is an essential tool in the design of complex structures. Today's capacities in the engineering field, notably in the area of nonlinear analysis, allow us to better understand structural behavior. The nonlinear analysis permits an almost endless series of analyses of a structure that takes into account its gradual dimensional transformation under load. They simulate the redistribution of forces within a structure as it deforms. Traditionally, if a tension member in a structure went slack its presence would be excluded from consideration. However, with nonlinear analysis, if the member is able to resist force after the structure has deformed under the load, then its capacity is considered.

COLUMBIA UNIVERSITY LERNER HALL
GLASS WALL AND RAMPS – STRUCTURING
ARCHITECTURE – A SYNTHESIS

This project is a demonstration that structure should not only be conceived as the most economic or efficient solution to an architectural problem; if thought of as a design element, structure can address architectural objectives while resisting loads. The design involves a total integration of steel structure and structural glass.

The hub glass wall and its supporting ramps make a transparent counterpoint in the composition of the Lerner Student Centre building by architects Bernard Tschumi and Gruzen Samton of New York. Its clearly visible steel structure and glass surfaces act as a foil to the two masonry clad wings of the building on either side. The structure spans between these two blocks, and the glass encloses the hub void between them. The articulation of the trusses and steel ramp structures expresses the activity and movement zone of the hub itself; these functional structural components – ramp wind beams, main trellis truss, suspension rods, and cantilever glass support arms – all animate the space.

The inclined arrangement of the ramps and truss is a logical consequence of the change in levels between the Broadway street level and the main campus level, which is half a typical floor height above it. The angular geometry of this arrangement is carried through into the layout of all of the components of the façade and the ramps. The glass grid follows the incline of the ramps, as do all of the support arms and fixing brackets.

The inclined façade truss is a simple triangulated trellis beam with tubes as compression members and rod ties as tension members. This truss partially supports the ramps, which are an intricate mesh texture of plates assembled diagonally. The inner edges of the ramps are suspended by a virtual plane of inclined ties from another, much heavier triangulated trellis truss at roof level. Each of these structural components are transparent in one way or another. The glass plane, with its own inclined grid matrix of joints, is fixed to the ramps with cantilever arms arranged as a series of 'x' points punctuating the elevation.

The glass is used structurally without glazing bars. It is a laminate of clear toughened glass units. It is fixed to the end of arm supports using bolted connections. Each panel supports its own dead weight and wind loads. The absence of glazing bars or mullions is critical to the clear reading of the composition of structural elements. A clear distinction is thus achieved between the steel structure and the pure transparent glass weatherproof surface. The glass is fixed using a system of bolts that incorporates a spherical bearing in the head of the bolt allowing a moment free connection to the glass at its holes.

Walking surfaces on the ramps are also executed in glass. They are made from laminated tiles with the upper sheet toughened and covered in an anti-slip treatment. A dust of tiny glass beads is laid on the top surface and then flamed to vitrify it to the surface.

The design also addresses visual expression of the critical functional details, which are carefully studied and drawn to express each specific function. They are designed to demonstrate how they work.

Each cantilever arm 'x' consists of two lower 'gravity' arms that support the dead weight of the glass and 'wind' arms that support the wind loads only. The reason for this configuration is to clarify the analysis of how the glass is to

63

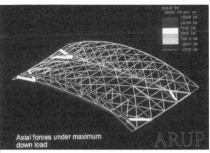

Axial forces under maximum down load

ARUP

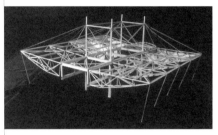

top to bottom:
Inchon Airport – triangulated ceiling panels
Inchon Airport – computer buckling analysis
Inchon Airport – model of Pagoda Roof module

Alfred Lerner Hall, Columbia University, Bernard Tschumi with Gruzen Samton (1999)
Engineer: OAP
Consultant: HDA
Computer model of elevation

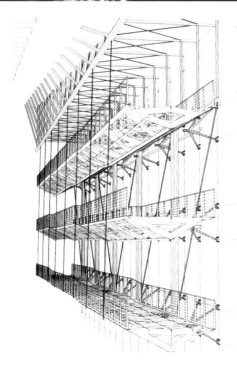

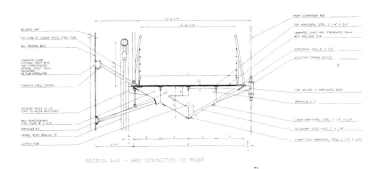

SECTION A-A - ARM CONNECTION TO RAMP

above top: Lerner Hall, interior as built

above: Lerner Hall, section through ramp

left: Lerner Hall, ramp design drawing

behave structurally and to allow the designers to guarantee that the glass can not be loaded in any other way than in the manner for which it is designed. Each glass panel is simply and independently supported, and any relative movement between the arms or between the ramps cannot be transferred into the glass as a load. This concept is rigorously carried through to all of the details. In the case of the gravity arms, the glass is supported on cast brackets at their ends. One lite is suspended from the bracket and the other rests on it. For the wind arms, the end bracket is used to fix a group of small articulated struts that can only resist wind loads perpendicular to the glass plane. They are free to rotate in all other directions, thereby guaranteeing that they cannot resist any forces in the plane of the glass. If, for example, the upper ramp deflects downward with a crowd of people, the glass panel suspended from it remains free to move downward slightly without pushing on the arm of the ramp below it. This principle is critical to the compositional idea, because it allows the glass to be fixed to each ramp independently and directly without any secondary framing, as would probably have been the case in a conventional glazing application.

The arms are hung from the ramps with a system of adjustment turnbuckles for correction of construction tolerances that can be achieved even if the glass is in place. This allows for fine tuning that could be necessary after the whole system has settled due to the dead weight of the glass.

The castings themselves are also equipped with adjustment devices for fine tuning corrections, and, in particular, angular correction to compensate for differences in arm angles. A spherical bearing at the core of each piece permits a rotational capacity. These adjustment devices are also used to correct for a slight non-alignment of the ramp slope with the glass grid, which is the result of the two mid-slope landings required by the New York building codes. The castings are important components of the design, because they resolve in a single piece the consequences of the geometric complexity. The casting process gives these key parts a unique identity specific to this project and allows them to express in an almost sculptural form the resolution of the overall geometric composition at a small hand-sized scale.

In engineering terms, though the main components, with the exception of the ramps, are simple and classic structural elements, their movements and interactivity require careful analysis. The analysis included 3–D electronic models of the design to evaluate the interactive behavior of the different components of the structure and, in particular, the relative stiffness of the two different trusses and the ramps that they support.

Full volumetric analysis was required to understand the complex geometry of the ramps themselves and the structural capacity of the tight mesh of small elements of which they are made. The design is based on the idea that every piece of steel is fully exploited for its structural capacity as well as its role as a support element for secondary finishes or cladding items such as handrails, glass support arms, glass floor tiling, etc. There is no distinction between any 'primary' and 'secondary' structure or framing; everything is 'primary.' Glass flooring can be paved directly onto the main structure and has no secondary framing.

Such an intricate interface between what are traditionally distinct trades requires a particular contractual arrangement to ensure that necessary coordination happens smoothly. Indeed, the design depends wholly on the success of these delicate interfaces to work. To help make this happen, the designers proposed that one contractor be globally responsible for all components in the glass wall and steel ramp design, and that all of it be let under one single bid package. Given that this type of work was not at all common in the United States, and particularly in New York, competition outside the United States was recommended. A French firm, Eiffel Constructions Metalliques, was selected as the winning bidder. This firm is principally a steel fabricator with considerable experience in structural glass as well.

Complications arising from a European steel company working

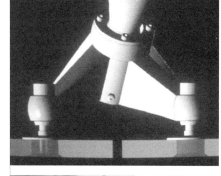

top to bottom:
Lerner Hall, gravity arms/wind arms
Lerner Hall, glass panel simply supported
Lerner Hall, X point
Lerner Hall, installation of glass panel

above: Société Générale, Paris, Andrault and Parat (1995)
Engineer: RFR with Hugh Dutton
left: Osaka Maritime Museum, Paul Andreu (2000)
Engineers: OAP and Tohata
Consultant: HDA

in New York using European product standards and measurement systems required significant effort and cooperation of all concerned. Beyond the issue of standards there was also a professional culture barrier to break. The tried and tested methods, practices, and contractual responsibility conventions in one country's construction industry are very different from those in another country.

OSAKA MARITIME MUSEUM AND
SOCIETE GENERALE GLAZED STEEL DOMES –
STRUCTURAL SKINS

In the two projects presented here, glass and steel work together as two parts of a single surface. Both are spherical surfaces using a spiraling radial Lamella pattern for the steel frame. In each case, the design of steel details is specifically adapted to the glass surface it supports.

SOCIETE GENERALE

The new Société Générale bank headquarters at La Defense in Paris by the architects Andrault and Parat consists of two towers rising from a forty meter high base plinth. The plinth contains the main entrance hall with a full height cylindrical atrium space topped by a thirty meter diameter glass dome centrally situated between the twin towers.

The stainless steel structure consists of a series of ribs spanning between a central compression ring and a perimeter ring beam. The steel ribs are triangular in section and vary in depth from 250 millimeter deep at the edge to 100 millimeter deep at the centre. The crossover nodes are designed as bolted joints to permit factory assembly and avoid welding on site without any visual thickening of the members.

Light falling on the polished stainless steel members, which are inverted isosceles triangles, would be reflected downward into the space and would thereby not create shadows on the profiles when viewed from below. Thus the structure would appear light and not in silhouette against the sky. The glazing gasket system is applied directly to the upper 'base' of the triangles.

The structure would have been more efficient if circumferential members were added in complete rings at the crossover nodes, thus creating a perfect triangulated grid-shell dome, but it was decided that the fluidity of the spiraling ribs would have been compromised, so the rings were left out. This means that the ribs function as arch members relying on their bending capacity to span from the center to the edge. The crossover connections, however, prevent the arches from buckling sideways, allowing the deep individual sections to be thin in plan.

The circumferential ring members would also have made glazing easier. This is because it is not possible to glaze the lozenge panels with flat planes given the spherical geometry. The ring could have provided a glazing bar forming a fold line, and the glass could be applied in planar triangular panels. Instead, the glass itself is made in folded panels that are bent along the circumferential line forming twin triangular planes, and no joint is visible at all.

OSAKA MARITIME MUSEUM

Contrary to the Société Générale project, the 73 meter diameter hemispherical Osaka Maritime Museum dome, designed with architect Paul Andreu, is a fully triangulated grid shell structure braced by an 'x' of steel rods. This 'x' also forms a point support for the glazing. Four glass panels are used to clad each lozenge of the dome structure. At the mid point of each, the rods cross over and a glazing support bracket supports the internal corners of the four sheets of glass

The dome glazing has a double role as necessary shading for the internal volume in addition to keeping the rain out. Osaka's climate is relatively hot, and the greenhouse effect of the entirely glazed volume would have made it intolerable for the users. The glass is a laminate with a perforated steel sheet incorporated in the interlayer. The density of the perforations in the glass vary as a function of the shading requirements for the internal volume. The annual solar exposure of the dome is plotted as a contour map projected onto the dome surface.

top to bottom:
Société Générale
Société Générale grid
Osaka construction
Osaka construction
Osaka grid

67

above: La Vilette Facades Bioclimatiques, Paris, Fainsilber (1986)
Engineer: RFR
left: 50 Avenue Montaigne, Paris, Glaiman, Epstein, Vidal (1992)
Engineer: RFR

Each contour represents a different density of perforation in the interlayer metal sheet, such that it is highly shaded at the top and more translucent towards the base where the sheet disappears. Views of the surrounding seascape are unhindered while the space is protected from sunlight coming from above.

STRUCTURAL GLASS

An integrated approach to design involves a structural exploitation of materials traditionally in the cladding domain, which requires a better understanding of the behavior of conventional cladding materials such as glass or sheet metal. Structure and skin become one and the same.

Rice's La Villette greenhouse façades with architect Adrien Fainsilber, one of the first projects to use the glass itself to its full structural capacity, is a poignant example. The array of toughened glass panels supports its self weight in each 8 meter x 8 meter bay, exploiting the glass's in-plane strength as well as each individual panel's capacity to resist wind loads without any aluminum framing. The resulting curtain of sixteen glass sheets is then braced using cable trusses that support the only loads it is unable to resolve itself, which are the overall wind forces.

The structural glass advances at La Villette depend on three principle technical achievements that set it apart from traditional glass wall design. First, the glass industry's innovation of toughened glass, which improves its long term performance and strength. Secondly, the development of nonlinear engineering analysis enabling the use of pre-tressed cable wind trusses. And third, the development of special articulated glass bolt attachments that achieve a predictable performance of the glass, even though it is being fixed to a relatively supple support system.

Glass panels can also be employed as primary structural members. In this case, sufficient care must taken in detailing the connections to take into account its brittle nature and sensitivity to cracking. Glass structures can be analyzed using computer finite element modeling, where the material or object is recreated as an electronic model simulating the material structural properties.

The appearance of the structural glass connections becomes an explicit tactile expression of their function. Beyond making the force lines themselves readable, there is the aesthetic potential of the details for their own decorative value. The cast stainless steel structural glass connections are modeled for visualization using computer graphics software to refine their shape. Once the final shape is agreed on, then the models are used as a basis for fabrication drawings and casting mold fabrication.

TECTONIC ARCHITECTURAL COMPOSITION

The work reviewed here is organized in a gradual progression from large scale structures to structural glass and its connections. From structure to structural skin. One might conclude that with such an approach the total architectural form and image ends up being determined by purely structural requirements. However, this is not the intent. On the contrary, it is to point out the potential design benefits when the various technologies involved in building are fully understood and composed as a conscious whole.

An integral approach to design requires a deep understanding of the technologies of architecture. We design with this technology. It is a critical tool of our design methodology. It is important to control it as designers.

There is a danger as architectural technologies become so complex and difficult that it is impossible for designers to master them. It is important not to be overwhelmed. Architects work at the beginning of the building process and can still remain in control at the level of first principles. There is a risk in the profession's growing tendency to flee responsibility and readiness to leave the resolution of the detailed work to the contractor. This means that we shall gradually lose the required skills, and clients will go directly to builders and engineers. In time the designer's role shall become less and less significant.

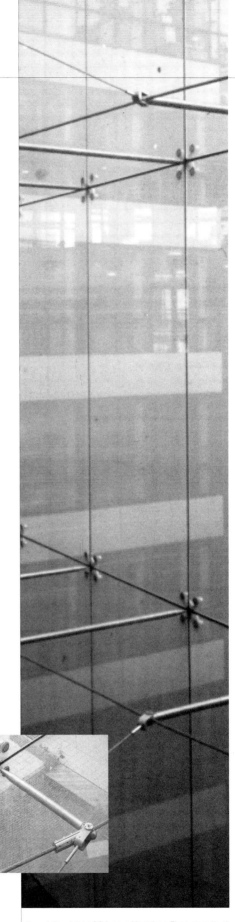

above, left and right: 50 Avenue Montaigne. The system developed at La Villette is also repeated on a larger scale on the 50 Avenue Montaigne project in the glazed curtain of 96 panels of glass 16m wide by 24m high.

Antonio Juarez

TOPOLOGY AND ORGANICISM IN THE WORK OF LOUIS I. KAHN

NOTES ON THE CITY TOWER

Louis Kahn and Anne Tyng's proposal for a new office building at the Philadelphia City Hall is a speculative project in its purest form – a forceful expression of ideas present in more subtle forms in actual built work, which, in turn, enlightens our understanding of that work. In fact, an examination of the City Tower reveals a pattern of planning in Kahn's previous and subsequent projects where either frameworks or clusters of cells, or a combination of the two systems is employed to organize space. The proposal is a visual record of the ideas Kahn and Tyng had been talking about, reading about, and sketching: growth, organicism, topology, structure, and monumentality.

Kahn's early preoccupations with structure surfaces in his 1944 paper, *Monumentality*, where he looks for 'a continuous structural unity worthy of being exposed,' and can be seen as preliminary ideas for what he will develop later with Tyng in the City Tower. As Kenneth Frampton suggests, Kahn's idea of monumentality can effectively be called 'structural monumentality.'[1] Tyng's interest in molecular structure is clearly manifest in the City Tower project, where structure is the language used to explore connectivity and growth at a monumental scale. Kahn's interest in topology and organicism is magnified in this project, which was an opportunity for him to reach beyond accepted dispositions for columns, beams and walls.

THE NATURE OF THE STRUCTURE

Kahn and Tyng published the final version of the City Tower as 'an exploration into the nature of a high-rising structure.'[2] The publication by the Universal Atlas Cement Company begins with text on the importance of voids in modern structures:

> In Gothic times, architects built in solid stones. Now we can build with hollow stones. The spaces defined by the members of a structure are as important as the members. These spaces range in scale from the voids of an insulation panel, voids for air, lighting

and heat to circulate, to spaces big enough to walk through or live in. The desire to express voids positively in the design of structure is evidenced by the growing interest and work in the development of space frames.[3]

The proposed building is described as the product of a constant search for order. This order, and the structure that delineates it, could not be concealed. As Kahn had written before, the nature of spaces and their making had to be identified.[4]

The tower is explained in the proposal as 'a gigantic wind resisting, weight-distributing space-frame consolidating the many needs of a central city location.' Kahn does not hide the wind-resisting frame but forcefully expresses it. His intent is to clearly show how the building was made – it was important that none of the levels of the construction process be erased. Kahn presented the project as a structural idea allowed to grow into a building, without being forced into a preconceived, purely formal notion.[5] (figure 1)

The structure is a precast, pre-stressed, concrete, triangulated strut frame, integrally braced by cross framing that intersects the column system every 66 feet. Each intersection is crowned by a capital 11 feet deep that houses storage, toilets and sub-stations for mechanical services. (figure 3) Conduits and pipe run through hollow columns. Intermediate level floors (up to 6 within the 66 foot vertical bays) can be moved up and down within the triangulated envelope to suit specific planning and sectional requirements. No two adjacent floors align in plan.

Triangulated membranes and arteries form 3 foot deep precast light-weight concrete floor slabs that can span up to 60 feet and harbor air conditioning, lighting, wiring and all piping. The continuous mechanical system affords flexibility in space division. A central core of vertical shafts, which houses stairs, elevators and air

ducts, rises through the building without disturbing its structural continuity.

Modernism required the separation of a tower's structure from its skin-- both elements had to be pure in their function. Instead, Kahn conceived of building skin as an intermediary element between interior and exterior- the beginning of the structural reaction against wind and gravity forces.

The proposal shows a permanent scaffolding of aluminum, which would secure the glazing panels and block sunlight, covering the entire exterior. From a distance, windows would dissolve into the flickering collage of the skin as a whole. The multi-plane form of the building sets up a range of positions for the sun louvers, which also break up and distribute wind loads. This purposeful design adds up to an intricate tracery texture modeled by changing color, light, and shade (figure 10):

> A lacey network of metal reflecting the color of the light and its complementary color of shadow would be seen by the passerby.' The shimmering quality of the building produced by the structure, the many planes, the multi-positioned sun louvers, the sun and the shade.[6]

FROM THE YALE GALLERY TO THE CITY TOWER

Many of the ideas for the City Tower originated in the Yale University Art Gallery (1951-53) (figure 4). The sketch Kahn made in the process of designing the Adath Jeshurun Synagogue (figure 5), after finishing the construction of the Art Gallery, represents an understanding of the frame as an organism with an integral, geometrical order. In her elementary school project Tyng 'increased the layers of the single layer tetra hedron/octahedron truss used by Fuller and Le Ricolais to 'grow' columns of the same geometry.'[7] The integral frame idea would later be developed in the tower by Kahn and Tyng, where the structure is understood as a continuous framework, instead of as a cluster of separate

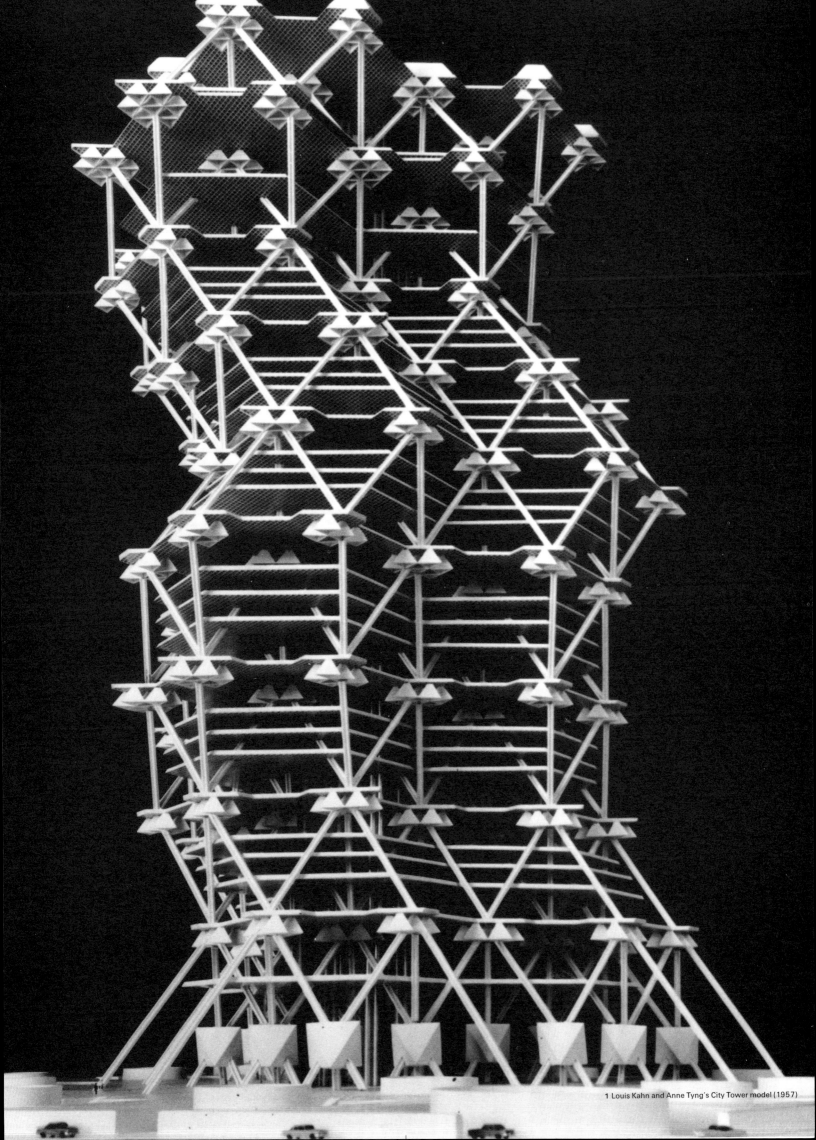

1 Louis Kahn and Anne Tyng's City Tower model (1957)

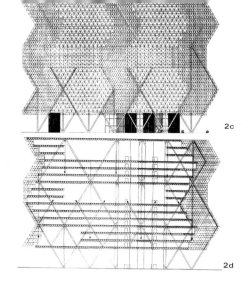

2c

2d

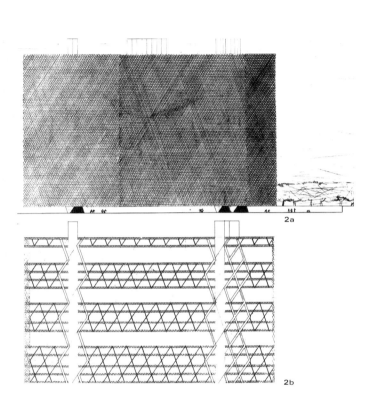

2a

2b

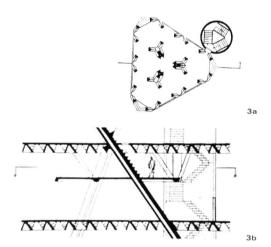

3a

3b

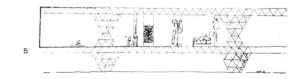

5

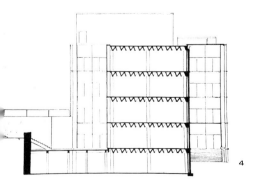

4

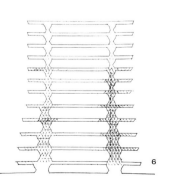

6

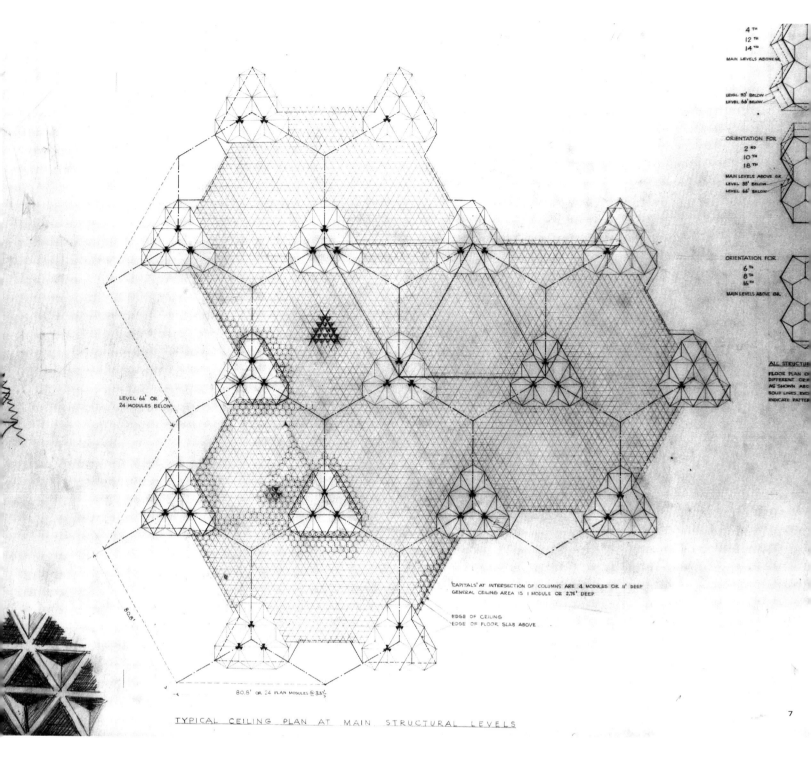

7

LEVEL 66' OR
24 MODULES BELOW

80.5'

80.5' OR 24 PLAN MODULES @ 3.37's

'CAPITALS' AT INTERSECTION OF COLUMNS ARE 4 MODULES OR 11' DEEP
GENERAL CEILING AREA IS 1 MODULE OR 2.75' DEEP

EDGE OF CEILING
EDGE OF FLOOR SLAB ABOVE

TYPICAL CEILING PLAN AT MAIN STRUCTURAL LEVELS

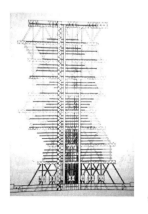
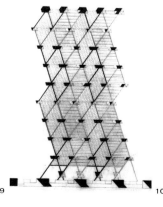

8

9

10

2a-b Elevation and section, first City Tower proposal (1953)

2c-d Elevation and section, second City Tower proposal (1953)

3a-b Plan and section of 'Hollow Capital,' final City Tower proposal (1954–57)

4 Section, Yale University Art Gallery, New Haven (1951–53)

5 Idealized section sketch, Yale University Art Gallery (1954)

6 Section sketch, tridimensional extension of the Yale University Art Gallery
tetrahedral floor slab

7 Typical ceiling plan at main structural levels, City Tower

8 Structural ceiling plan, structural floor plan and intermediate floor plan, City Tower

9 Final section, City Tower (1954–57)

10 Study of exterior skin, City Tower

elements as in other Kahn's projects of the 50's. The Adath Jeshurun Synagogue drawing can also be interpreted as a postscript of the earlier art gallery, or some sort of recognition of what the project should have been. Kahn noted when he made that sketch that the structural order implicit in the tetrahedral floor slab of the recently finished Art Gallery should also have been extended into the columns:

> *A tetrahedral concrete floor asks for a column of the same structure.* [8]

However, in the building as it was made, the construction system of the floor was not actually a space frame, but a conventional floor slab in which the beams were inclined, and the hollow spaces between the concrete tetrahedrons allowed the utilities to be exposed. The value of the project as a space frame is more its intention than its reality, and that intention is pushed further in later projects.

In the mid-50's, after the Art Gallery was finished, Kahn became severely critical of it. The tetrahedral floor slab adequately housed ducts, lighting and acoustic utilities while protectively 'harboring' those beneath it, but the concrete columns did not work with the whole. At that moment, it became clear to Kahn that it was illogical to place a triangular grid within a rectangular building. The absolute continuity of the geometrical order, without any break, was central to his thought. He demanded absolute integrity of the structure and insisted that a building should clearly show how it was made and serviced.

These developing intentions would be fully explored during the design of the City Tower, in which Kahn and Tyng derived forms by extending the triangular space-frame vertically. A three dimensional extension of the Art Gallery's tetrahedral floor slab is the basis for early sketches of the City Tower (figures 6, 19, 20). Although all of the versions of the Tower use the triangular geometry, the later version reflects a much clearer structural principle and hierarchical order (figure 2). The main difference amongst the designs is the external presence of the space frame and its relationship with the enclosure. In the first project, the glazed walls do not clearly express the major structural order against the forces of wind, which is so important in the others. The development of the tower design can be described as a progressive liberation of the glazed skin from the traditional conventions regarding prismatic office buildings. In the series of proposals, one can see increasing interplay between enclosure and structure, ending with the glazed skin becoming part of the structure in the last version.

THE HISTORY OF AN UNBUILT NOTION OF GROWTH: THE CONTEXT OF THE CITY TOWER SPACE FRAME

In projects surrounding the City Tower proposal Kahn and Tyng invesitgated the occupied space frame idea from different approaches; while Kahn thoght of it as occupied by mechanical services, Tyng introduced the idea of a space frame occupied by humans. While Kahn was working on the Yale Art Gallery, Tyng was designing an addition for her parents' house using large scale tetrahedral geometry (figure 13). Tyng refers to her parents' house as 'the first built habitable

total space frame' and the tower as 'the first conceptual tower structure that was a totally triangulated habitable, space frame.' Kahn later used the tetrahedral frame in the roof of Clever House (figure 14). Tyng's Wolworth Tyng house uses the new geometry in a more extended way, encompassing the whole building instead of just the roof. However, Clever House presents a clearer distinction between the two tectonic orders that Frampton calls earthwork and roofwork and develops a more gradual connection to the ground.[10] The roof can be read as an exploration of Tyng's organic geometry, while the massive elements in contact with the ground are closer to Kahn's interest in the physical materiality of the 'beginnings' of architecture. As in the Trenton Bathhouse, (figure 12) the walls and roof have independent structural forms.

If Tyng defines architecture as 'the art of giving form to number and number to form,' that is to say, the possibility of giving sensible reality to numerical order and vice versa, Kahn's way to give physical presence to his ideas was fused with his reflection on the contruction process, the experience of material, and his ideas about space.[11]

The remainder of Kahn's search for approaches to the hovering or habitable structural frame occurred in unbuilt projects, where the strongest structural ideas lie in the intermediate stages of design.

The Trenton Bathhouse that was actually constructed represents a minimal part of the entire proposed complex. The main part of the project, the Community Building, was never built. One scheme for this building uses a spatial grid composed of octagons and squares, more complex than previous grids using the sole tetrahedral element. The elevation (figure 16) clearly shows ideas about the natural growth of structure that also occur in the City Tower.

A proposal for the Bryn Mawr Dormitory (figure 15) shows a three-dimensional grid of interlocking octagons and squares forming the stepped-back volume of five floors. This octagonal grid is similar to the one used for the Community Building in Trenton, but it is more developed three dimensionally. The cells in Bryn Mawr are not only juxtaposed on a horizontal

11

plane but combined in an organic frame, very close in concept to that of the City Tower. Tyng prepared most of the material in this first stage of the project.[12] The similarity of this version of the building to the DNA models developed by James Watson and Francis Crick has been suggested. For that reason, this scheme was called 'the molecular plan.'[13] Although an ingenious solution for the problem of the multiplicity of dorm rooms, it was not satisfactory for the public spaces. Kahn finally decided on a very different solution, paying more attention to the public courts. Tyng remembers that Kahn rejected the first scheme because he 'did not like the zig-zagging facade of the rooms.'[14]

Tyng's devotion to molecular form came to fruition in her scheme for the the General Motors Exhibit (figure 17) at the 1964–65 New York World's Fair, which is based on the four fold carbon atom bond. Individual pavilions, in the shape of halved tetrakaidecahedrons form a semi-circular cluster, which is supported by inflated forms derived from the geometry of the cluster and anchored down by cables. This scheme was rejected by Kahn, but it is evidence of the intensity of Tyng's investigation into organic form, which was a presence in his office.[15]

TOPOLOGY AND GROWTH

As reflected in the title of the Universal Atlas Cement Company brochure, 'A City Tower: A Concept of Natural Growth,' the notion of 'growth' seems to be central in the City Tower, as well as in other projects realized during those years.[16] The Adath Jesurum Synagogue and the Adler House (1954) are two projects that epitomize Kahn's ideas toward organic form, and they sit at the two poles that underlie the City Tower organicism: 'branched' and 'cellular' structure.

From one project to another, throughout his career, these two extreme models fix the limits of Kahn's work: the natural growth of the space frame and the addition of space units. Kahn's work can be seen as an interplay between these two poles: the continuous framework vs. the clustering of elements.

The City Tower seems to reflect both extremes: on the one hand, it is generated from a tetra-octahedronal tree-like structure as a whole; on the other, the connectivity between the geometric cells is also a concern in the spatial conception of the tower. This duality, expressed with the most strength and clarity in the City Tower, is a thread that runs through all of his work.

There is an approach to the building as a living being, as an organic structure. Kahn's own organic approach can be compared and related to two main references. The first one is a scientific discipline: Topology, through the influence of the French engineer Robert Le Ricolais. The second refers to the notion of 'growth' and D'Arcy W. Thompson's ideas on biology in his book 'On Growth and Form,' which comes to Kahn through the influence of Tyng and her interest in the geometric principles of form.

Topology is the branch of mathematics that studies properties of geometric forms that remain constant under continuous transformations. Two figures are topologically equivalent if one can be obtained from the other by stretching or curving without cutting it. This property has caused topology to be called 'rubber sheet geometry,' since a square can be transformed into a circle, but not into a ring. Ideas of opened and closed, connected or disconnected are central to this discipline. Topology is also the science of connectivity in the realm of form.

Topological ideas were central to Robert Le Ricolais' thought. As a 'mathematician of structures,' Le Ricolais was the first to introduce Topology as a tool for mathematical structural analysis.[17] In the fall of 1953, Kahn received a letter from Le Ricolais, who had seen the project for the City Tower in Perspecta and told Kahn about his coming to teach at the University of Pennsylvania in 1954. In that issue of Perspecta appeared the famous statement by Kahn about 'the hollow stone'[18] that houses a building's systems. A parallel thought from Le Ricolais' mathematical approach to structures appears when he states that his goal was hollowing the solid, in the paradoxical conclusion that 'the art of structure is how and where to put the holes.'[19] Le Ricolais would teach courses in experimental structures in tandem with Kahn's design studio.

11 Model of elementary school project, Anne Griswold Tyng
12 Trenton Bathhouse, Jewish Community Center, Erwing Township, New Jersey (1954–59)
13 Walworth Tyng House, Cambridge, Maryland, Anne Griswold Tyng (1951–53)
14 Clever House, Cherry Hill, New Jersey (1957–62)
15 Model of Erdman Hall, Bryn Mawr College, Bryn Mawr, Pennsylvania (1960)

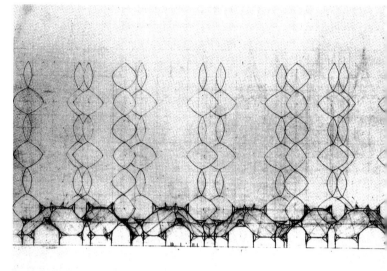

16

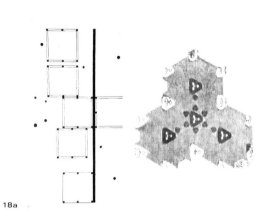

18a

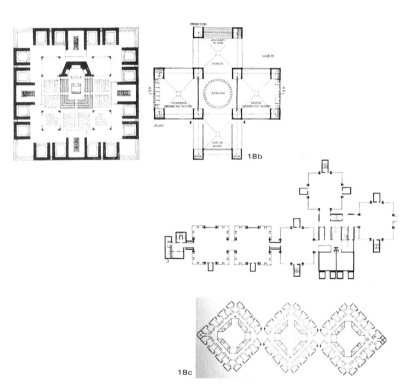

18b

18c

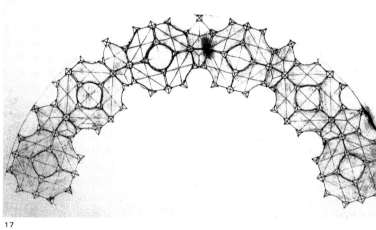

17

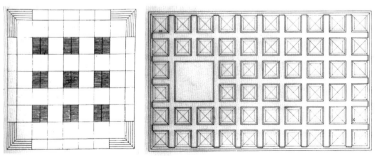

18d

In 1955 Le Ricolais wrote an article called Topology and Architecture that opened with the following quotation by Cyril Stanley Smith, then director of the Chicago Institute of Metals: 'How could Architecture, which deals with connections, ignore Topology, which by itself is the science of connectivity?'[20] Actually, what Kahn understood as form – 'conceptual patterns without dimensions' – was very close to some kind of 'topological order' in the project.

For Le Ricolais, the realm of structures and poetics was based on the same quality: 'arrangement,' or 'topological organization.' Creative energy is only liberated in 'disposition,' not 'composition,' which is based only on visual considerations. Arts and Techniques are grounded in this idea:

It is really just a matter of 'arrangement'. Physics, with electrons, Poetry, with words. Everywhere wild energies are at hand, so to speak, ready to break loose. No doubt, in most cases our perceptions are obtuse, and to discover these arrangements, something or someone has to remove a veil.[21]

Le Ricolais' notion of 'arrangement' in considering form as a more open way of analysis than 'composition' also explains what Kahn understood as Form. Kahn's projects can be analyzed following Le Ricolais' suggestion that what constitutes the project is not the external form, but its internal topological arrangement.

Kahn's desire seems to lie in seeking out the formal structure of the project. This means that the origin of the project can be traced beyond any specific formal solution. What Kahn means by 'Form' can be understood as a flexible disposition or arrangement, an open form organizing space. The nature of the building, what the spaces 'want to be,' is rooted in the relationships between spaces, in their internal connections or disconnections, and in their proximities and separation, but not in the concrete form.

Many of Kahn's projects clearly show 'connectivity.' There are clusters of cells, basic elements following different topological patterns. Sometimes they are merely juxtaposed; other times they are connected or interlocked. They also constitute a kind of synthesis between the addition of unconnected elements and the natural growth of the structure. The total autonomy of the cells interacts with a proposal for totality when their structures connect or intersect. Even in three-dimensional terms, the connection reveals the nature of the structure in the City Tower. The capitals crowning the intersections of the triangulated strut frame were called the 'knuckles' of the structure. Kahn tells us with these ideas that a definitive part of the project it is not in the spaces themselves, but in the way the spaces relate to each other or grow together according to topological laws.

The connection with D'Arcy Thompson's idea of growth is more explicit than others. Kahn had Thompson's book and became excited with discussions about it at his office. Tyng, who more thoroughly went through Thompson's ideas, points out that Kahn was always interested in connection to nature and that he was motivated by Thompson's drawings, which related natural and man-made products. She also remarked that Kahn's own drawings of natural elements such as people and trees, with their intense vitality, show his connection to nature. [22]

These ideas connect Kahn with the general context of the architectural debate in the 50's and later. After Bruno Zevi's Towards an Organic Architecture (published in English in 1950) many different attitudes were labeled 'organic' and recognized as critiques to rationalism. Broader than the Wrightian interpretation of the concept, Alison and Peter Smithson's ideas of 'growth and change,' Fumihiko Maki's Investigations in Collective Form, and Reyner Banham's Megastructure reflect successive readings of organicisms metaphor. Some of the drawings for Kahn's project of the Adath Jeshurun Synagogue (figure 20) are not far from Maki's definition of megastructure as a large, harboring frame that houses the functions of the city.[23]

Referring to the idea of growth in the Tower, Tyng explained some of their intentions as a non-literal representation of natural principles. Linked to Kahn and Tyng's notion of growth is the idea of hierarchy:

...a unique opportunity to express hierarchical shape as well as hierarchical quantity that can res-onate with human scale and vision is presented by the multi-storied tower. Although one may try to count the number of floors in a high building such as the World Trade Center in order to know objectively how many stories there are, the subjective sense of scale or of levels of identity through the clusterings of twos and threes is not there. The plan is repeated unchanged in the vertical dimension as an extruded two-dimensional pattern. There are no clues for the intuitive perception of its scale. In the proposed City Hall Tower for Philadelphia on which I was associated with architect Louis I. Kahn from 1952 to 1957, clues for scale were intuitively rather than consciously integrated into its design. The three-fold hexagonal plan of the structure rotates in vertical increments every 66 feet. These undulating shifts of level result from the natural completion of the triangulated space-frame in its upward helical movement. Hierarchical expression occurs in variations in floor level between the main 66-foot structural levels, in the hollow triangulated 'capitals', high enough for a person to stand in, and the three-foot-deep hollow ceilings of octahedron-tetrahedron geometry. In this project, hierarchical expression of structure is integrated with hierarchy of quantity and of shapes in triangle or hexagon.[24]

The plans grouped under the category 'patterns of topological growth' (figure 18) show Kahn's interest in the notion of growth, linked to the idea of connectivity and in harmony with geometric principles. In 1959, on the occasion of Frank Lloyd Wright's death, Kahn wrote:

Wright gives insight to learn that nature has no style, that nature is the greatest teacher of all. The ideas of Wright are the facets of this simple thought. [25]

However, assuming Kahn's organic statement that 'man through his consciousness senses inside of himself all the laws of nature,' at the same time he admits an essential difference between the conscious and the unconscious.[26] Kahn asserted that architecture is not only the expression of natural, organic forces, but also comes from conscious Inspiration, an impossible to elude desire-to-express, because 'nature does not build a house, nature does not make a locomotive, nature does not make a playground. They grow out of a desire to express.' [27]

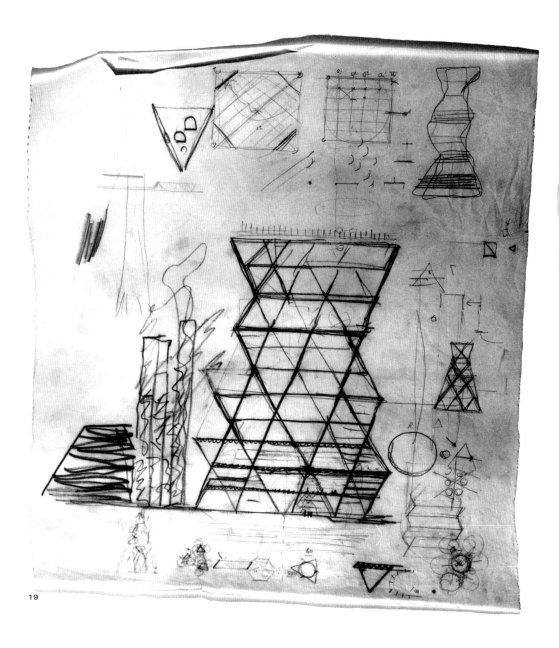

19

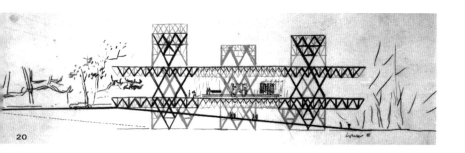

20

21

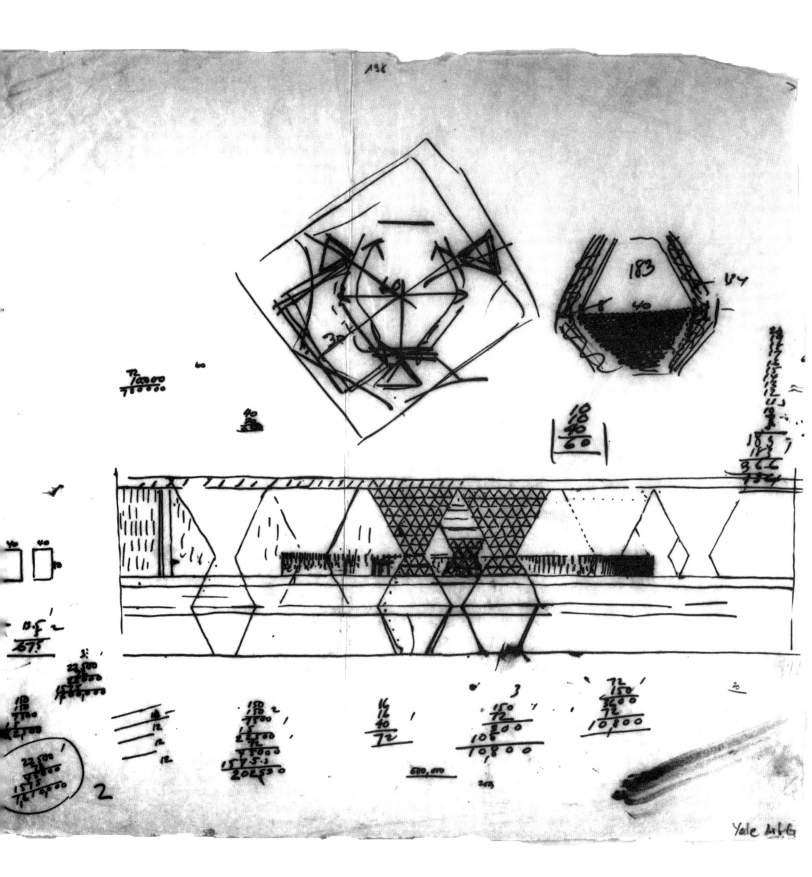

1 Frampton, Kenneth, 'Louis I. Kahn and the French Connection', *Oppositions 22* (Fall 1980), pp. 21-53.

2 Kahn, L. I. and Tyng, A. G., 'A City Tower: A Concept of Natural Growth' Universal Atlas Cement Company, United States Steel Corporation Publication 110, no. ADUAC-707-57 (5-BM-WP), New York, 1957.

3 Ibid, First published in Kahn, L. I., 'Towards a Plan for Midtown Philadelphia', in *Perspecta 2*, The Yale Architectural Journal, 1953, pp. 10-27. Reprinted In LATOUR, A. (ed.): Louis I. Kahn: writings, lectures, interviews, Rizzoli International Publications, Inc., New York, 1991, pp. 28-52.

4 Kahn, L. I., 'Towards a Plan for Midtown Philadelphia', in *Perspecta 2*, The Yale Architectural Journal, 1953, pp. 10-27. In Latour, A. (ed.): *Louis I. Kahn: writings, lectures, interviews*, Rizzoli International Publications, Inc., New York, 1991, pp. 28-52. Also published later in KAHN, L. I. and TYNG, A. G., 'A City Tower: A Concept of Natural Growth' Universal Atlas Cement Company, United States Steel Corporation Publication 110, no. ADUAC-707-57 (5-BM-WP), New York, 1957.

5 Two years after the publication of the final project for the City Tower, at the conclusion of the CIAM in Otterlo, Kahn made an allusion to the Seagram Building, criticizing its lack of structural principles. This statement, without being an explicit allusion to the City Tower, can certainly be interpreted as the justification Kahn would have given to such a structural typology chosen for his building. See Kahn, L. I., 'New Frontiers in Architecture, CIAM in Otterlo 1959'. In Newman, O., *New Frontiers in Architecture: CIAM in Otterlo 1959*, Universe Books Inc., New York, 1961. Reprinted in LATOUR, A. (ed.): Louis I. Kahn: writings, lectures, interviews, Rizzoli International Publications, Inc., New York, 1991, p. 96.

6 Kahn, L. I., quoted by Ronner, H. and Jhaveri, S., Louis I. Kahn: *Complete Work 1935-1974*, Birkhauser, Basel and Boston, 2nd. edition, 1987, p. 33. and Kahn, L. I. and Tyng, A. G., 'A City Tower: A Concept of Natural Growth' Universal Atlas Cement Company, United States Steel Corporation Publication 110, no. ADUAC-707-57 (5-BM-WP), New York, 1957.

7 Tyng, A. from unedited version of response to this article 1999.

8 Kahn, L. I., quoted by Ronner, H. and Jhaveri, S., Louis I. Kahn: *Complete Work 1935-1974*, Birkhauser, Basel and Boston, 2nd. edition, 1987, p. 76.

9 Tyng, A., interview by Alessandra Latour, in LATOUR, A., *Louis I. Kahn, l'uomo, il maestro*, Edizioni Kappa, Rome, 1986, p. 51.

10 Frampton, K. *Studies in Tectonic Culture: The Poetics of Construction in Nineteenth and Twentieth Century Architecture*, MIT Press, Cambridge, Massachusetts; London , England, 1995.

11 Tyng, A., 'Resonance Between Eye and Archetype', Via 6, 1983, p. 47.

12 Brownlee, D., LONG, D.: *Louis I. Kahn: In the Realm of Architecture*, The Museum of Contemporary Art (Los Angeles), Rizzoli, New York, 1992, p. 353.

13 Katherine Elizabeth McBride, president of Bryn Mawr College since 1942, who primarily dealt with Kahn during the design of the project, dubbed this scheme 'the molecular plan'. In BROWNLEE, D., LONG, D.: *Louis I. Kahn: In the Realm of Architecture*, The Museum of Contemporary Art (Los Angeles), Rizzoli, New York, 1992, p. 353.

14 Tyng, A, note to editor 1999.

15 Ibid

16 Kahn, L. I. and Tyng, A. G., 'A City Tower: A Concept of Natural Growth' Universal Atlas Cement Company, United States Steel Corporation Publication 110, no. ADUAC-707-57 (5-BM-WP), New York, 1957. and In the chapter 'The Mind Opens to Realizations', in Brownlee, D., Long, D. D.: *In the Realm of Architecture*, Rizzoli, New York, 1992, p.50-76.

17 Sabini, M., 'Between Order and Form. Fragments and Idea of Architecture', in *Rassegna 21*, March 1985, pp. 14-22. and Le Ricolais, Robert, 'Expose on Structural Researches', Institute for Architectural Research, University of Pennsylvania, in 'Le Ricolais', Box LIK 56, Louis I. Kahn Collection, University of Pennsylvania and Pennsylvania Historical and Museum Commission. See also review of 'The Work of Le Ricolais'. Notes on 'Tension Structures, Inc. Background Material on Tension Structures'. 'Le Ricolais', Box LIK 56, Louis I. Kahn Collection.

18 The first proposal of the City Tower was published in *Perspecta 2*: Kahn, L. I., 'Towards a Plan for Midtown Philadelphia', in Perspecta 2, The Yale Architectural Journal, 1953, pp. 10-27. In LATOUR, A.

(ed.): Louis I. Kahn: writings, lectures, interviews, Rizzoli International Publications, Inc., New York, 1991, pp. 28-52. Tyng refers to Le Ricolais letter in Tyng, A., interview by Alessandra Latour, in Latour, A., Louis I. Kahn, l'uomo, il maestro, Edizioni Kappa, Rome, 1986, p. 51.

19 Le Ricolais, Robert, 'Expose on Structural Researches', Institute for Architectural Research, University of Pennsylvania, in 'Le Ricolais', Box LIK 56, Louis I. Kahn Collection.

20 Sabini, M., 'Between Order and Form. Fragments and Idea of Architecture', in *Rassegna*, March 1985, pp. 14-22.

21 Le Ricolais, R., 'Matières', in *Via 2*, 1973, p. 111.

22 Tyng, Anne, G., interviewed by the author. Philadelphia, February 14, 1996.

23 Maki, Fumihiko, 'Investigations of Collective Form', The School of Architecture, Washington University, a special publication, no. 2, St. Louis, June 1964.

24 Tyng, A. G., 'Resonance Between Eye and Archetype', *Via 6*, MIT Press, 1983, pp. 61-63.

25 Kahn, Louis I., 'Statements by Architects on Frank Lloyd Wright', *Architectural Forum* 110, no. 5 (May 1959), p. 114.

26 Kahn, Louis I., 'Silence and Light,' Lecture at the ETH in Zurich, February 12, 1969, in Wurman, Richard Saul, ed. *What Will Be Has Always Been: The Words of Louis I. Kahn*, Access Press and Rizzoli International Publications, New York, 1986, p. 61.

27 Kahn, Louis I., 'University of Cincinnati, College of Design, Architecture, Art and Planning,' (1969) in Wurman, Richard Saul, ed. *What Will Be Has Always Been: The Words of Louis I. Kahn*, Access Press and Rizzoli International Publications, New York, 1986, p. 75.

I welcomed the essay's general strategy, the way it juxtaposes a quite personal account of two spaces with definitions and reflections that are very much indebted to Heidegger. The trajectory of the essay is indicated by the sequence of words that appear in boldface in the latter: **structure; frame; enframing; we are caught in a tradition of progress, commonly known as the metaphysical tradition, yet we no longer have a larger view of where we are going; we need not push on blindly with technology, nor simply rebel helplessly against it; verwindung; to weaken the strength of the enframed world.** No one familiar with Heidegger will find this sequence surprising. And though I do not favor the expression 'commonly known as the metaphysical tradition,' I do think that we face no more significant task today than to show how it is possible to say 'yes' to the technological world without losing our soul. Ms. Fontein provides us with some welcome pointers.

The two buildings discussed in the main part of the article help to make more concrete what is discussed in the quite literally marginal observations on which I have commented so far. In the first section the 'building for hire' becomes a figure of our modern world, the world of Heidegger's *Gestell*. There is the suggestion that ironic or subversive strategies are necessary to make such a structure genuinely habitable; and that they would be necessary also to live a fully human life in this modern world.

The second building discussed, the Carleton University School of Architecture, complements the first: it offers an example of how to 'reveal and twist the 'enframed logic' of technological imperatives.' Key here is the obtrusive column that , even as it accepts, 'twists' the structural frame and renders it explicit in its presence. The rectilinear structural system is engaged in a kind of counterpoint by the wanderings of the air ducts and the electrical system, and of course by the human occupants of the school. The concrete structure is said 'to stand as a mirror, 'the other' against which life is set.' Here is another place where I would have wished for more discussion. Is 'mirror' the right word here? The ambivalence of this 'other,' too, deserves more discussion.

The most questionable part of her presentation here is the seemingly easy movement from 'structure,' to 'frame,' to 'enframing.' The German *Gestell* 'enframing' unfortunately does not derive from the German for 'frame' – *Rahmen*. This lets the reader wonder to what extent the points made here trade on associations that work only in English. I would have welcomed at any rate a fuller discussion of these terms. But perhaps it is in the nature of such quickly moving suggestions to raise a multitude of questions and to open up a whole host of issues.

Karsten Harries is Professor of Philosophy at Yale University. He has published widely on art and architecture including a number of articles for *Perspecta* the most recent being "Context, Confrontation, Folly" for *Perspecta 27*. His most recent book is *The Ethical Function of Architecture*. His next book will be *Infinity and Perspective*.

The 'integrated design' ideal championed by Hugh Dutton is not the Holy Grail of high tech façades, but rather a reductive form of modernism. The works cited as examples of 'integrated design' are all commendable achievements, but it is simplistic to maintain that building structure and cladding structure are somehow elevated to a higher art form if one is inseparable from the other. The dichotomy of structure and cladding has existed since the neo-Gothic architect Sir Gilbert Scott defined the term 'curtain wall' in the 1850s, and has generated one of the primary dialogues of architectural form ever since. The literal integration of structure and cladding is therefore ironically regressive; it is one valid approach, but, in my view, far too limiting as a governing design principle.

The pyramid, Le Grand Louvre, by I.M. Pei is cited by Dutton as an example of the presumably conventional, i.e., non-integrated design methodology. In fact, Pei's firm worked closely with the engineers to design the layering of glazing and structure in order to satisfy very real and demanding performance criteria.

In the ambitious and innovative point-supported glass wall of the Lerner Hall project, cladding and structure are indeed integrated; in designing the bridges to support the glass, the need for an interstitial curtain wall structure is eliminated. The irony, of course, is that the bridge structures and the cantilevered dead load supports for the glass have become so massive that the net effect of transparency and lightness is compromised. Would it have been indefensible to have bridges floating independently of the glass wall, and the glass independently suspended on thin tensile elements? Is such a non-integrated approach really too 'conventional'?

A contemporary example of the alternative is the new planetarium for the Rose Center for Earth and Space of the American Museum of Natural History, by James Stewart Polshek Architects and engineer Weidlinger Associates. Here, the larger architectural goal was to articulate the objects within, and therefore to minimize the overall structure of the glass enclosure. The resulting design, with an interstitial structure to carry the point-supported glazing, was realized with the concept not to integrate structure and cladding.

If point-supported glazing is to be employed, presumably for lightness, transparency, or even dematerialization, then scale is an essential determinant in the choice of detailing strategy. The glass wall of Lerner Hall, itself only a portion of the north elevation, is simply too small for its ambitions. An analogy might be the gothic cathedral's seeming weightlessness despite its tracery of heavy limestone ribs: reduce the scale of the space and buttress spans by half or more, and the desired effect is lost. By contrast, the success of the Osaka Maritime Museum and the Societé Générale steel dome projects is due in part to their larger scale.

Finally, a word about 'structural glass,' an expression used throughout Dutton's article to describe point-supported glazing. The term implies that glass is being used structurally, when in fact it is simply being supported in a different way, and is no more structural than conventional two- or four-side edge supported glass. Integrating the words 'structure' and 'glass' is, however, a convenient metaphor for the premise of Dutton's article.

Robert A. Heintges is Associate Professor (Adjunct) of Architecture at Columbia University Graduate School of Architecture, Planning and Preservation. His firm, R.A. Heintges Architects Consultants, has consulted on over fifteen million square feet of curtain wall, cladding, and specialty glass façades around the world.

ARCHITECTURE WITH A LIFE OF ITS OWN

Antonio Juarez's article offers an interesting distinction between 'organic' growth expressed in the proposed City Tower and other Kahn projects based on the clustering or addition of space units. The distinction should not be understood as 'organic' Tower versus 'non-organic' clustering or addition of space units. They both embody principles of organic growth – one more vertical and the other more horizontal accretions. In both cases units of form are involved, some tetrahedron/octahedron and other cubic. All lie within the space-filling fourfold ordering of the 'Simpler' of the five Platonic Solids – cube, tetrahedron and octahedron – while the non-space filling 'Higher' Solids – dodecahedron, and icosahedron – have five-fold ordering. The Five Platonic Solids are the only regular forms possible in three-dimensional space, in each of which all the faces are the same and all the angles at which those faces meet are the same. They represent the dice of the universe – with an equal chance of landing on any face – and are the basis of all the infinite variety of natural or synthetic matter.

The architecture of Wright, and especially Gaudí before him, expresses connections between geometry within us – the DNA molecule in 1953 and the hemoglobin molecule in 1964 – and the extraordinary geometries found far our in space are all forms that give life. In the close packed density of black holes and in trailing wisps of stardust, recognizable bilateral, rotationally helical, and spiral geometries are being found.

Kahn and I experienced our own breakthrough in exploring the direct expression of natural triangulated space-filling geometry, extending our vocabulary of architecture beyond cubic or orthogonal networks.

I believe the proposal for the City Tower is the first concept of a totally triangulated tower harboring all its spaces within continuous geometry. The structural members act simultaneously as both columns and beams, lightening the structure by optimizing on the multiple directions of connectivity to resist earthquake and wind stresses. The Tower's resistive undulation appears to be in motion with a life of its own. Our explorations freed Kahn to go beyond any style of architecture power and living energy in original expressions of organic monumentality. Our explorations freed Kahn to go beyond any style of architecture to the beginnings of form as a universal timeless resource, giving his architecture power and living energy in original expressions of organic monumentality.

IN RESPONSE

Anne Griswold Tyng is an architect based in Philadelphia and a Fellow of the American Institute of Architects. She collaborated with Louis Kahn on a number of projects including the Philadelphia Tower. She is the editor of *Louis Kahn to Anne Iyng: The Rome Letters 1953–1954*.

Seagram Building, New York City, Ludwig Mies van der Rohe and Philip Johnson (1958)

IN PERSPECTIVE: SKIN

Modernism has consistently divided buildings, new or old, into load-bearing-wall and frame-and-curtain-wall structures, and the frame structures themselves into the skeleton and the skin. It is easy to find examples that defy this classification: the Baths of Caracalla seem to be neither wall nor frame, as does the typical wood platform house. The frame – skin dichotomy itself is simply

an abstraction imposed on a far more complex reality.
Edward Ford *Details of Modern Architecture, Volume 1*

From the time of Francis II the architectural form diminishes more and more in the construction, leaving visible the geometric character, like the bony framework of the emaciated invalid. The fine lines of art

make way for the cold, inexorable forms of geometry. An edifice is no longer an edifice; it is a polyhedron.
Victor Hugo *Notre Dame de Paris*

Until the end of the eighteenth century construction was carried out with methods that evolved from those used in the High Middle Ages and the Renaissance. The expressive

traditions of these periods conceived of the integration of construction and architecture in essentially the same way. But suddenly, between the eighteenth and nineteenth centuries, it became possible to use iron as a construction material (first cast iron, then various types of steel), and very quickly this material began to be manufactured in pieces of prismatic wholes that were then assem-

Lever House, New York, Gordon Bunshaft of Skidmore, Owings and Merrill (1950–52)   John Hancock Tower, Boston, Henry Cobb of I.M. Pei & Partners (1966–76)

bled to form the structure of the buildings. It is by now a commonplace to point out the importance of this conceptual shift, which allowed us to think of the structure of a building as a skeleton partially free of its walls, and which made architectural space independent from construction method in a way unknown until that time.... The need to clarify other primary aspects of architecture

seems to have made us forget an elemental thing: architecture is also construction. A work has not been well conceived unless thought has been given to how it will be constructed. The methods of construction have in themselves extraordinary inspirational and expressive value. Every type of structure is

intimately linked to certain building methods, and these methods can be read in the finished product. It is not enough to resolve functional problems and give them spatial form. We must also build those spaces so that their expression will be conditioned by the methods and materials that we use to construct them. Spatial conception, form, and materials must constitute a whole; they must be

unified in the creative process after having dwelled in the architect's mind. Construction will always be indiscernible from architecture. It is its flesh and bones.

Eladio Dieste "Some Reflections on Architecture and Construction"

Economy is achieved by means of repetition and pattern. Thus we speak of a structural framework or grid, the delineation in three dimensions of neutral space, which stands ready to be finished to suit a particular program. The grid is a skeleton waiting to be fleshed out.

Lucie Fontein "Reading Structure Through the Frame"

Apparently the neutral grid of space which is enclosed by the skeleton structure supplies us with some particularly cogent and convincing symbols, and for this reason the frame has established relationships, defined a discipline, and generated form. The frame has been the catalyst of an architecture; but one might notice that the frame has also become architecture, that contemporary architecture is almost inconceivable in its absence. Thus, one recalls innumerable buildings where the frame puts in an appearance even when not structurally necessary; one has seen buildings where the frame appears to be present when it is not; and, since the frame seems to have acquired a value quite beyond itself, one is often prepared to accept these aberrations. For, without stretching the analogy too far, it might be fair to say that the frame has come to possess a value for contemporary architecture equivalent to that of the column for classical antiquity and the Renaissance. Like the column, the frame establishes throughout the

SKELETON

like the vaulting bay in the Gothic cathedral, it prescribes a system to which all parts are subordinate.
Colin Rowe "Chicago Frame"

Skeleton construction permitted flexibility in scheduling construction of a tall building.

Once the steel framework was in place, work could proceed without the necessity of slowly moving upward until the structure's full height was reached. In the 1890's at least one Chicago building was enclosed in masonry from the top down.
Cecil D. Elliot *Technics in Architecture*

Besides specializing forms in relation to materials and structure, modern architecture separates and articulates elements. Modern architecture

is never implicit. In promoting the frame and the curtain wall, it has separated structure from shelter. Even the walls of the Johnson Wax Building are enclosing but not supporting.
Robert Venturi *Complexity and Contradiction in Architecture*

Chicago Civic Center, Skidmore, Owings and Merrill (1963–65)

Herman D. J. Spiegel

SITE VISITS:

An Engineer Reads Le Corbusier's Villas

Many architects avoid thinking about structure. They prefer to ignore gravity, wind, seismic, or thermal forces. But to disregard these real forces is to miss architectural opportunities. Instead of ignoring the physical necessity of structure, Le Corbusier used it to create architecture. At the same time, he is not a slave to structure; he didn't force structural regularity for the sake of purity or economy. Instead, he manipulated structural elements for architectural ends – depicting gravity in one place and defying it in another. He made peace with structure by facing it and understanding it thoroughly. The resulting virtuosity allowed him to manipulate structural ideas as easily as he would formal ones.

In a way, Corbusier's approach to structure has an ancient Greek sensibility. In that pre-statics world, no one had a clear understanding of structure, but the architecture shows a captivation with the visual drama of loads and strain. Gravity was awesome. Corbusier was equally enthralled by these forces, but he understood structure so well that he could levitate it.

MAISON JAOUL

More than some of Corbusier's whiter residences, Maison Jaoul looks like it is about structure. The exposed masonry facades do not lend themselves to strict formal analysis but beg to be read as essays on how loads travel through a building to its foundations.

top: At Maison Jaoul, formwork board lines shift direction at arches, and windows are placed under bond beams
at left: Bearing wall and bond beam
previous page top: Interior of Maison Jaoul. Neuilly-Sur-Seine, Le Corbusier (1957)
previous page bottom: Interior of Villa Savoye. Poissy, Le Corbusier (1929-31)

top to bottom:
Center beam accepts tie rods for Catalar
arches on either side
Concrete caps staggered
Concrete caps aligned

Maison Jaoul appears to have grown out of three structural devices: the bearing wall, the bond beam, and the Catalan arch. Corbusier understood them and expressed them. His longitudinal concrete bond beam works against three sets of forces at once; gravity, thermal expansion/contraction, and thrust are addressed by the beam's depth, top and bottom surfaces, and width, respectively. The beam takes the gravity loads of the bearing wall, roof and third and second floors, knits the masonry together longitudinally, and resists the continuous thrust of the interior arches between the tie rods. The beam is large, so it is economical to reinforce. It is exceptionally efficient in all directions – laterally, vertically, longitudinally, economically, and architecturally.

Corbusier oversized the depth of the bond beam, and, in doing so, depicts on the exterior the full depth of the interior floor, arch, and tie rod assembly. The impact structurally is that the beam is deep enough to allow huge liberties to be taken with the placement of openings in exterior walls and the sizing of interior spaces, because it can supply enough bending, shear, and deflection resistance to span over the widest openings. This early structural decision gives him the architectural freedom to shift elements around, pop openings in, do whatever he wants. The masonry is indeed a bearing wall, transporting all load down to the foundation. But the

three continuous beams truly solve most of the structural concerns.

It looks effortless, because it is. The fact that a structural parti enabled him to depart from convention makes the fenestration forceful instead of flippant; the jumping windows exhibit a command of structure, not an affront to it.

The beam is working longitudinally as a bond beam as well. Its top and bottom surfaces adhere to the masonry through friction, preventing the bricks from spreading apart over the years and ending up on the ground, which is their natural inclination. Of course, there are bond beams in every brick structure, occurring at every floor level, but the convention is to hide them behind exterior brick facing. Corbusier engages the bond beam architecturally and structurally by exposing it and asking it to bear gravity load and resist thrust as well.

The three beams receive rods that tie the two concrete arches spanning between them. Thrust is delivered continuously along the spring line of the arches, and the beams act in bending laterally between the ties that take the thrust out. Corbusier threads the rods through the beam, anchors them with bolts and washers, and then hides them with those little concrete caps. In order to simplify construction for the builder, an engineer might work out a regular spacing for the ties and line those knobs up one right over the other. Not Corbusier, He did line them up once to let us know that he's aware of how it is normally done.

The oversized section of this bond beam also accommodates the depth of the arch from spring line to crown plus concrete fill and ceramic tile. There is just enough beam depth left underneath the spring line of the tiles to accept the tie rods, which are centered precisely at the location of thrust transfer. Corbusier played with the arches themselves as well, choosing a stacked bond for the tiles instead of the traditional staggered as more commonly used by Antonio Gaudí and Eduardo Gaustavino.

The two roof arches and three beams form a structure that is stable and balanced when just the dead and uniform loads are considered. But add non-uniform live loads (snow, earth, and plantings on roofs), and the structure may become unbalanced. Because the two arches have unequal spans but the same vertical rise, the imbalance resulting from non-uniform loading allows tension to intrude into the arches, which basically want to remain in compression. Corbusier and his engineer did what I would do – provide enough dead load in the roof arches and size and reinforce the three beams for the worst case scenario. On a small building project this is the most economical approach.

Corbusier used concrete formwork to write a layer of commentary over his arch and beam system. This project was constructed before plywood was commonly used in Europe, and the typical board formwork system provided him with a palette of narrowly spaced lines. At the short façades, where the arched vaults terminate and the two arches are rendered in concrete, he destroyed any expression of the existing horizontal forces pushing against each other at the crown of the arch. A lot of designers would want to clearly emphasize the compressive forces, but Corbusier puts vertical lines on one side of the crown and horizontal lines on the other, and at the spring line he does the same. He completes the subversion by, on one end elevation, placing a window under the center beam. The patchwork of board lines breaks up the massive beams along their length, and, over many of the windows, vertical and horizontal lines deny the spanning action of the concrete they mark.

Corbusier liked to cantilever canopies, which means that no columns muddy the structural picture. He put that slender drainpipe close to the wall and then curved it out just above the ground instead of running it all the way down to drain below grade – it is clear that it does not provide support.

At Jaoul there is a clear delineation of working structure and veneer. Corbusier sorted out

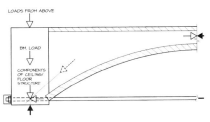

above clockwise:
Unequal arch spans
Patchwork of board lines
Cantilevered canopy with drainpipe
Diagram of stresses when tie rod meets
bond beam
Tie rod hits spring line
at right: Staggered fenestration

Longitudinal, bearing brick walls
alternate between stretcher and
header courses, producing a sturdier
construction. Transverse, non-bearing
brick walls are all stretcher courses.

90

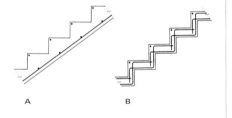

A   B

top left: Center beam 'spans' past painted pier
top right: Stairway and Plumbing
above: Concrete stair reinforcing:
A conventional vs. B Corbusier

panels and bearing wall by material. The façades are assembled of masonry, and the resulting gaps are filled in by glazing or wood panels. Inside, some of the working structure is made to look like veneer. The interior concrete columns and piers are dematerialized with bright colored paint on one face, allowing the center beam to read as if it were spanning the entire length of the house.

The sculptural, stepped underside of the interior concrete stair required a more complicated formwork, steel reinforcing fabrication/installation, and concrete placement than a conventional sloped soffit. If Corbusier's stair is reinforced with 1/2" diameter #4 bars, the effective depth is only 2.25" to 3.5", which adds further to the expense and creates much more work for the contractor. Nevertheless, the stair is a delight to see, and, as it strays from the conventional, more fun to work out. And as Corbusier has so economically resolved the major structural issues, the stairs are a negligible blip on the economic screen.

Although not apparent to my eye, Corbusier did labor over the mechanical and plumbing articulation as well. Madame Jaoul told me that she didn't understand why he spent so much time working these systems out and painting pipes different colors, especially since the results were so mundane.

On the whole Maison Jaoul is a beautifully conceived and executed tour de force.

VILLA SAVOYE

Compared with the obvious presentation of structure at Maison Jaoul, where exterior expresses interior, the structural story unfolds more subtly at Villa Savoye.

The beauty of the Villa Savoye's structure lies in its column grid. When establishing a structural bay size, it is common to space columns as far apart as economically possible (usually spans of 18'–24' or more), and to think that fewer columns means more design freedom. But sometimes this strategy backfires. The problem is that once that grid is set, there's no changing it without a struggle. With every column removal comes the possible addition of a large transfer beam and, without fail, coordination issues to solve among all the consultants. Unless the architecture will remain as rigid as the structure, sometimes it makes sense to start with comfortable spans instead of maximum spans. This generally was Corbusier's approach. At Savoye, he established a grid of five columns in each direction set at about 15'6" on center, a spacing so comfortable that the grid can easily be violated. Integrating the columns into the architecture becomes an artistic and practical process instead of a tortured one.

From the exterior, Savoye's columns are presented on a regular five-by-five grid. Driving from the northwest and circling around the south of the house back to the north entry, the

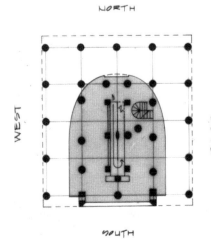

top sequence: Automobile approach to Villa Savoye, sequenced from left to right

above left: Interior columns jump off grid to form entry portal

above right: Exterior grid implies column behind front door

below left: First floor plan

below right: Second floor plan

(Column sizes are exaggerated for clarity in both plans)

left: Center ramp looking toward top landing – lozenge shaped column in foreground allows visual velocity that greets visitor upon entering to continue.
above: Beam and teardrop column at roof deck

grid registers strongly in your mind. The first view of the house by car is of the north elevation; five white round columns frame the shadowy entrance. Driving past the west elevation you then see five white round columns that stand out against the green garage. On the south elevation you come across two round columns at the corners and two trapezoidal columns at the quarter points, and, if the curtain is drawn, you can make out an interior round column that is placed on grid. Circling back to the north and pulling up under the porte cochere, you must drive through the grid, two round columns on your left and five on your right. The sequence of views is experienced quickly, and the image of a rigid five by five grid is forcefully impressed upon the visitor.

Corbusier stuck to this grid on the exterior but destroyed it completely inside, beginning right at the front door. The seemingly relentless exterior grid suggests an interior column centered on the other side of the entrance. But as soon as you open the door, you see two columns replacing the one you'd bump into had he left it on the grid. Study the ground floor plan and it is clear that this move is only the beginning. There are eight freestanding interior column grid points, and Corbusier leaves only one column in place; he replaces the other seven implied by the grid with seventeen off-grid columns, located to suit the architectural needs of both floors. Once inside the front door, look overhead and you see the transfer beam that carries the second floor column above and allows the first floor columns to jump off grid. This beam is notched

clockwise: firebox masonry changes direction
Almost cantilevered table
Cracked transom glass
Columns at ramp - looking toward entry
Beam and column

right through the front door transom glass– a straightforward class move, but not even Corbusier could pull off that glazing detail. Note the cracks that emanate from the inside corners of the glass on each side of the beam.

However, the architectural move that necessitated the rearrangement of the most first floor columns is the long ramp leading to the second floor at the heart of the plan. Here he freely reconfigured the columns to allow for the extended slab penetration centered right on a grid line. Instead of three columns on one grid line, he placed ten columns on three.

Whenever a hole is punched in a slab, there's a problem around the edges of the hole, where the continuity of the reinforced concrete has to be maintained. Corbusier just popped in columns with beams around the edges and solved the structural problem immediately. An engineer's delight – lots of columns to grab on to quickly for short, simple little spans. And he had no hang-ups about consistency; most of the columns are round, but if he had to fair in a window or a wall, he'd square the column to simplify detailing.

Beams are usually visible at Savoye, but not always. Some are hidden in exterior walls. Beams are sometimes oversized to match column dimensions and simplify the formwork.

One beam in particular, bracing the top of the wall at a horizontal opening to the roof deck, is made into an architectural feature. Its bottom flange tapers to reflect the horizontal force it's resisting – deepest in the middle, tapering back as it passes the teardrop columns, and ultimately matching the thickness of the walls at the far ends, (see dashed lines on second floor plan). It looks like a bending moment diagram. The beam below the opening doesn't taper, but where it joins the wall the top flange is notched. Bending is no longer the issue, and ample cross section remains to transfer shear stresses to the square columns at each end.

Walking through Savoye, one continues to encounter jewels of structural play. To me, it is evidence of an architect thoroughly engaged with structure, and proof that understanding structure brings more architecture.

On the firebox, masonry is laid in a manner that implies the direction of air flow that makes the fireplace work – horizontal on the firebox and vertical where the flue shoots up.

A table just inside the entrance is cantilevered off a substantial column and helped by a slender leg, creating a startling contrast.

At the stair a thin pipe column supports the railing, and there is a sliver of space where the stair curves around it. Corbusier wanted to make clear that this pipe column does not support the stair in any way – he prevented it from acting as a structural parasite.

Corbusier was able to employ structure, but what about today's practitioners? What is fair to expect of them when they encounter structural

94

clockwise:
Beam tapers according to bending stress
View of beam from below
Notch detail of beam
Pipe column at stair

AUTHORS NOTE: The Editors of this journal
are to be commended for their foresight and
bravery for producing an issue of *Perspecta*
devoted to structural engineering.

engineering issues? Today's opportunities lie in the relationship between engineer and architect– one in which the two disciplines truly overlap will be the most fruitful for design. Architects have the program; engineers have natural forces. I'm happy to see more architects integrating and reasonably accepting both! It is the responsibility of engineers to offer original as well as established structural ideas, but architects can get the most out of their engineers if they are able to speak their language somewhat, to understand bending moment, shear, and deflection and to know basics such as 'bending is the most expensive stress.' Gaudi stated this many years ago, discussed and debated it with his colleagues, and was very proud of what he felt was his superior structural prowess. Corbusier, as I understand it, read every book on concrete that was available to him. Clearly it is not possible to say that their creative efforts were hindered by this allied knowledge.

Unfortunately, the message in today's American architecture education is that structure is a pragmatic necessity, not an intrinsic part of the design process to be manipulated creatively. I have been retired from teaching for the past seven years, and if I am wrong in my assumption I would love to be corrected. Time allocations are involved; there are only so many hours in a student's day, and there are more disciplines jockeying for those hours than can be fully accommodated in a three year Master of Architecture program. Only the design faculty can change this situation, since they drive the priorities of architecture schools. The challenge is to convey to students that facility with structure contributes to design facility. To get to the point where they can design with structure, architects really do have to crunch some numbers, because you cannot just intuit or talk it. It takes work to get such an understanding, but it is necessary for pulling off either a structural tour de force such as Maison Jaoul or the reserved structural cleverness at Villa Savoye.

Round and square columns at stair

MATERIAL, WORK, AND RESISTANCE
Alan Organschi

Vaulted interior space, House in Litchfield, Connecticut

THE EDITORS WANTED TO KNOW HOW A YOUNG
FIRM WORKING ON SMALL SCALE PROJECTS
MIGHT DESIGN WITH STRUCTURE. WE ASKED ALAN
ORGANSCHI TO REFLECT ON THE STRUCTURAL
INVESTIGATIONS THAT OCCUR IN THE DESIGN AND
CONSTRUCTION OF THE HOUSES BY GRAY
ORGANSCHI ARCHITECTS, THE OFFICE HE RUNS
WITH LISA GRAY.

In making buildings, architects necessarily define the relationship between architecture and its structural formation. They deploy material and methods of assembly and generate work, in the form of human and mechanical labor, to answer the physical demands of the spaces they design. I'm intrigued by the effect of this symbiosis of form, stuff, and work on the measure and texture of the spaces we inhabit.

We've recently completed two small houses and a bridge. The projects are quite different in their use, their spatial character, and their relationship to their sites, but they share a common constructional premise. All three were conceived, in whole or large part and for varying reasons, as prefabricated structural assemblies. The necessary synthesis of architectural conception and construction strategy allowed us to explore, at an elemental level, the nature of each building's structure, its material composition and the agency of its production.

When we conceived of using curved laminated beams to form the vaulted interior space of the house in Litchfield, we were compelled by the idea of the stresses acting within each member. Above and beyond the typical bending stress of roof loads we saw the considerable potential energy bound up in the deformation that was required of the roof timbers to create the shape of the room. We began to reflect on the character of that deformation, the relationships among the wooden plies within the laminated timber, and the material attributes of each ply.

Wood is a fibrous material. Its structural value is based not only on the strength of the individual fibers in the wood or the size and orientation of the bundle of fibers but also on the degree to which those fibers are uninterrupted by flaws such as knots, checks, or cracks.

The lamination of smaller boards to create larger members serves two possible purposes. One is to build a better, more stable, more efficient, and more readily analyzed structural timber. This is accomplished through the culling, grading, and re-assembly of individual boards or laminations. In this way, in a simple bending member, for example, those layers with the fewest flaws are laid up along the beam's tension and compression edges, and those with the most flaws are grouped in the center where the primary forces of the tension and compression are smallest. This reconfiguration, in which the relationship of successive laminations within the cross section of the member is evaluated and adjusted, suggests the second purpose: the shifting of the longitudinal relationship of the laminations, i.e., the sliding of layers against one another to create curvature in the member. The ability to fix the relative position of the laminations, usually with glue, guarantees the rigidity and bending resistance of the larger member.

Typically, in the industrial process of glue-lamination, the glue is allowed to squeeze out from between the layers so that when cured, the member must be 'resized' or surfaced to its final specified dimension. This final step in the process nearly erases the distinctions among laminations: gaps between layers are filled; the presence of glue joints is almost eliminated. The finished 'glulam' becomes a simulation of a solid timber.

Rather than suppressing the distinction among plies, we chose to articulate the individual laminations and the resistance to the forces of horizontal shear necessary in the connection between each layer. To avoid the a-tectonic reading of the curvature produced by industrial glue lamination, we chose to make a dry lamination that was fixed in its shape by a pattern of shear bolts that ran along the length of each beam. We used rough band-sawn ash boards of inconsistent width and eased their edges slightly to exaggerate the joint between successive layers. As a result, the highly legible stacking of layers, the irregularity of the face of the beam, and the emphasis of the mechanical fasteners became artifacts of the beam assembly and a description of material resistance.

House in Litchfield, view from the east

In retrospect, I see that our impulse in that house to articulate the particular character of the material within a structural member became a kind of model for the structural and spatial elaboration of the building itself. It reflects, I think, our interest in creating a structured object, a desire to identify and develop an underlying constructional and structural motivation for any tectonic form and its associated space. By dissolving the envelope of the house and articulating the structural relationships among its constituent parts, we felt that we were creating an internal mechanical argument for the simplicity of the building's external volume. Whether elemental, at the scale of material and detail, or compositional, within the scale of a room or even landscape, we saw the relationship of structure to architecture as an artifact of the construction process, a residual description of why the form of the building exists.

We developed this predilection in our workshop, where we first made cabinetry and furniture. Those early small projects provoked a series of increasingly focused questions about the basic nature of the working of material. Typically, in architectural and structural design, because of the scale of an architect's responsibilities and the logistical complexities of even the small architecture of houses, structural materials are consumed as prepackaged products. The structural characteristics of wood, for example, are determined by the dimensioning systems inherent to manufacturing processes of the timber and

North elevation showing offset cladding

lumber industry and the grading apparatus and structural performance data that they provide. In design and construction at the compact scale of furniture, however, one develops a primary relationship to the material characteristics of wood. Not only its species, but the relative position of a board within a tree trunk, the history of its growth, the way it is sawn, dried, and even stored, are all questions with enormous bearing on its workability and structural suitability.

Our current work in the studio has shifted from the scale of furniture to that of small buildings. In producing parts and prototype assemblies and coordinating the prefabrication of components of the projects we design, we've continued to engage the construction process as a medium for architectural exploration. We have come to see the problem of inserting an architectural object into an existing terrain as physically akin to the problem of developing a piece of joinery. But by making this leap in scale, while maintaining a control of the material and structural elaboration of our work, we've inadvertently sidestepped the professional, commercial, and industrial standards for small building construction. It's forced us to face a lot of questions about the feasibility of designing architecture as one might a cabinet assembly. Ultimately, I think, our goal has been to address these problems not as technical hurdles, but rather as the source of an architectural language.

By exploring the character of material and its

assembly as a foundation of structural elaboration, we face, in our work, the inevitable issue of time and cost. The exacting investigations of an integrated method of design and construction that small scale affords the cabinet maker seem hopelessly rarified within the context of buildings. And though the idea of integrating structure and construction into the process of architectural conception and the language of building is so basic to our profession as to seem commonplace, the difficulty of achieving it in the demanding economy of contemporary building is nearly insurmountable. Despite the promises of our education and the romance of our professional history and traditions, architects are faced everyday with the fact that the sector of our society that has most successfully reintegrated architectural design, structural engineering, and construction is the American commercial building industry. Here economies of scale and long histories of product development have produced building systems of almost unmatchable economic refinement. Dimensioned assemblies, pre-engineered structural members with code-compliant connectors, cladding, and fenestration systems, all define what's economical and builderly in architectural design today.

That a building might convey a system of resistance to structural forces or describe the order of its assembly runs counter to the intention of commercial light construction. Like the industrially glue-laminated timber, which

obscures the residue of its manufacture through the machining of its surface, the structural envelope of the western platform frame, the revolutionizing construction system of postwar America, conceals the order of its assembly in the layering of its wall. Within a vapor tight six and a half inch wall thickness are compressed a building's interior and exterior finish systems, vertical load bearing structure, lateral shear resistant structure, insulation, electrical wiring, plumbing supply and waste lines, and, often, heating and ventilation ducting. Any lateral structural load that cannot be absorbed by the panelized sheathing of the vertical building envelope or by stiffening interior partition walls is transferred into a similar horizontal sandwich in the floor which serves as a shear diaphragm. From a structural and constructional standpoint the economy of the system lies in its capacity to absorb and conceal difference and error. From an architectural standpoint, the tendency to absorb constituent parts into an apparently monolithic assembly is indirectly proportional to its capacity for articulation, particularity, and distinction. Meaning is typically conferred upon it as stylistic reference through distinctions in roof slope and geometry, wall height, and trim detail. The apparent homogeneity of the 'stick framed' wall has created a kind of universal architectural homogeneity in the new American landscape where structural ideas are limited to episodic or anecdotal luxuries like the grafting of the a-func-

Construction of laminated beams and stressed skin panels
Fabrication of laminated beam in Architect's workshop

View of dual structure – frame and stressed skin

100

tional 'decorative truss' or the hyperfunctional steel 'W' section onto the hermetic enclosure of the platform frame.

While my tendency is to want to articulate structural relationships in our buildings, to let the architecture convey the complementary physical workings of structural resistance and manufacture, I'm wary of the extremes of icono-clastic formal or structural exhibitionism that that approach might engender. The pitfall there, I believe, is the objectification of the structural system at the expense of an architectural idea. The solution lies instead in the analysis and reconfiguration of current building practice, the teasing of larger architectural ideas from the tightly knit technical formulations of industry.

In the stick-framed wall, for example, the action of plywood sheathing, whose cross-lami-nation of graded and glued veneers transmits and absorbs directional loads, provides racking resis-tance within the sheet, and confers that resis-tance to the line of studs in the wall. The lamination of plywood reiterates the laminary character of the wall itself, as if the material resistance of the sheet is repeated thematically throughout the structure of the building. It is a model of structural interdependence, the shunt-

House in Washington, Connecticut
Gaps between materials widen to frame windows and doors

House and workshops in Washington, Connecticut

ing of varying kinds of forces through appropriate material components of a building envelope.

The endoskeleton of the house in Litchfield relies on those principles of interdependence and exploits the structural relationship between stud and sheathing at a magnified scale. We felt it important to emphasize the sequential transformation of the house's twelve ashwood ribs and articulate their role in the deformation and curvature of the house's south wall. We freed the building interior of the bracing members typical to the freestanding frame of traditional barn construction and instead absorbed the lateral racking forces of the wind in the structural lamination of the building's insulating sheath, a sandwich of two 'skins' of oriented strand board on an insulating core of expanded polystyrene. The tectonic distinction between frame and enclosure that unfolds as you experience the house is a distinction not of structure and skin, but of two interdependent components of structural resistance. The ash ribs alone, like studs in a wall, are structurally incomplete. Without the stressed skin sheath, they would collapse.

The serial arrangement of ash ribs, uncomplicated by diagonal interconnections, more immediately and forcefully expresses the mechanics of the house's assembly. Each rib was placed,

plumbed, and propped. The panels were then applied. Those steps of assembly, like the lamination and bolting of plies in the arches, reinforced our conception of the interior space and mirrored the structural function of the building.

In looking at the house now, I'm struck by the fact that the reading of the building as an assembly of interdependent yet discreet elements was most forcefully conveyed at the scale of the landscape through the formation of a seemingly small structural detail. By placing the ash ribs to bear directly on the 10" foundation wall and leaving the stressed skin panel sheath to overhang it by the full thickness of the panel and the dimension of panel standoffs, we created a condition of discontinuity at the junction between the base and superstructure of the building. Like a shadow line that at once articulates and forgives the irregularity of a joint between two different materials, the break between the prepared ground of the site and the prefabricated building that we erected there emphasizes the transition between different structural systems and telegraphs the interruption in construction concept and method. That overhang, essentially a simple manipulation of the building section, significantly altered the relationship of the house to its immediate ter-

rain and the quality of its placement on the land.

That small discovery has since prompted us to explore this intersection of structural systems more fully. The generic wall section of the contemporary American stick framed house marks this transition between foundation and wood frame with a pressure treated wooden sill plate at about 8" above the surrounding grade and only a slight offset between the exterior surfaces of concrete and the siding above. As a matter of function, the detail minimizes the destructive effects to wood of soil and moisture and clearly delineates the scope of both the foundation and framing subcontractors' responsibilities. It is technically undemanding, universally applicable and, therefore, ubiquitous. It is indifferent to the land on which it sits and ambivalent about the building it supports.

We began to explore this line where distinct structural and material systems meet, when we were offered the opportunity to build with stone in a project for a small house, workshop and garage. We split the buildings into three material and construction components: a heavy masonry wall that formed the perimeter of the building complex, prefabricated 'glulam' timber frames, and an enclosing system of panels that, as in the Litchfield house, provide directional racking resistance to the timber frame. In the stone masonry, we deeply recessed the mortar joints in an effort to suppress a more typical reading of surface pattern and to instead emphasize the weight and bearing of each individual piece and the history of the system's assembly. Small chink stones fill any irregular open joints and facilitate the placement, fitting, and balance of larger stones and transfer the force and weight of each stone to the bed of stones beneath it.

Like the chinked gap between two irregular surfaces of adjoined stone, we treated the connection between the masonry walls, extrusions of the buildings' foundations and the wood panel enclosures – prefabricated and erected on site – as a mediating gap between two materially incompatible systems. At some points that gap is literally just that, a separation between the rough edge of masonry and the finished edge of the panel. Elsewhere it widens to form an entryway, a line of windows, or the space of a balcony. The structural frame bridges the space between the enclosing systems of masonry and prefabricated panel as struts and braces, making connections to the stone that are specific and mechanical. From the forest and meadows that surround the building, the masses of masonry are legibly distinct from the relatively light wood members that spring from it to form the interior spaces of the house.

Although we deployed the industrially produced wood components and hand-laid stone work as physically and conceptually distinct systems, I now see their essential similarity. Whether a craft like the laying of stone, in which the accumulated skill and judgement of the artisan endows an object with a particular character, or an industrial process like the glue lamination of timbers, in which the refinement of repeatable steps in a method guarantees the uniformity and reproducibility of a product, the method and order of assembly endows a physical artifact with dimension and syntax. The work that underlies the production of an architectural object suggests the complementary nature of structural resistance and building manufacture. Material, by itself, is architecturally inert. It lacks an inherently appropriate application or proportion. But the capacity of material to be worked and manipulated – like its capacity to resist stress – is elemental to architecture and its structural form.

We've worked again with curvature and laminated wood since developing the structural members for the house in Litchfield. The deck panels of a bridge we designed to carry construction vehicles across a small stream explore both the structural capacity and expressive potential of industrial glue lamination. A local wetland regu-latory agency had demanded that the construction of any crossing have a demonstrably minimal impact on the stream's delicate floodplain, so we proposed to crane into place from the stream's upper banks six prefabricated timber planks. To maintain the curvature of the road that serves it, we formed the panels as 'glulam' arches that were then laid on their sides. With the lamination laid up in this axis, each panel acts as a composite slab, in which each lamination transfers and spreads the heavy wheel loads of construction vehicles laterally to adjacent laminations through the continuous structural glue joints that bind them together. We determined a 10 $^{3}/4$" depth as the minimum section modulus required for the member to resist the axial load of the 10-ton vehicles that were to use it. Our glue laminator's limit for the width of a single layup was 60". Two of these planks, laid side by side, provided sufficient width for a single traffic lane and reiterated the wheel tracks of the small access road that serves the bridge.

The two bolt-laminated wooden rails that line either side of the bridge were developments of the arches in the Litchfield house, but the structural action is quite different. In our prototype studies of the earlier project, we had come upon the potential flexibility of a laminated member without a continuous glue line and wanted to exploit that elasticity here as a possi-

Bridge in Washington, Connecticut

Shock absorbent laminated beam

ble shock absorber. By separating each layer by the thickness of a large fender washer, the lamination would allow the individual 2" x 4" plies to deflect within their elastic range. That distortion would absorb energy from the impact of a wheel strike and shed load through the bolts into the steel connectors and the member as a whole. We were particularly excited by the curb detail, because, unlike the bolt laminations in Litchfield, it wasn't necessary to produce formwork for the bending of the member. The bridge's deck panels, already in place, provided a template for the curb's arc, a jig for the assembly of the rails.

In working out the problems of building structure, architects bind their invention of form and space to the experience of inhabiting architecture. At one level, the construction of the bridge and its wheel curb is merely a technological solution to a relatively simple structural problem. But we felt that it simultaneously conveyed a broader idea about one's movement through a landscape and, in detail and execution, an attitude about the relationship of a building to the terrain of a particular place. I think that the means are always embedded in the end, and I believe that the character of the spaces we imagine are inextricably intertwined with the processes by which we form them.

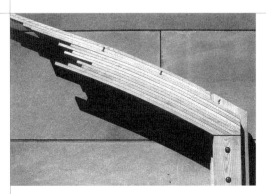

Prototype of laminated beam for house in Litchfield

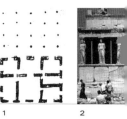

Peter D. Waldman

NUMBERS IN THE NIGHT

STRUCTURE AS THE SYNCOPATION OF GRAVITY AND ORIENTATION

3   4   5   6   7

105

ON REPOSITIONING

On that first terrific night, Crusoe had to choose between a cave or a tent; he chose both

– Daniel Defoe, *Robinson Crusoe*

For thirty-nine years I have sketched structure syncopated by night. As a student I would jot down parti diagrams in my bedside sketchpad, deceiving myself into thinking that structural clarity was achieved by a few bold lines representing emphatic walls, or by what I took to be the converse, a cartesian forest of columns. (Wall and Column – the struggle would characterize my work ever since.) Lying there supine,* the day's upright, calm, rational thinking would melt into the mattress and become turbulent. I would fall asleep by recounting the possible combinations of walls and/or the syncopation of grids. These iterations entered my dreams, where they became tortured, endless, morphing possibilities. Numbers were supposed to stabilize the day's production. But they became unstable at night as their permutations haunted my unconscious world. The endless shifting around of structural paradigms choreographed movements for my body – vertebrae rolling back and forth according to a nightmare's diagram

For many of those years I would wake up exhausted but relieved that daylight had returned to restore reason – the relief would be tainted, however, when I examined the night's sketched productions, which could only be read as confrontational marks and erasures. Reason's tyranny compelled me to hide the evidence in an adjacent closet, for it revealed a topographic imagination – unresolved, fragmentary, incomplete, frictional linea occultae carved into the toothy paper of my pad. But, perversely, at a certain point,** I decided to take confidence in the utility of my own nighttime markings and now delight in reading structure as a volatile element in the design process.

Conventional wisdom perpetuates the passivity and immutability of structure achieving static resolution. The alternative is to celebrate the ongoing evidence of dynamic and competing loads.

Conventional wisdom perpetuates structural paradigms as singular (walls or frames, caves or tents), complete and authoritative unto themselves. The alternative is to think of structure as contingent, incomplete, in stress if not failure, vulnerable and certainly oppositional if not multiple, as in the model of the megaron.

*The body itself transposes structure according to a syncopated meter: vertical by day, horizontal by night.

**An example of an acceptance of mutable structure was my own re-positioning within polemical contexts - it is a story of caves and tents. At Princeton in the '60's one generation was taught that modern architects were obliged to build with light, but precise structural armatures. A decade later, another generation was taught that architects had obligations to reestablish the benchmarks of the known world and, as such, should no longer explore the extension of space with frames but reconfirm the finiteness of rooms with substantial walls. Slow to learn or resistive, as a young teacher during the '70's I offered an alternative model to the polarized students, an intentionally ambiguous structural diagram of two systems (wall and frame, or cave and tent) in frictional and evasive engagement (megaron). This image of the megaron (figure 7) borrowed from enduring teacher Michael Graves in 1969 is now returned in gratitude.

1 sketch by Le Corbusier
2 Caryatids, Erectheum, Acropolis, Athens
3 cave: Neolithic Hut, Mycenae
4 tent: Native American wigwam
5 cave: General Assembly Building, Chandigarh,
Le Corbusier (1956)
6 tent: Maison Domino, Le Corbusier
7 megaron
8 View from the south of Parcel X, North Garden, Virginia

9 a   9b   9c   9d

106

ON LANDSCAPES OF AGGRESSION

In the beginning God created Heaven and Earth, and all was without form – Genesis

Ever since *Genesis*, architecture has been conceived as both physical and temporal, metering the space between heaven and earth, ephemeral vapors and the topographic imagination, ultimately establishing the recurrent paradigms of Eden and Jerusalem, the cyclic garden and the resistive city.

The world as construction site was the first structured place before cities, buildings, or gardens; structure in its incompleteness was there first in its progressive state. The moment it was finished – when Paradise became a walled-in garden – it was abandoned.

Structure is first to negotiate with the world of nature. Only then does architecture fix a world within. Structure is the precondition to enclosure, to dwelling within architecture. It is also the last evidence of occupation; when the enclosure dissolves, structure remains as a ruin. Concrete pours and steel erections create the walls and columns that will one day remain to mark the site as having been inhabited. The syncopation of structuring acts by a myriad of makers, fabricators who are neither initial designers nor eventual users, establishes the construction site as one of fundamental political authority rarely considered today. Those who dwell in ongoing, enduring work help define building structure as a generative verb.

Building is then considered here as a verb, as an instrumental deformative act. Building is manifested through successive territorial transformations, Semperian Landscapes of Aggression, conventionally known as the short-term construction site and pessimistically perceived as the long-term scarring of earth.

Starting with foundations, structure is the frictional character in a Spatial Tale of Origins, engaging both concentric gravity and eccentric orientation and persisting as a ruin to retell the story.

Gravity is invariant, constantly pulling vectors to the center of the earth. Orientation is temporal, yet recurrent, inscribing each day with its own specific arcs marking sunrise, high noon, and sunset. Both factors are grappled with when structure negotiates with nature. Gravity and orientation are then the only benchmarks agreed upon by the Engineer and the Gardener who provide the constituent characteristics of an architect.

9 Four Progressive sections through Parcel X beginning with the East cave-like elevation (a), moving west every 26 feet (b, c) and ending with the diaphanous frame (d)
10 The Maison du Weekend employs primitive and contemporary structures of great mass and ephemeral lightness. Paris, Le Corbusier (1935)
11 Ronchamp in part is a tent, which looks like a cave, part rubble of the former sanctuary, part gunnite over a veiled steel fabric, with a heavy concrete cloud of a roof floating on point supports
12 Plan and section of the Chapel of Notre Dame du Haut, Ronchamp, Le Courbusier (1951-53)
13 Genesis – Construction of the Earth

10   11   12   13

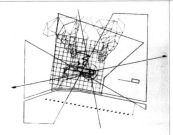

14

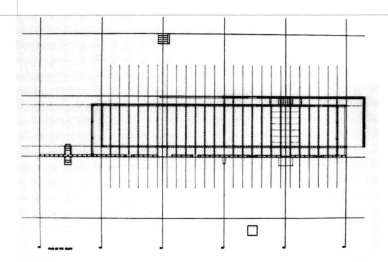

15

The 3.84 acre Parcel X sits at the margin
of a still vast pastoral landscape. It was
already marked long before map-makers,
surveyors, and soil-samplers came to
project their scars upon its surface.
Geological origins were recorded in
massive oblique granite ridges – these
ravines are the source of one of the most
generous wells in Albemarle County,
which is fed by a constellation of cisterns.
To this parcel have journeyed two
nomads, one with a ruler, the other
with a compass. They seek to prepare the
ground, to tend a garden, and eventually
to engage the earth.

16

17

14 Site Plan of Parcel X
15 Plan of the ruler
16 Plan of the compass
17 Composite plan

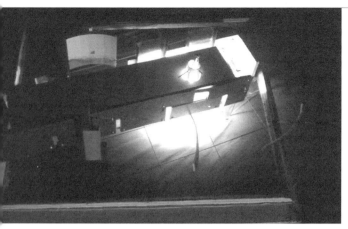

a

b

c

d

e

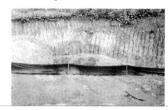

ON SPECIFICATIONS FOR CONSTRUCTION

The first architectural act is to break the ground; the second is to raise structure vertically to the sky – Semper

I read Specifications for Construction as instructions for alchemy, strategizing the soiling of foundations before eschatological finishes are burnished. They define architecture as the collaboration of Engineer and Gardener.

The sixteen divisions of the Specifications are prefaced by a section enumerating the Preconditions of the Site before construction. The preconditions of Parcel X record a site already full, not empty, of geological fissures and colluvial soil where ancient forests of vertical tulip poplar trees are metered by split rail fences.

The first eight divisions of Specifications for Construction determine the strategic repositioning of trades for the material and temporal metering of space. Yet the final eight divisions of Specifications for Construction retreat from this frictional process with provisions for external and internal finishes, as if to stabilize or fix the now objectified artifact.

But visceral structure is appreciated most in terms of the lingering construction site. It is an architect's privilege to bear witness to the growing structure over time and refer to the accreted process when understanding the building as it stands after Specification 16: the product of eons of local geology, centuries of local history, and months of local labor. The architect can see in the building individuals from the past, repeating routine, familiar tasks.

Building as a verb, as an ongoing phenomenal process, is in crisis if one accepts the notion of substantial completion; with the assemblage of a checklist comes the assumption that structures are invariant and, thus, should not creak or leak. There are alternatives to the impoverished and pretentious architecture that values more the resolution or stabilization of structure over stress scars and watermarks. I suggest an architecture that celebrates the instrumentality of structure in action. The Spatial Tale of Origin recounted in Specifications for Construction should begin and end with yet another eschatological beginning, always in water and watermarks, soil and stain, darkness and encrusted patina, fire and ash, secret springs, manholes, and volcanic eruptions.

f   g   h   i

Construction of Parcel X:

On the first day, a tent is pitched not far from the pre-existing well. A campfire establishes the ash traces of man's first nightmare.

The second morning begins the process of clearing the site as a staging area for construction. At noon a plinth is extended along the full southern edge of the site. That evening at the western boundary X-bracing records the setting of the sun in the brittle surface of this first *parterre*.

The third morning begins the process of erecting a steel framework based on a 26-foot meter, which gives another measure to this now cleared and leveled site. A fireplace is erected to the south, and to the north a totemic marker establishes the construction precinct.

On the fourth day a shield is erected to challenge the southern exposure. Steel studs, copper siding, and Hope's doors become an incessant backdrop. Thereupon an armature of eye hooks and guide wires collaborates with wisteria vines to mask this pretentious straight edge.

On the fifth day a new terrace is formed by a framed plane hovering above the previous plinth. From this rooftop one can recover the horizon previously denied by the undulating topography. Late in the day, glass curtain walls seal off the east and the west with unsentimental anonymity, while a glass block panel of equal size makes the northern exposure prismatic.

On the sixth day a man-hole reveals the secrets of the cistern below; a study is perched above; a volcanic lens points south; and the ground begins to heave. On that sixth night the nomads dream of how similar the first move was to the last.

On the seventh day a wall rises to the north where the totemic stake once distinguished within from without.

18 The initial retaining wall splits to frame a gap as it emerges from the ground to permit the summer solstice morning light to enter the basement of Parcel X. Then shining steel studs, before they are enclosed with the copper skin, cast magical shadows for a brief moment in collaboration with the adjacent stand of ancient tulip poplars. This magic is merely represented now by the regular markings of the burnished standing seam sleeves that meter the copper shield from sunrise to sunset.

LESSONS LEARNED

Reading structures as products of both the permutations of immutable Numbers in the Night as well as the visceral choreography of the Construction Site is an apology for Parcel X, a temporal encampment where the steel frame creaks and the concrete walls display stress cracks; structure groans when it is harnessed to an architecture that holds a covenant with the world again.

22 Parcel X – view from the West

Parcel X Design Team
Architects: Peter D. Waldman, Architect;
Joe Atkins, Pat Byrne, Dave Ackerman, Robert Corser, Todd Ray,
Design Team; Robert Corser, Model Maker
Consultants: Robert Corser, Structural; Robert Corser and
Todd Ray, (the landscape within)
General Contractor: Ace Constuction Company

In the nomadic North American condition, one can never tell if your next move is to be your last. Precautions should be taken to secure both day dreams and night-mares; ancient flues must guard deep cisterns; household goods must be kept at a distance while the pre-conditions of the site punctuate the campsite of Parcel X from within. This Genesis of Revelation is the ancient rite of all Nomads who know that the City and the Garden have origins in the Oasis.

Parcel X – The insistent horizons of
the floor and roof are in contrast to the
oblique section of the site. The
copper shield is an unrelenting ruler
with the character of a fine tooth comb.
The Volcano is also a tent encamped
once again upon the site. The hearth is
a grotto, outrigger ark beneath the
kaleidoscopic box, which merely frames
the sun and the moon.

19 Ceiling Skylight – volcano and/or tent
20 Cross bracing looking East up to the
volcano /attic
21 Cross bracing looking North to
basement cave below

111

19

20

21

on SITE VISITS
Grant F. Marani

On reading Herman Spiegel's essay, what came to mind were two articles written some 50 years ago by two then young British Turks: Colin Rowe and James Stirling. Their essays, respectively "The Mathematics of the Ideal Villa" and "Garches to Jaoul," approach Le Corbusier's work from different directions but arrive at a similar position – one of respect and admiration for the rich complexity and rigor of his work. At Cornell, where Rowe taught for over twenty years and Stirling was a more than frequent visitor, their essays became touchstones for a generation of students' understanding of this

influential architect's work. For Professor Rowe, the 'white' work was a paradigm, an intellectual game open to the erudite formal analysis within which he would revel; for his practitioner friend, Sir James, the materiality and sheer gravity of Le Corbusier's work, evident in the 'rustic' Maison Jaoul, was a return to sensual architectural fundamentals he deemed missing in Corbusier's earlier work.

Like these two articles, Professor Spiegel's essay inspires readers to revisit Le Corbusier. His sweeping yet straight forward opening statement, 'Many architects avoid thinking about struc-

ture,' is surely the voice of a stately, experienced engineer. The insights that follow articulate how this aversion was not so of Corbusier, who masterfully manipulated structural realities to reinforce architectural ends. In this way Spiegel's argument resembles Kenneth Frampton's: true architectural concepts do not eschew structure.

What is refreshing about this essay is its language and structure; straightforward and clear, it provides a counterpoint to the conventionally fashionable obfuscative analyses so prevalent in recent architectural writing. What is enjoyable about this essay

is the sheer delight this engineer evokes when describing Corbusier's work. Using Le Corbusier as an exemplar of an architect steeped in the classical tradition, who also delights in the 'visual drama of loads and strain' to create architecture and 'depicting gravity in one place while defying it in another,' Spiegel speaks more to the realm of poetics than mere calculation.

Grant F. Marani is an associate partner at Robert A.M. Stern Architects. He is also an associate (adjunct) professor of design at the Columbia University School of Architecture, Planning, and Preservation, where he coordinates the housing studio.

on MATERIAL, WORK AND RESISTANCE
Eeva–Liisa Pelkonen

The work of Gray Organschi Architecture is known for its fine material and tectonic sensibility. The buildings are often, at least in part, produced in the office workshop. The projects built so far speak about the care and precision the firm gives to their work, as well as about clients who are willing to invest in such quality.

Organschi, a trained carpenter and furniture builder, is at an interesting turning point in his career where after having now executed small residential work, bigger work is on its way. Along with an increase in scale and a shift from private to public and institutional clients comes an intensification of pressure, and a problem always latent in building becomes more immediate: how to maintain high quality against the now stronger forces of budget and schedule.

Understanding the word 'resis-

tance,' which appears in the article's title, is key to understanding how Organschi starts to address the issue of cost in his text. The word can be read as both a technical and critical concept. Overtly, Organschi employs the former usage: 'resistance' refers to structural forces and their formal outcome. Also implied in his text is an argument which uses the word critically: architectural form and structure should be resistant to socio-economic forces. One could make a connection with, for example, Kenneth Frampton's argument that certain types of structure and form – unique, well crafted, and sometimes expensive – can be used to resist the economic imperative which results in so much of the built environment being generic, badly made, and cheap.

Both readings suffer from what I would call a 'purity problem.' Decisions

of structure and materiality cannot and should not be bracketed to pertain only to structural problems. Total resistance of socio-economic forces in the field of architecture is neither possible nor desirable. I would thus encourage mediation and negotiation between architectural structures and what could be called 'reality structures.' Here I would argue for the use of mass produced elements and materials, even cheap material alone or along with hand-crafted elements. It is through this negotiation that we can expect the work of Organschi and Gray to gain new richness and present new challenges.

Eeva-Liisa Pelkonen is Assistant Professor (Adjunct) in Architectural Design at the Yale University School of Architecture and a design partner at Turner Brooks Architects. She has written extensively on 20th century European architecture and is the author of *Achtung Architektur: Image and Phantasm in Contemporary Austrian Architecture*.

IN RESPONSE

on ON NUMBERS IN THE NIGHT
Edward Allen

Many years ago, while still a student, I formulated a goal for myself that I still believe to be a worthy one: That each building I design should be more fascinating at the time of its completion than at any time during its construction. This has proven to be difficult if not impossible to achieve. A partially-finished building reveals countless Piranesian wonders and mysteries that are later concealed, and possesses the inherent tension and multiple imagined possibilities of a creative work-in-progress. How can one retain and reveal for the enjoyment of the occupant and onlooker the endless, constantly changing thrills of construction?

Peter Waldman addresses much the same question. His prose, open-ended and inconclu-

sive, leaves numerous dangling, highly-charged, spark-spewing conductors of thought to which the architecturally savvy reader can connect to be jolted out of the terminal complacency that threatens us all. He celebrates the incomplete, the unstable, the 'under construction,' as distinguished from the complete, the stable, the well-studied, the fully resolved. His sentences caress and curl about such restless words as 'shifting,' 'syncopation,' 'frictional,' 'vulnerable,' 'struggle,' 'turbulent,' 'tortured,' 'fragmentary,' 'incomplete,' 'volatile,' 'dynamic,' 'temporal.' His buildings are true to his words. His own house, Parcel X, with its creaky steel frame and cracked, honeycombed concrete, is as far removed from the forced, funereal per-

fection of the Farnsworth House, as is his preoccupation with the transient phenomena of construction from Mies's compulsive pursuit of dead, static resolution.

Waldman, like I, in his career-in-progress as gardener and engineer, has found it maddeningly difficult to transform the ever-shifting, always-provocative terrors and delights of a building under construction into long-term virtues of an inhabitable building. It isn't enough for a building to leave a few stones lying about, as Stirling did in his Stuttgart Staatsgalerie, or to spill a pile of bricks, as SITE did in some of its retail buildings. Neither is it enough to celebrate in exquisitely finished hi-tech details the necessities of structure and

mechanical services. Somewhere out there, waiting to be discovered but virtually unattainable, is a way of building in which the risky, heady euphoria of experiment and artisanry remains, sometimes restless and unsettling, sometimes cumulative and reassuring, to give a building's occupants new insights each day, in perpetuity, into the work of making and occupying architecture.

Edward Allen is the author of *Fundamentals of Building Construction*, *Architectural Detailing*, and the co-author of *The Architect's Studio Companion*. He has taught design studios and technology courses for 25 years at many schools including Yale and MIT.

Architecture being in its perfection the earliest, as in its elements it is the first of all arts, will always precede, in any barbarous nation, the possession of the science necessary either for the obtaining or the management of iron. Its first existence and its earliest laws must, therefore, depend upon the use of materials accessible in quantity, and on the surface of the earth; that is to say, clay, wood, or stone: and as I think it cannot but be generally felt that one of the chief dignities of architecture is its historical use, and since the latter is partly dependent on consistency of style, it will be felt right to retain as far as may be, even in periods of more advanced science, the materials, and principles of earlier ages....Metals may be used as a *cement*, but not as a *support*.

John Ruskin *The Seven Lamps of Architecture*

IN PERSPECTIVE THE APPEARANCE OF SOLIDITY

Despite the manifold difficulties in achieving a monolithic construction, it remains perhaps the most popular conception of good building among all young architects and not a few older ones, not least because it has been a tenet of Modernism almost from its inception....Contemporary architecture is divided into two groups who consider conventional contemporary building systems either too light or too heavy. On one side are those who feel that only the functionally excessive is adequate and who strive to achieve this goal through real mass – through massive, monolithic walls of masonry or concrete – or through the appearance of mass by artificially thick yet hollow walls or by stone veneers striving to retain the appearance of a traditional stone configuration. For their opponents, who must include the majority of the High Tech architects, no configuration is too complex, no quantity of labor too excessive, no quality of material too dear, if the result is the style that comes from economy of means.

Neither of these offers an easy direction to pursue. The pseudo-vernacular, which so conspicuously demonstrates the structural roles of a wall while so conspicuously concealing its role as insulator and vapor and pressure barrier – as an environmental envelope – is an odd choice indeed for a profession so naturally dedicated to environmental concerns. Those who have sought to achieve the appearance of the massive stone wall without the reality have perhaps fooled only themselves.

Edward Ford *Details of Modern Architecture, Volume I*

Monadnock Building, Chicago, Daniel H. Burnham & John W. Root (1884–1890)

But the moment that the iron in the least degree takes the place of the stone, and acts by its resistance to crushing, and bears superincumbent weight, or if it acts by its own weight as a counterpoise, and so supersedes the use of pinnacles or buttresses in resisting a lateral thrust, or if, in the form of a rod or girder, it is used to do what wooden beams would have done as well, that instant the building ceases, so far as such applications of metal extend, to be true architecture.

John Ruskin *The Seven Lamps of Architecture*

One advantage of painted architecture is that the laws of statics do not take full toll; they need only appear to apply. Inside the frame of the painting, architecture may divest itself of its rigid, cautious rectangularity. As it is compressed and flattened into pictures, it is made free. A dimension is relinquished and a freedom is gained; a reasonable exchange. I use the word exchange because I want to suggest some kind of bargain struck within an established economy. This economy affects all sorts of transactions between wishes and fulfillments, but the cost increases with the extent of that fulfillment. We all recognize this crude precept that permits us to wander freely in the imagination while opting for a confining security in reality.

It is the application of this same formula for localized indulgence that leads to the parceling of architecture into businesslike and gamelike aspects. The business is to make stable structures, and the game is to invoke illusions that make the building appear to contradict its own necessarily stable constitution. [The painter Francesco] Salviati's 'capricious and ingenious inventions'* are easily assimilated because they are understood to be fictions. When a comparable caprice is realized in stone, its status is not so clear. The game has gone further, perhaps too far. There *is* masonry that defies its own material constitution and the pull of gravity; there is building that escapes the straight line and the circular arc.

Robin Evans *The Projective Cast: Architecture and its Three Geometries*

*The words used by Giorgio Vasari to describe Salviati's Palazzo Sacchetti frescos.

The Getty Center, Los Angeles, Richard Meier (1984–97)

118

INTRODUCTION

Behind any discussion of buildings or other structures lurks the largely ignored issue of how designers and builders think. Architectural theoreticians have always analyzed design thinking for its formal implications, but it is only recently, and from outside the field, that anyone has attempted to examine the act of making form and structure in space as a thought mode. What building technology and its thought form are, however, has never been clearly defined, neither in Semper's much-cited *Der Stil*,[1] Viollet-le-Duc's *Entretiens* or *Dictionnaire raisonné de l'architecture française...*, nor in Sigfried Giedion's influential *Mechanization Takes Command*.[2] Philosophers have not contributed to a definition of technology in building either. The weaknesses in Martin Heidegger's article "Die Frage nach der Technik"[3] are not surprising, since Heidegger had no professional connection with or knowledge about technology. Ludwig Wittgenstein should be more useful to us, since he had trained as an engineer and participated in the development of an, albeit unsuccessful, airplane propeller. He also designed and built a building that Adolf Loos admired, his sister's house in Vienna. Wittgenstein knew how technologists think, but he too left us neither a clear definition of technology nor an examination of its role in our thinking. He did, however, discuss the related concept of progress throughout his philosophical career.[4] Walter Benjamin and Roland Barthes[5] were others who occasionally wrote about technological subjects. But they did not define the thought form that gives us technology either.

It has only been recently that Subrata Dasgupta,[6] coming from a background in computer science and engineering, has begun to discuss how technological invention occurs as distinct from evolution, while Antoine Picon[7] and Ulrich Pfammatter[8] are examining how aspects of technological thinking influence engineering and architectural education. Nevertheless, we still have no clear idea of what it is that distinguishes the technological mode from other forms of thinking.

A HYBRID OF ANALYTICAL AND MATRIX THOUGHT

There are myriad variations in thought, of which three, the scientific, the artistic, and the technological, interest us here. The practitioners of science, the arts, and technology are complex humans who cross borders between many categories of thought, and we must therefore carefully distinguish between the thought mode and the profession. We can, however, say that the underlying interest of natural and social science is to discover knowledge or gain insight, while in art it is to create objects that fulfill non-physical, intellectual, or psychological needs, and in technology it is to make objects that primarily satisfy physical requirements. Technological thought, which this last group employs, is a hybrid mode that combines the 'matrix'[9] or contextual form of intuitive thinking, which is the prevalent form usually associated with artists, and analytical thought, which underlies scientific method.

All thinking is linear in nature and pathbound. However, matrix thinking is bedded in a multidimensional field of choices. Like analytical thinking, it can follow the linear pathways of logical sequences bedded in a context of parallel, converging or diverging tracks. But it can also make associative 'leaps' from one linear track to another or from one level of thinking to another. This gives matrix thinking a personalized character, since the apparently discontinu-

Tom F. Peters

TECHNOLOGICAL THOUGHT IS DESIGN'S OPERATIVE METHOD

ous path a thought process takes depends on the thinker's innate proclivities and conscious priorities, which are largely dependent on the individual's intellectual and associative makeup. Its unstable flexibility makes this form of thinking adaptable and powerful, especially when it is coupled with analytical thought. Matrix thinking, for which there is a long tradition in all cultures, strongly influenced scientific and humanist thought – the Industrial Revolution's dominant models – from the beginning to the middle of the nineteenth century.

While technologists concentrate on objects, purely analytical thinkers deal with abstractions, that is concepts, hypotheses, and theories. Scientists, a group that typifies the most formalized type of analytical thinkers, are of course very much influenced by matrix thought, especially when they generate or speculate on their problems, but scientific method, which, in contrast to the ancient field of analysis, is a Renaissance development, remains rigorously analytical. It stays within clearly delineated boundaries and is constructed to be independent of the thinker's personal or even cultural value system. It uses processes that anyone must be able to replicate to provide unambiguous answers to questions. Builders and other technologists are makers rather than analysts, but they do use analytical method in a limited way to examine quantifiable design aspects and help control the process of design synthesis. Nevertheless, they need to go beyond analysis in order to design. Their use of matrix thinking is not random. It follows methods that have never before been clearly defined.

Design, construction, manufacture, and assembly are linked processes. Since these processes are connected by causality more than by concept, builders rely on accumulated experience, on subjective criteria based on personal and cultural values to help them forge the links and define relationships between design and process. In contrast to the scientific method, a technolog-

ical method's correctness lies ultimately in the functioning of the object, not in its abstract logic. That is why technologists are more concerned with subjective experience than with epistemology, the objective method of knowledge. This also explains why unschooled inventors continually try and invent the perpetuum mobile in spite of its proven impossibility. Science, they argue uninformedly, has been proven wrong before; there is no reason why it will not be proven wrong again. This argument can certainly apply when the parameters of a problem change, but not, of course within a given framework.[10]

While building the Eddystone Lighthouse off the southern coast of England in 1756, John Smeaton introduced scientific method to design by analyzing how hydraulic cement worked chemically.[11] Smeaton's goal was technological rather than scientific; he wanted to build a better object and not merely provide new insight into the nature of cement. In fact, Smeaton finally stayed with a natural hydraulic cement and did not use any artificial cement based on his analysis. Although his intentions were technological rather than scientific, his results, published in 1791, sparked interest in the nascent field of material science. Materials researchers (Pasley and Tredgold in England or Vicat and Treussart in France)[12] expanded on Smeaton's work, while others, like the creators of analytical engineering theory (Eytelwein in Prussia, von Gerstner in Austria, Navier in France, and Hodgkinson in England)[13] analyzed other materials and structures, discovered their properties, and ultimately increased our structural knowledge. These researchers did want to provide better knowledge of building materials for practitioners, too, but this was not their primary focus.

Eddystone Lighthouse off the coast of southern England, John Smeaton (1756)

Builders describes those who are actively engaged in some aspect of the actual building process. The term can include civil and structural engineers, architects who build, contractors, and sometimes developers. There are many in the building professions today, both in Europe and in North America, who are trained as architects, but have expanded into becoming builders. It is a term that is more comprehensive. I think particularly of the growing group of 'design-build' people, a type common in most of Europe (perhaps excepting France, Sweden, and Denmark) but until recently not in the United States. They can be one person or small enterprises, like Simon Ungers or the 'Jersey Devil,' or large firms. They are capturing an ever increasing segment of the market and taking control of the whole process of making architecture once again in the United States. However, a builder may simply be a contractor as well. A builder's medium is the building, and his or her concentration lies in the process.

Designers describes those who design buildings and environments but who are not directly engaged in building them. Designers also create plans for industrial objects, cars, and the like. It is not confined to the building world. I use it in this article, however, to designate architects. I rely on the traditional American understanding of who architects are – those who design and then pass their drawings on to contractors, developers, or fabricators for realization. Their chief professional medium is the plan, not the building, and they concentrate on the product. The term does not apply to most analysts, theoreticians, or historians, and certainly not to those who do 'talketecture.'

Britannia Bridge over the Menai Straights,
Wales, Robert Stephenson and William
Fairbairn (1850)

As an example, Eaton Hodgkinson's dispute with Robert Stephenson over the time he took to analyze the novel, hollow-box beams for the Conway and Britannia railway bridges 1846–1850 was directly related to Hodgkinson's scientific concerns. Hodgkinson was not at all willing to be hurried, and his goals were diametrically opposed to those of the owners and the contractors building the bridges. Stephenson, as chief engineer of the London–Holyhead Railway Line, was bound by contract to push the deadline for opening the line as far forward as possible. The goal, of course, was to begin earning a return on the shareholders' capital investment quickly. William Fairbairn, who manufactured the beams and headed the research effort, had solicited Hodgkinson's participation on the design team. He was a practical technologist and an industrialist, and, embarrassed by the dispute, he felt caught between the needs of science he understood, and the railway's directors and their chief engineer whom he understood equally well.[14]

Henri Navier had formally incorporated scientific method into building thinking seventy years after Smeaton's pioneering use of it, but the ramifications of what he had done hadn't yet manifested themselves throughout the industry. What Navier had done was develop analytical structural models that were independent of scale and material and codify analytical statics. Navier defined live-loading on bridges for instance as a unit of 200 kg/m^2 to replace the previously used, predicted site-specific load. This allowed engineers to compare different spans and loading conditions objectively, and thus scientifically, and to abstract quantifiable characteristics that they could then apply to a range of specific cases.[15] While this made physics useful in understanding and predicting structural behavior, Navier hadn't defined the relationship between theory, construction, and erection. Scientific thinking certainly helped builders understand technological behavior, but it could not help them design or build.

THE INTRINSIC DILEMMA

Analysis is a tool we use to examine and optimize predetermined design aspects, but not to create an object. Builders, architects, and engineers need associative matrix thinking, the other half of technological thought, to create structures or processes. The resulting hybrid thought form is a continuous balancing act.[16] Only those of us who practice it and balance between associative synthesis and analysis realize that homo sapiens and homo faber are one and the same in technology. It is not a Jeckyll-and-Hyde with shifting characteristics, but a Janus with two faces and a single brain. The fluid, almost formless relationship creates tension, even stress. Science and design follow different goals that coexist in an uneasy relationship in technology. It can be characterized as an unstable intellectual equilibrium that works to create useful solutions. Creative people find this exhilarating, while those who exclusively practice the one or the other find the ambivalent duality disturbing. The ceaseless balancing act between the analytical and the synthetic sides of technological thought demands more flexibility than either component on its own. Calatrava's work attempts to make this unstable equilibrium visible. Sigfried Giedion's fascination with transformable furniture reflected this inherent ambivalence fifty years ago,[17] and more recently Antoine Picon has discussed it from another standpoint as a technological preoccupation with 'movement.'[18]

The most curious feature of technological thought is that hard technology, the analytically driven part of this thought mode, cannot be 'digested' by matrix-driven 'soft' technology. The two cannot be reconciled or synthesized through a dialectic process either, because they are not opposites; they are intrinsically other in nature. Hard technology remains a foreign body imbedded in the contextual matrix, and this is what causes the un-relievable, yet self-regulating tension that drives modern creativity. The fact that there can be tension between a mode of thought and one of its parts – a tenuous balancing between two so unequal partners – is a curious characteristic of technological thinking. Equilibrium, whether stable or unstable, is usually between roughly equivalent partners. In this case, it is not, and that's why technological thought is so unusual. It works quite differently from a traditional dialectic relationship. It is this unique characteristic that Dasgupta and Chandrasekaran have tried to define.[19] Builders use this balancing to meld theories of form and perception, analytical methods of science and mathematics, and practical processes for dealing with humans and materials into tools for manipulating the environment. Because of the tenuous equilibrium it manages to sustain, technological thought crosses the boundaries between the ideal and the pragmatic in many ways. It is inclusive, open to external influences, and it has several aspects that are evaluative rather than quantifiable. The principle of equilibrium is reflected in the special role that issues of scale, system, and procedural thinking play in technology, and it makes technological thinking unusual and dominant.

SCALE

One of the principal differences between the 'hard' and the 'soft' components of technological thought lies in their divergent concept of scale. This is reflected in their different use of professional vocabulary. 'Small' means less to an analyst, to whom a 'detail' is a 'hierarchically minor and subordinate part,' while to a designer a 'detail' is a 'small-scale problem,' small in size but not lesser in importance. Misunderstanding this difference can lead to structural failure. The 'O-ring' gaskets that failed on the space shuttle Challenger in 1986 for instance, were a vital small-scale problem, not a minor part. The NASA engineers apparently knew that the rings were faulty and tried to warn the project managers, who, because many of them were not technologically trained, failed to understand that the 'small part' that worried the constructors was crucial, not 'minor.'[20]

True technologists have the field experience to know that details are crucial. They work comfortably in the both realms of theory and practice, a milieu that has origins in a nineteenth century shift in Parisian education. The industrially oriented Ecole centrale des arts et manufactures, founded in Paris in 1829, crossed this boundary and bridged the distinction between scientific experiment and technological practice. The school's founder, Auguste Perdonnet, and his group of disaffected engineering practitioners reacted to the intellectual bias and the drift of the Ecole polytechnique toward abstract, scientific thinking by linking engineering theory and practice to manufacturing and assembly processes.[21] Others soon followed their lead to found innovative architecture and engineering schools in Karlsruhe, Stuttgart, and Zurich. Together they spread technological thinking throughout the building professions and even influenced the older builders' academies in Prague, Berlin, Manchester, Schenectady and West Point, New York, and even the Ecole polytechnique itself. Based on the new thinking propagated by the Ecole centrale from which he graduated in 1854, Gustave Eiffel successfully developed a component assembly system for his

bridges and the tower that hinged on issues of scale, while another graduate, William Jenney, became deeply involved in the development of the tall-building frame.

SYSTEM CONCEPT

Like 'detail,' the word 'system' also means different things to the analyst and the technologist. It builds on the understanding of the role that scale plays in structure and form. To both, it is the principle that governs relationships between parts and the whole, but the analyst understands it as the hierarchical organizing principle that distinguishes the primary from the subordinate, while the designer-builder usually understands it as a layered or sequentially organized, yet non-hierarchical kit-of-parts. While both are sequentially organized in terms of their manufacture and erection, hierarchical systems have relative value assigned to their elements and components, whereas layered systems do not.

Even the earliest nineteenth-century English iron bridge builders did not design solely from the whole to the part, but the other way, too: from the part to the whole. They developed standardized sets of prefabricated members and connections out of the process of iron casting from 'below' so to speak, while they designed the overall form from 'above.' They used a reciprocating method that is typical of technological design, balancing back and forth between different scales, each design decision influencing the next step in circular feedback loops throughout the design process.[22] This method made the detail as important to them as the whole and it changed both their thinking and their use of

Garabit Viaduct over the Truyère,
France, Gustave Eiffel (1884)

language. The act of balancing or reciprocation implies equilibrium, and the bridge builders' design method reflected the unstable equilibrium that exists in their technological mode of thinking. Engineers above all regard equilibrium as the goal of their design thinking. But it is not limited to engineers alone. Designers like Calatrava, Norman Foster, Renzo Piano, Peter Rice, or Jörg Schlaich have tried to express this in visual form.

The reciprocating, iterative, balancing method also occurs elsewhere in technological thought. Its clearest manifestation in building may have been in Hardy Cross's moment distribution method, the first useful method for calculating three-dimensional, moment-resistant frames for tall buildings. Cross's method balanced bending moments and deflections from node to node, back and forth throughout three-dimensional frames until equilibrium was achieved. It presaged the iterative way computers work and gradually became redundant when computer programs began to supplant it in the late 1950s.[23]

PROCEDURAL THINKING

The early iron bridge builders' preoccupation with equilibrium as both an intellectual and a structural phenomenon led to their understanding of design, manufacture, and assembly as dynamic processes. Giedion's and Picon's thoughts about the dynamic principle in technology span half a century and confirm an ongoing concern with this aspect of technological thought. The procedural aspect of system thinking has its roots in military thought. The basic elements of this thought mode are strategy and tactics, aided by logistics.[24] Military campaigns try to reach a goal defined by politicians (if armies have anything to do with defining the goals of their actions, they become dictatorships). Military thinking concentrates exclu-

sively on procedural matters and not on the product, and it led nineteenth-century builders to develop standardized relationships between structural members.

The main material they used to achieve this change was iron. Both the material and iron components are manufactured away from the building site, so instead of constructing their structures from the materials, they began to assemble them from industrially manufactured parts. This was a drastic change. Construction implies putting together, creating, changing, and manipulating interfaces and connections by altering components. Assembly, on the other hand, is one degree removed from manufacture. It implies fitting together without alteration. This means that components arrived on site ready to use with no adaptation needed.

As a result, designers began to stress the connections between components, and this is what distinguishes industrialized building from the pre-industrial. The principles of industrialized building spread quickly from iron to traditional materials. The standardized connections and members that builders developed through system and process thinking gave rise to economical, repetitive component manufacture. The new assembly and connection techniques

gave rise to concepts like monolithic structural behavior, mass prefabrication, and structural redundancy. These concepts, in turn, gave us our modern building systems. Eiffel's construction system, a design-matrix of structural constants and variables, carried the idea of building system to maturity at the end of the nineteenth century. His simple and yet sophisticated catalog of wrought-iron parts, connection rules, and erection sequences for the Garabit Bridge (1884)[25] and his tower (1889)[26] paved the way for modern steel-bridge and high-rise construction. It also spilled over into our general culture through instructional toys like Erector Set and Lego.[27]

Builders develop intellectual strategies to support their system-approach in design. The associative characteristics of matrix thinking lead them to transform or to translate information from one format to another. Transformation remolds information within the boundaries of a field, while translation crosses borders and moves it from one field to another. Both forms are characteristic of matrix thinking since they rely on non-predictable, and therefore seemingly illogical, 'leaps' in thought processes. Transformation and translation are strategies implemented by 'creative misunderstanding.'[28] Where misunderstanding occurs inadvertently, it is a flaw as the example of the Challenger accident showed. But where it is consciously manipulated as 'creative misunderstanding,' it becomes one of the methods matrix thinkers use to create. Creative misunderstanding is a personally and culturally determined phenomenon, not an abstract, analytical one.

There are many examples of both transformation and translation in building. In 1818, the engineer Marc Brunel observed how a salt-water mollusk called 'pipeworm' or terredo navalis drilled through ship timbers and translated the process into the first mechanical tunneling

Garabit Viaduct detail showing
the Eiffel kit-of-parts system.

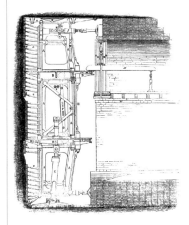

Cross-section through the Tames Tunnel sheild, Marc Brunel (1824–43)
The shield was a translation of the way a marine mollusk drills from a biological format into mechanical terms.

shield for the Thames Tunnel in London (1824–1843). Cultural border-crossing can foster the translation process, too. While working on Robert Stephenson's Victoria Bridge over the St. Lawrence River in Montreal (1854–1859), site engineer Arthur Helps noticed that the British mechanics who had emigrated to the building site in North America seemed able to build more reliable machinery than those who had stayed in the component factory at home.[29]

Another common strategy in procedural thought is 'divida et impera' or 'divide-and-conquer.' It demonstrates a combination of analytical and synthetical skills in technological thinking and shows how the combination of the two is more than the sum of the parts. This method is in a way 'political,' since it strategizes the analytical process. The strategy consists in dividing problems with conflicting requirements into their constituent parts, solving the components serially, and then reuniting the results into an overall solution.

Richard Turner designed the Palm House in London's Kew Gardens (1846–48) as a rigid frame that can expand and contract with temperature changes. In order to solve the novel problem with its conflicting requirements of stiffness and flexibility Turner separated the function of his purlins into three distinct layers. The first and largest were the structural purlins. Turner designed them as tension rods running through tubular spacers that post-tensioned the webs of the structural arcs. The second layer of thinner ones was balanced above the first and carried the glazing panels, and the third layer, composed of the thinnest purlins, stabilized the glass mullions. Turner formed flexible joints or discontinuities between each of these layers. Since the secondary purlins were too thin to carry on their

own, Turner welded them to struts fixed to the primary spacer tubes. These struts were so thin and flexible that they served as articulations between the two layers. At their ends, the secondary purlins were bolted to the top flanges of the structural arcs with an offset lag, and this too gave them additional flexibility. Finally, the third purlin layer, that ran still farther out and con-

nected the glazing mullions above the arcs, had no direct connection to those below.[30] By means of all these 'semi-fixed' connections and discontinuities Turner created an adaptable yet rigid structure. It was complicated, but it has survived the past 150 years well. Today, French designers practice similar 'divide-and-conquer' strategies in high-rise glazing techniques.

Builders have long used similar decoupling mechanisms in processes too. When a procedural bottleneck threatened to disrupt the roof assembly of the London Crystal Palace in 1850, the contractor Charles Fox accelerated the process by decoupling the linear erection sequence from the frame's modular geometry. His mobile glazing staging ran in the gutter-purlins from module to module over the entire length of the roof and obviated the need for time-consuming and labor-intensive scaffolding. Robert Stephenson carried this tactic one step further into the design process. While building the Conway and Britannia Bridges (1846–1850), he saved construction time by using a primitive

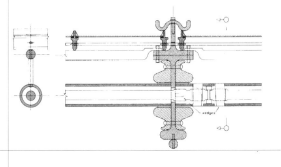

top to bottom:
Palm House, Royal Botanical Gardens at Kew, England, Richard Turner (1848)
Detail of the first two purlin layers during restoration of the building in 1988.
Cross-section and elevation of the three purlin layers

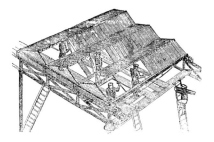

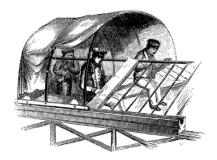

top: Crystal Palace, London, Joseph Paxton and Charles Fox (1851)
The manual assembly of the roof glazing module led to a bottleneck in the erection process.
bottom: Crystal Palace. Fox rationalized the assembly of the roof glazing by inventing a glazing cart that rolled in the gutter-purlins, making it a linear process.

form of critical-path method to decouple and then coordinate the experimentation on the iron tubes, the design of the structural system and erection of the masonry towers in parallel. The critical-path method is based on the military concepts of strategy, logistics, and tactics, and it provided builders with a useful tool to solve problems with continually shifting, linked parameters and unanticipated occurrences.

LANGUAGE AND THE DIVERSIFICATION OF TECHNOLOGICAL THOUGHT

For all its distinctiveness, there is no single form of technological thought. It is a continually developing mode, not a codified entity like scientific method. It takes many variant forms that the professions that use it continually modify to suit their needs. This is how it has come to influence older forms of thinking like scientific, artistic, or humanist thought. Even two fields as closely related as architecture and structural engineering have developed distinctive variants. One of the most important differences between the two stems from the fact that engineers today generally use the abstract and analytical language and notation of mathematics to develop their designs, whereas architects employ the more matrix-based visual language and graphic notation. The separation began with the introduction of analytical statics in the early nineteenth century by Navier and others.

The result is that today engineers and architects are conditioned to see different things in the same object. Engineers instinctively translate what they see into an abstract model and fre-

quently ignore the visual aspect, while architects attempt to recognize a formal logic or pattern and commonly block out non-visual concepts. An engineer looks at a complicated node in a trussed structure and sees a 'point,' an abstract diagram denoting the convergence of forces, where tension and compression ideally come together along axial trajectories. An architect, on the other hand, tries to discern a visual pattern, a recognizable structural geometry in space. The engineer tries to abstract structural qualities and override the visual impact while the architect strives to stress the visual often to the detriment of intellectual comprehension.[31]

The engineer sees a 'simply supported beam' in Squire Whipple's 1841 bow-string truss because it exerts only vertical forces and no thrust on its supports, whereas the architect sees an arch with a tie rod. Such different views of the same object vary over time too. A century ago builders saw the bowstring truss as an erection procedure. They called it a 'suspension bridge' because the primary member, the deck, is suspended from the arch. 'Beam,' 'arch,' and 'suspension system' are all correct interpretations of the object. Our knowledge of the object and its naming is inherent to our thinking, not implicit in the object itself. Each viewpoint we develop depends entirely on what we consider to be the most important issue, and the name we give it depends on the mix of analytical, design, and procedural thought modes prevalent in the segment of the building profession we occupy at the time.

There is an incipient method hidden in this example, and that is the potential for a quick and subtle shift in the way we view an object. This shift is another characteristic of matrix thinking and typical both for the divergence of the architectural and engineering variants of technological thought and for technological development generally.

Squire Whipple called his invention a suspension bridge because what he saw was an overlay of kingposts with all their members in tension, radiating down from the arch to carry the deck. The overlay method was the way designers developed ever larger and heavier

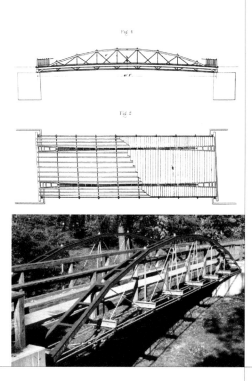

top: Bowstring Truss patented by Squire Whipple (1841)
bottom: Whipple Truss at Union College, Schenectady, New York.

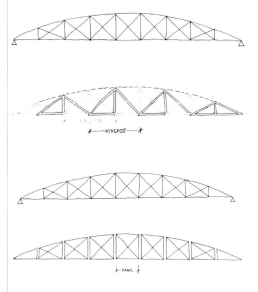

top to bottom:
The Whipple Truss as an 'overlay' of over-
lapping kingposts.
Zuoz Bridge over the Inn, Maillart (1901)
Tavanasa Bridge, Maillart (1905)
The Whipple Truss as a panel system.
A Town Truss (lattice bridge) under
construction showing the components
and connectors.

structures in the pre-industrial and early industrial era before the concept of system spread.[32]
Carl Culmann saw Whipple's bowstring truss on
his celebrated voyage of industrial espionage
to the United States in 1850. Whipple had
designed his bridge as overlapping kingposts,
but Culmann intentionally misunderstood
Whipple's idea creatively and saw iterative
panels. He shifted his viewpoint half a module
and 'invented' the concept of the modern truss.
Others were making similar shifts. This subtle
translation may have seemed minor at the time,
but it was a detail in the true technological
sense, a small-scale change of great import to the
development of subsequent truss theory and
construction practice. It is this kind of shift that
changed the Western world's way of seeing
structure. And as a result, it irrevocably changed
our nomenclature, and with it our concepts.

We find shifts in viewpoint at key moments
of change throughout technological history.
Robert Maillart experienced one such shift in his
viewpoint when his first independent structure,
the small Zuoz Bridge over the Inn River in
Switzerland, twisted slightly and cracked its
spandrels across the calculated direction of the
shear stresses in 1901. Any normal engineer
would have been horrified and have decided to
strengthen the spandrels next time so that the
failure could not recur. But Maillart shifted his
viewpoint and did the opposite. Since the bridge
had not collapsed he argued, the cracks proved
that the spandrels were not transferring shear
and must therefore be extraneous. So when he
designed his next bridge, the Tavanasa Bridge in
1905, he omitted them and created a distinctive
new bridge type. The method he used in this
transformation process was an inversion of logic.

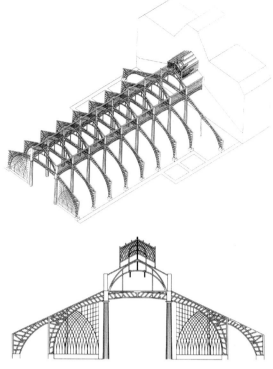

clockwise from left:
Sayn Foundry, Bendorf, Germany, Karl
Ludwig Althans (1830)
Axonometric drawing of the cast-iron
structure showing the façade and
clerestory truss configuration.
Sayn Foundry framing section.

THE SAYN FOUNDRY

The intellectual shift, the principle of inversion, and the creative role word meanings play are some of the ways translation and transformation work in technological design. The medium they use is creative misunderstanding, which depends on interpretation. Karl Ludwig Althans built the Sayn Foundry in Bendorf, Germany in 1830.[33] This building is one of the still unrecognized icons of nineteenth-century iron construction. The multi-leveled complexity of this machine-building is astounding due partly to the way Althans used transformation in structural innovation. The gantry crane that carried molten iron from the furnace mouth to the casting floor rests on a fishbelly truss. The fishbelly truss was an unknown structural form in 1830,[34] so in order to invent it Althans had to overlay other structural and non-structural models familiar to him. The underspanned beam, long known in wooden construction, was one. Gothic tracery was another, and he used that to transfer shear between the top and bottom chords. But the model that really demonstrates transformation is Althans's use of a gigantic, laminated carriage spring made of crucible steel for the lower tension chord. We can follow Althans's observation of the way a carriage spring transfers bending in the middle into tension at the ends, but it is difficult to follow his highly personal leap of creative misunderstanding from the spring to the truss chord. We can only wonder at the high caliber of Althans's invention when we remember that the very concept of a truss still lay twenty years in the future.

Another of Althans's transformations by means of creative misunderstanding was his use of cannonballs, one of the foundry's products, as ball bearings for the swiveling derrick cranes, which rotated around the columns of the casting floor. Again, ball bearings were only patented in France twenty-seven years later in 1857.[35] It appears that ball bearings may have originated in nautical tackle arrangements,[36] but other than that, Althans had nothing in machine construction to build on as a model, and we can only speculate on the observation he must have made that initiated the translation process. He certainly could never have designed his cranes the way he did without ball bearings.

Althans probably used both linguistic interpretation and overlay to design the façade and clerestory of his casting hall. Although the tracery reminds us visually of Gothic church design more than anything else, the clue to the translation process is the spread of knowledge at the time about the prefabricated and standardized wooden bridge system Ithiel Town had patented in the United States in 1820. The novel characteristic of Town's truss was that he used a single timber cross-section and only one type of connection, the dowel, called 'treenail' in timber construction. This vastly simplified its manufacture and erection. European engineers immediately grasped the construction potential of Town's idea and soon transformed it from wood to iron in Ireland around 1845, and in Switzerland and Germany in the mid- and late 1850s.[37] But two decades before they did that, Althans reformulated the Town truss into a shear panel and a bracing mechanism. The foundry hall had to withstand heavy dynamic live loads rolling back and forth and swiveling to and fro on the brittle, cast-iron framework. Althans braced his frame laterally with surrounding masonry walls. However, the exposed glazed front needed further stiffening. The crisscrossing 'tracery' of the Town truss served his purpose well. And the small panes of glass Althans inserted in the interstices of the truss transformed it into a partial shear membrane, not a wall, but a planar structure that resists in-plane forces. Althans did the same for the clerestory, which connects the heavily loaded nave columns and transfers thrust generated by the swiveling cranes and the hall gantry the whole length of the nave to the furnace block at the back of the building. In yet another innovative maneuver, he transformed the characteristic doweled crossings of Town's diagonals into monolithic castings, and shifted his connection points to the interface between the panels, a masterful feat of creative misunderstanding. This shift in connection technology is paralleled by Culmann's later shift from the traditional way of regarding bridges as incremental overlays of simple king-posts, queen-posts, and slanted struts to our way of looking at them as a panel system.

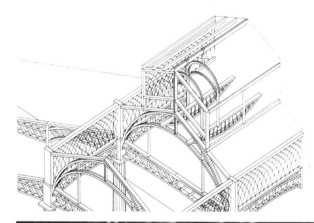

top to bottom:
Sayn Foundry, drawing of the
gantry crane from above.
View from below of the fishbelly truss supporting
the gantry crane in front of the furnace mouth.
View of clerestory trusses before restoration.

left: Sayn Foundry. Detail view showing
the connection between the cast-iron
truss panels.
right: Sayn Foundry. Detail of the
façade showing truss configuration
with glass infill.

CONCLUSION

Technological thought is a subtle thought form that developed its current level of complexity over the past two centuries. Its hybrid and fluctuating nature is an unstable equilibrium of its unequal parts – analytical and matrix thinking – and it is primarily this characteristic that causes the creative tension designers need and that distinguishes it from other thought forms. Technological thought crosses intellectual, professional, and cultural borders and borrows freely from other thought modes, like military thinking, whose basic concepts of strategy, tactics, and logistics have become some of its strongest characteristics. Technological thought translates and transforms ideas, concepts, and solutions using methods and strategies such as thought shift, divide-and-conquer, or inversion by creative misunderstanding. Its inventiveness and flexibility make this thought mode adaptable to many situations and, as a result, technological thought and especially the variants it developed in building have gradually infiltrated most other forms of thinking and disciplines, including such abstract fields as the philosophical discipline of aesthetics. It is not by chance that computer programmers and hardware developers both call their abstract configurations and their physical assemblages of electronic modules 'architecture.' Nor is it surprising that biologists 'engineer' genetic solutions or statesman 'engineer' agreements or social contracts. Today, natural and social scientists, artists, economists, businesspeople, soldiers, politicians, and humanists have adopted many more aspects of technological thinking than they acknowledge. This is precisely what makes technological thought the premier thought mode of our age, intimately connected to the creation and development of new concepts.

Sayn Foundry.
Detail of the derrick crane showing cannonballs as ball bearings.

1 Semper, Gottfried, *Der Stil in den technischen und tektonischen Künsten, oder praktische Aesthetik: ein Handbuch für Techniker, Künstler und Kunstfreunde.* 2 vols. (Frankfurt a.M.: Verlag für Kunst und Wissenschaft, 1860 / Munich: Bruegmann, 1863).

2 Giedion, Sigfried, *Mechanization Takes Command: A Contribution to Anonymous History.* (New York: Oxford, 1948). In spite of its methodological weaknesses, this book is still one of the early issue-oriented (rather than biographical) studies in the history of technology. It reaches a little higher than a chronology of invention and poses several overarching questions. Other historians who discussed building technology like Nicholas Pevsner or Carl Condit used technological material as part of their historical argument without defining it either.

3 "Die Frage nach der Technik," published both in vol. 1 of *Vorträge und Aufsätze,* 3 vols. (Pfullingen: Neske, 1954), and *Die Technik und die Kehre* (Pfullingen: Neske, 1962). In German this article is simplistic and not very original in its treatment of technology. It has been rendered opaque and complicated in the two English translations: *The Question Concerning Technology, and Other Essays,* translated with a brief introduction by William Lovitt (New York: Harper and Row, 1977), and *Basic Writings: Nine Key Essays, Plus the Introduction to Being and Time.* edited, with general introduction and introductions to each section, by Davis Farrel Krell (New York: Harper, 1977). It attained notoriety through its use of convoluted conceptual definitions, unusual in English but clear in German. According to a note in the Lovitt translation, Heidegger gave four lectures on the topic with the titles: Das Ding, Das Gestell, Die Gefahr, and Die Kehre. It was the second that evolved into "Die Frage nach der Technik." (Thanks to Gordon Bearn, Lehigh University, and Steven A. Moore, UT Austin for this information.) See also Rudolf Carnap's critique of Heidegger's thinking and language in "Ueberwindung der Metaphysik durch logische Analyse der Sprache" in *Erkenntnis,* 2, 1932, trans. in *Logical Positivism,* Alfred Jules Ayer, ed., (New York: Macmillan Free Press, 1959). (Thanks to George Reisch, University of Chicago, for this information.)

4 Wittgenstein did not deal with technology directly, but he did deal with the nefarious influence of the analytical method of scientific thought on culture in *Vermischte Bemerkungen* (Frankfurt a.M.: Suhrkamp, 1977), and there are references to the negative cultural impact of the concept of progress in his earlier *Philosophische Bemerkungen* (Frankfurt a.M.: Suhrkamp, 1981), written after his return to Cambridge in 1929, in *Philosophical Investigations/Philosophische Untersuchungen* (New York: Macmillan, 1953) and in *Ueber Gewissheit* (Frankfurt a.M.: Suhrkamp, 1969), no. 131. (Thanks to Gordon Bearn for this information.) See also Peters, Tom F., *Building the Nineteenth Century* (Cambridge, Mass.: MIT, 1996), pp. 26–33 and further references throughout that text for the relationship between the concept of progress and technological thought.

5 Barthes, Roland, *La Tour Eiffel* (Paris: Delpire, 1964).

6 Dasgupta, Subrata, *Technology and Creativity,* (London: Oxford, 1996). Dasgupta is concerned with how ideas come about, what constitutes invention.

7 Picon, Antoine, *L'invention de l'ingenieur moderne: l'école des ponts et chaussées, 1747–1851* (Paris: ENPC, 1992), and *La formation polytechnique* (Paris: Dunod, 1994).

8 Pfammatter, Ulrich, *Die Erfindung des modernen Architekten: Ursprünge und Entwicklung der wissenschaftlich-industriellen Ausbildung* (Basel: Birkhäuser, 1997).

9 *The Oxford English Dictionary* defines matrix in this sense as 'a place or medium in which something is 'bred,' produced, or developed.' The term 'matrix' is preferable to Edward de Bono's "lateral" because it describes intuitive thought's multidimensionality in contrast to 'vertical' thought's linear nature. See *The Use of Lateral Thinking* (London: Cape, 1967).

10 Peters, Tom F., *Building the Nineteenth Century,* op. cit., Mont Cenis Tunnel, pp. 136–141.

11 Smeaton, John, *A narrative of the building and a description of the construction of the Edystone* [sic] *Lighthouse with stone...,* (London: Nichol, 1791/93/1811/13), pp. 102–123, Part 3, Chapter 4 'Containing EXPERIMENTS to ascertain a compleat Composition for WATER-CEMENTS, with their Results.' However, Smeaton did not always use chemical analysis in his experiments, see his observations on a 'reddish, or brownish stone' on p.118.

12 See: Pasley, Charles William, *Observations on limes, calcareous cements, mortars, stucco and concrete, and on puzzolanas, natural and artificial* (London: Weale, 1838); Tredgold, Thomas, *Practical Essay on the Strength of Cast Iron, intended for the assistance of engineers...* (London: Taylor, 1822); Vicat, Louis-Joseph, *Recherches expérimentales sur les chaux de construction, les bétons et les mortiers ordinaires* (Paris: Goujon, 1818); Treussart, Clément-Louis, *Mémoire sur les mortiers hydrauliques et ordinaires* (Paris: Carilian-Goeury, 1829)

13 Eytelwein, Johann Albert, *Handbuch der Mechanik fester Körper und der Hydraulik: mit vorzüglicher Rücksicht auf ihre Anwendung in der Architektur...* (Berlin: Lagarde, 1801); Gerstner, Franz Joseph von, *Handbuch der Mechanik.* 3 vols. (Vienna: Sollinger, 1831 / Prague: Spurny 1832 & 1833); Navier, Claude Louis Marie Henri, *Rapport à M. Becquey...et Mémoire sur les ponts suspendus* (Paris: Imprimerie royale/Carilian-Goeury,1823); and: *Résumé des leçons...* (Paris: Didot, 1826), 2nd. expanded, 2 vol. ed. (Paris: Carilian-Goeury, 1833-1838); Hodgkinson, Eaton, "On the transverse strain, and the strength of materials" from *Memoirs of the Literary and Philosophical Society of Manchester,* 2nd. series, 4 (1824): 25, "Theoretical and experimental researches to ascertain the strength and the best forms of iron beams" from *Memoirs of the Literary and Philosophical Society of Manchester,* 2nd. series, 5 (1831): 407, *Experimental Researches on the strength and other properties of cast iron,* Forming a second part to the fourth edition of Tredgold's *Practical Essay...* (London: Weale, 1846).

14 Peters, Tom F., *Building the Nineteenth Century,* op. cit. pp. 168–170.

15 Peters, Tom F., *Transitions in Engineering* (Basel: Birkhäuser, 1987), pp. 52–53, & 111–112

16 Quite similar to Dasgupta's "The Hypothesis Law of Maturation," quoting B. Chandrasekaran's 'propose-critique-modify' strategy. Dasgupta, op. cit., pp.66–67.

17 Sigfried, op. cit., especially in part 5: "Mechanization encounters human surroundings," but also in the rest of the book, as chapter titles like "Mechanization and Death: Meat" suggest. Giedion was himself a border-crosser between mechanical engineering, his first profession, and art history, which was his chosen professional field.

18 Picon, Antoine, "Toward a History of Technological Thought," *Technological Systems and Technological Thought,* Robert Fox ed., (Amsterdam: OPA, 1995).

19 Dasgupta, op. cit., pp. 66–67.

20 The Challenger accident has become a cultural preoccupation in many ways. See for instance Tufte, Edward, *Visual Explorations* (Cheshire, Conn. Graphics Press, 1997).

21 Pfammatter, op. cit., pp. 103–104.

22 Dasgupta, op. cit., pp. 67–68.

23 See: Cross, Hardy, *Continuous Frames of Reinforced Concrete* (New York: Wiley, 1932, 1950).The conceptual importance of Cross's seminal method was recognized by the Institution of Structural Engineers in London, who awarded Cross their gold medal in 1958.

24 According to the *American Heritage Dictionary,* strategy is the science or art of military command as applied to the overall planning and conduct of large-scale military operations. Tactics is the technique or science of securing the objectives designated by strategy. Logistics is procurement, distribution, replacement, and maintenence of material and personnel. See also Clausewitz, Carl von, *Hinterlassene Werke des Generals Carl von Clausewitz über Krieg und Kriegführung.* 10 vols. 1-3 Vom Kriege. (Berlin: F. Dümmler, 1832) (English ed., 1873).

25 Eiffel, Gustave, *Mémoire sur le viaduc de Garabit, Description, calculs de résistance, montage, epreuves et renseignements divers par G. Eiffel, Président de la Société des ingénieurs civils.* 2 vols. (Paris/Liège: Librairie Polytechnique, Baudry, 1889).

26 Eiffel, Gustave, *La tour de trois cents mètres.* 2 vols. (Paris: Lemercier, 1900).

27 The cultural importance of the English Meccano (1906), or Erector Set (1912), as it came to be called in America, was pointed out by Svante Lindquist in 1990 in a talk at the annual meeting of the Society for History of Technology in Cleveland. Henry Petroski discussed the American variant in "The Toys That Built America," *American Heritage of Invention and Technology,* vol. 13, no. 4, Spring 1998, pp. 40–45. Lego "automatic binding bricks" date from 1949. The system was developed and registered as Danish patent 92683 in 1958.

28 The term 'creative misunderstanding' was coined by William J. J. Gordon in his book *Synectics: The Development of Creative Capacity* (New York: Harper, 1961, 1991), and used by George M. Prince in *The Practice of Creativity: A Manual for Dynamic Group Problem Solving* (New York: Harper & Row, 1970), and Harold Bloom in *A Map of Misreading.* (New York: Oxford, 1975). See also Peters, Tom F., "An American Culture of Construction," *Perspecta* 25 (New York: Rizzoli, 1990)

29 Helps, Arthur, *Life and Labours of Mr. Brassey, 1805–1870* (London: Bell and Daldy, 1872), pp. 206–207.

30 For details of this and the following examples: see: Peters, *Building the Nineteenth Century,* op. cit.

31 See also: Peters, Tom F., "Architectural and Engineering Design..." *Bridging the Gap* (New York: Van Nostrand Reinhold, 1990).

32 See Hauri, Hans, "Thoughts on the historical methods for dimensioning bridges," in Peters, Tom F. ed., *The Development of longspan bridge building.* 3rd. ed. (Zurich: Verlag der Fachvereine, 1981) pp. 153–157.

33 Custodis, Paul-Georg, *Die Sayner Hütte in Bendorf* (Cologne: Rheinische Kunststätten, 1980): 241; Peters, Tom F., *Building the Nineteenth Century,* op. cit., pp. 211–218.

34 The type first entered professional awareness in 1835–1840 in the wooden and cast-iron bridges of the Hanovarian builder Georg Laves (1788–1864), while its inversion, the bowstring truss, had appeared in Guillaume-Henri Dufour's (1787–1864) work in Geneva ca. 1830 (Peters, Tom F., *Transitions in Engineering,* op. cit., pp. 186, 192–193, and in Whipple's 1841 patent.

35 Patentedby Courtois, Tihay, and Defrance, see: Darmstaedter, Ludwig, *Handbuch zur Geschichte der Naturwissenschaften und der Technik...,* 2nd. ed., Berlin: Springer, 1908.

36 Thanks to Stephen M. Houghton, Chinese University of Hong Kong, for this information that stems from an article in *Old Gaffer's Journal.*

37 The Royal Canal Bridge on the Dublin–Drogheda Railway in Ireland 1845 was a singular case. (See Pottgiesser, Hans, *Eisenbahnbrücken aus zwei Jahrhunderten* (Basel: Birkhäuser, 1985) p. 118. But Karl von Etzel's (1812–1865) Rhine Bridge at Koblenz, 1856, and his Sitter Bridge near St. Gallen and Aare Bridge at Berne, 1857–1858, as well as Karl von Lentze (1801–1883) and Rudolf Eduard Schinz's (1812–1858) bridges over the Nogat and Vistula at Dirschau, 1858–59, popularized the form in iron. As a matter of interest, the architect F. A. Stuler, mentioned earlier, consulted on the Dirschau Bridge.

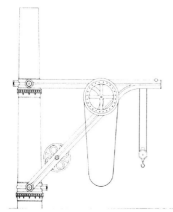

Sayn Foundry, drawing of the derrick
crane attached to a nave column.

BUILDING MYTHS:

THE 'EVOLUTION' FROM WOOD TO IRON IN THE CONSTRUCTION
OF BRIDGES AND NATIONS

NOTICE

Sheep are not allowed to cross this bridge.
They must go through Camps Lane to 9th North

BEN. D. LUCE

Jorden River Bridge, Salt Lake City, Utah

Gregory K. Dreicer

The complete knowledge of a machine as an object tells us nothing about it as a machine.

Michael Polanyi, *Personal Knowledge* (1958)

Engineers and historians have constructed our understandings of structural design out of 'great divides': practice versus theory, wood versus iron, unsophisticated versus advanced, Europe versus the United States. 'Practice,' 'wooden,' 'unsophisticated,' and 'American' represented one side of a mythical divide that helped propel personal, institutional, and industrial competition in the nineteenth century. This became historical explanation in the twentieth. With a better understanding of the divides, architects and engineers will have a sharper picture of the forces that continue to drive design and the justifications made for design decisions.

We need a bridge, not a divide, to understand a history that includes the full gamut of cultural and physical forces, including nationalist fervor, creative genius, capitalist greed, a yearning for professional prestige, and tension and compression. Examining the effect of these forces on bridge design will reveal much about the origins of the frameworks that undergird our world. It will also give us a better idea of what a culture is and isn't: what it means for a thing or a person, or a group of things or a group of people, to be labeled 'theoretical,' 'iron,' 'sophisticated,' and 'European.'

Using a nineteenth-century structure, the lattice bridge, as a touchstone, I will examine three interlocking myths held dear by historians of building: evolutionary theory as explanatory device, the hierarchy of wood and iron, and the influences of nations on the development of structure.

Connecticut River Bridge, Springfield, Massachusetts, Charles Hilton (1874)

Cologne Bridge, Cologne, Germany Hermann Lohse (1855–58)

If an engineer builds a structure which breaks, that is a mischief, but one of a limited and isolated kind, and the accident itself forces him to avoid a repetition of the blunder. But an engineer who from deficiency of scientific knowledge builds structures which don't break down, but which stand, and in which the material is clumsily wasted, commits blunders of a most insidious kind.

William Cawthorne Unwin, Professor of Hydraulic and Mechanical Engineering, Royal Indian Civil Engineering College (c. 1889)

UNNATURAL SELECTION

Construction has rarely been considered culturally significant, so most records of nineteenth and twentieth century building have been tossed into the garbage. Engineers' histories typically consist of anecdotes leavened by a belief in natural selection – a belief adopted by the professional historians who read their writings. Today, to the extent that there is *any* prevailing theory of development of civil engineering structures such as bridges, it is evolutionary. The term 'evolution' often surfaces in the titles and introductions that establish the theoretical foundations of these histories.[2] While evolution appears merely to create an orderly history out of disorderly reality, it is more than an ordering device. It is like a great work of science (really, technology) fiction, within which structures and building processes are causally connected from the beginning to the end of time.

Engineers used evolutionary theory to defend practices, hide uncertainties, and legitimize mistakes. For example, Theodore Cooper (1839–1919), an engineer known as the author of standard bridge specifications, and the designer of a bridge that collapsed catastrophically during construction, believed that:

The intelligent investigator does not decide upon the merits of any developed system by the failures which are necessary steps in its development. Without variations and failures there would be no evolution or survival of the fittest.[3]

Herbert Spencer's widely read philosophy and his phrase 'survival of the fittest,' so meaningful to late nineteenth century industrialists, seemed to allow engineers to justify the death of train passengers in bridge collapses, if that's what it took for the 'fittest' bridge system to 'evolve.'[4] A bridge type must be fit to survive, but evolution-minded engineers rarely noted that the meaning of 'fit' can vary enormously according to context and whom you ask. It may depend on the price of labor, the width of a river, or the decision of a king.[5]

Historians of technology have produced a body of work that supports nineteenth century engineers' self image as agents of evolutionary progress. Swiss engineering professor Jules Gaudard began his 1892 text on bridge construction by stating, 'Under the hand of man, things

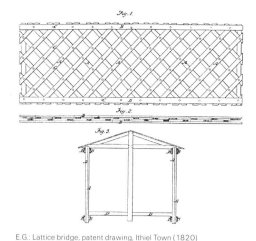

E.G.: Lattice bridge, patent drawing, Ithiel Town (1820)

Worm fence (depicted 1787)

Diagonal bracing of ship frames, Robert Seppings (1806 – 1811)

seem to come to life, join with his aspirations, and, like him, struggle for existence.' When writing his 1979 dissertation on the 'evolution of truss bridge design,' George Danko stated, 'The early railroad systems were, in fact, experimental laboratories in which the simple truss was allowed to develop. Different models were tried and the most successful design survived.' Engineer Henry Petroski recently claimed that 'with the increasing production and application of iron in the nineteenth century, trusses naturally evolved into a plethora of types and styles employing the new material.' To building historians, Darwinism was a Siren, and they headed toward the rocks.[6]

Natural history cannot explain the networks of people, ideas, and artifacts behind an engineering structure. The history of the lattice bridge reveals a decidedly unnatural creation.[7]

An 'improvement in the construction of wood and iron bridges' was registered with the U.S. Patent Office in 1820 by Ithiel Town (1784 – 1844), an architect, bridge engineer, and builder. His invention, consisting of frameworks of diagonally intersecting planks, became a pro-

totype for the long-span truss systems developed during the nineteenth century. Over waterways and valleys, from Alabama to Bavaria to Russia, builders erected what came to be known as 'American bridges.' Compared to existing frame systems, the lattice possessed a uniformity and rectilinear clarity that made it one of the earliest engineering pinups of the railway age.

The lattice bridge, designed for quantity production, became the Model T of industrial structures. It inspired engineers to create the wood and metal truss frameworks that became fundamental engineering structures. Theorists consequently developed standard methods of analysis.[8]

Natura non facit saltum ('nature makes no jumps') was a favorite Latin saw of Charles Darwin.[9] Gradual bit-by-bit emergence is central to his theory. Does it hold for building? Was the lattice bridge just a small step? It appeared to be a long jump to most observers. It meant a switch from massive stone arch construction as well as wood and iron translations. It challenged fundamental beliefs about building materials, redundancy, durability, safety, appearance, and time. It was apparently conceived by combining struc-

tures, ideas, and processes that could be found in a fence, a ship frame, or a garden trellis. Yet the amalgamation was startlingly novel in both conception and physical form.

When Darwin wrote, 'almost every part of every organic being is so beautifully related to its complex conditions of life that it seems as improbable that any part should have been suddenly produced perfect, as that a complex machine should have been invented by man in a perfect state,' he implied what many now believe about technological objects – that they become perfected through evolution.[10] Darwin's analogy points to the decidedly technological character of evolution, whose mechanical processes of variation and selection are often noted. Evolution proceeds autonomously: nature's slow-going assembly lines deliver species.[11] In clarifying a natural process, evolution made biology 'mechanical' and thereby scientific. When the analogy was then re-applied to its source – human activity – it made technological development mystical: individual designers had reasons for their actions, but as a group they became agents of autonomous progress.

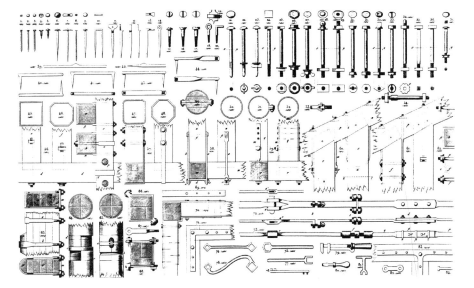

Iron hardware for 'wooden' structures (1837)

When we no longer look at an organic being as a savage looks at a ship, as something wholly beyond his comprehension; when we regard every production of nature as one which has had a long history; when we contemplate every complex structure and instinct as the summing up of many contrivances, each useful to the possessor, in the same way as any great mechanical invention is the summing up of the labour, the experience, the reason, and even the blunders of numerous workmen; when we thus view each organic being, how far more interesting – I speak from experience – does the study of natural history become!

Charles Darwin, *Origin of the Species* (1859)

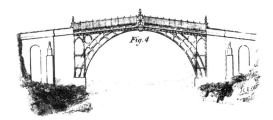

Iron bridge, Coalbrookdale, England
Abraham Darby III, iron founder (1779)

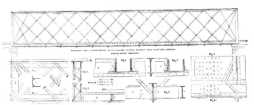

Bridge near Canestota Station, New York, Charles Hilton (1864)

Sigfried Giedion observed fifty years ago that 'evolution is now used interchangeably with progress,' and this is still true.[12] Bridges and buildings are always becoming more sophisticated; steel is superior to iron, which is superior to wood. The social Darwinist conception of evolution presupposes that the evolving object or system is heading toward a goal of improvement.[13] It reinforces popular belief in the autonomy and inevitability of technological development – a history in which things keep getting better.

But there is no ideal building or bridge design; there are always many choices. Designers must confront a technological (also known as a cultural, physical, economic, political) environment that they interpret and manipulate to make an invention succeed. For an architect, it is a matter, as Le Corbusier pointed out, of first formulating the question.[14]

THE NATURELESSNESS OF MATERIALS

In order to explain bridge development, historians have classified bridges by appearance: by types of forces (tension or compression); by designer (hero-genius); by location; by size (the bigger the better); by chronology (in which 'firsts' are all-important); and by material. The ideas behind these classifications are rarely examined. Size and scale are only two of many measures of significance, and chronology may reveal little about kinship. Grouping by material, a practice taken from engineering textbooks, may result in skewed conclusions: one finds pronouncements such as, 'the iron truss came soon after the iron arch.'[15] An examination of design conceptions rather than material manufacture reveals that the relationship between an iron arch bridge and an iron truss bridge was not direct. Before chaining systems together, one must understand the reasons behind their emergence.

The fact that a bridge was 100 percent iron is not necessarily significant for the history of structures. In fact, the first 'all-iron' bridges may be considered the least interesting, because they were imitations of existing structures. The so-called first (cast-)iron bridge, built in Coalbrookdale, England, around 1779, was based on stone construction, with details that duplicated wood connection technology. Yet this 'first' has been trumpeted as a remarkable British achievement and major advance in bridge building for two hundred years. While it may have served as an inspiration, this was an advance in some respects similar to the substitution of metal for wood in doorknob manufacture. Coalbrookdale is a monument to the belief that iron made civil engineering modern.[16]

But here is a shock: a critical selling point of the lattice bridge was that no iron was used. Although Town stated that the whole bridge could be built in iron, he deliberately invented and built bridges that included no iron. It was made of uniform size parts: plank and wooden pegs. Iron was considered a disadvantage rather

The first crude stone missile begat the spear,
which begat the arrow and then the bolt,
the bullet, and so on to Star Wars. Human volition seems to have less to do with this development than do the potentialities inherent in the
objects themselves.

Mihaly Csikszentmihalyi, *Why We Need Things* (1993)

Lattice bridge, Europe (location unknown)

than something positive – it was expensive, difficult to manufacture, it failed without warning, and it rusted. An essential part of the solution to early-nineteenth-century bridge deficiencies and a key to the modernization of bridge building lay in the development of a structural system – in wood.

The lattice system, moreover, was greater than the sum of its wooden parts: the sides of the bridge could be built on land and subsequently moved into position. This prefabrication saved time and money not just in the building of one bridge, but in the construction and maintenance of thousands. The lattice bridge as an epochal industrial structural design, however, went unrecognized by historians. An important reason for its dismissal was its material. In the iron age, a 'wooden bridge' was a species low on the evolutionary scale of engineering. It hardly merited mention:

> The construction of the first railroads greatly
> affected the development of strength of materials by
> presenting a series of new problems (especially in
> bridge engineering) which had to be solved. The
> materials used for building bridges were then stone
> and cast iron. [17]

So began a discussion of iron tubular bridges by Stephen P. Timoshenko, professor of engineering mechanics at Stanford University when he wrote *History of Strength of Materials* (1953), a standard reference on the subject. Yet thousands of railroad bridges were built of wood. Timoshenko represents wood as a material of the past, the stuff of craft, provisional and cheap, although he does note that early metal bridges were 'similar' to existing wooden ones. [18]

The classifications 'wooden' and 'iron' in this context require re-examination, because many of the most well-known 'wooden bridges' of the eighteenth and nineteenth centuries had tons, literally tons, of iron, in the form of critical parts such as bolts, straps, and suspension rods. Iron played an integral role in

these bridges, just as wood was central to the design of 'all-iron' bridges.

Builders seesawed between wood and iron. Around mid-century, the New York and Erie Railroad decided to replace its iron bridges with wooden ones after the collapse of an iron bridge patented by Nathaniel Rider; it seems that the railroad owners' financial interest in wood had something to do with it. [19] In a mirror-image action, the Compagnie de l'Ouest in France replaced its wooden arch bridges with cast-iron arches, in order to secure them against sabotage. (The oak and pine arch bridge at Asnières [1836], which carried three important rail lines to Paris, required major reinforcing and was burned during political upheaval of 1848.) [20] These were local movements in which 'evolution' encountered politics and not infrequently stalled or went into reverse. By 1854, wood had been banned for railways in the German states, although some engineers continued to use it, and by 1863, both wood and cast iron had been 'removed from the field of investigation: the former by negation, and the latter by direct condemnation.' [21] Inflammability and maintenance issues were 'obvious' reasons to reject wood, although only as obvious as local conditions; one historian reports that wooden railway bridges were common in the United States until the 1890s. [22]

As wooden bridges were rejected by the railways, the importance of the type of knowledge required to build with wood diminished. Because wood fails with forewarning, the carpenter could learn through observing and repairing his own work. The engineer using iron did not ordinarily have this opportunity, because iron breaks with no or little warning and does not lend itself to direct evaluation. He became more dependent on the manufacturer and mathematical calculation for the security of the bridge. The manufacturer became responsible for creating a material which met a specific stan-

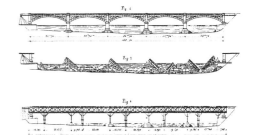

Bridge, Asnières, France, Karl Etzel (1836: destroyed 1848)

dard; this standard was established by testing, which usually was done independently of the bridge designer. This 'liberation' of engineers from the material was an important factor in allowing the mass-construction of bridges.[23]

The professionalization of engineering coincided with the development of structural wrought iron.[24] Engineers imbued iron with the aura of progress and science, and it was upon iron and the methods of analysis developed at the time of iron's introduction that engineers maintained their status. The 'evolutionary' substitution of iron for wood in structures was accompanied by the lowering of the status of the carpenter – and the raising of the station of the iron engineer, who possessed a different kind of knowledge. As historian Joachim Radkau explains, craftsmanship and feeling for materials were still important, before iron and industrial building and after, but with iron 'human skill was pushed to the edge of the technologists' consciousness.'[25] Engineers knew, in any case, that to maintain their professional status, they needed to distinguish themselves from the fabricators and contractors whose participation in iron construction was essential.[26]

Iron is considered the classic material of the 'industrial revolution,' although lumber was no less an industrialized product, no less the stuff of 'revolution.' Many considered wood suitable for temporary structures or for nations on the other side of the 'great divide:' for less complex, less civilized societies. As historian Carl Condit asserted: 'Wherever wood was plentiful and industrial techniques less advanced than in Western Europe, timber construction was bound to be the natural choice.' For him, wood framing belonged to a 'vernacular tradition' – it was unscientific, practical.[27] From the evolutionary viewpoint, the wood-wielding inventors, builders, and engineers who developed our industrial technologies were primitives.

THE NATURE OF NATIONS

Technology was – and is – regarded as a defining element of national culture. Observers from Europe therefore examined 'American' technology at least as carefully as they examined American citizens. Like the naturalists and geologists who studied North American plants, animals, and rocks, engineers and entrepreneurs came to the United States to explore technology that could be of use to them. That a sparse population had built an enormous infrastructure within a few decades made the 'new World' an obligatory object of study. The missionaries of industry who stalked the latest inventions were as much technologists as promoters, politicians, proselytizers, and prophets.

The political and economic importance of transportation networks meant that many technological tourists scrutinized Town's lattice

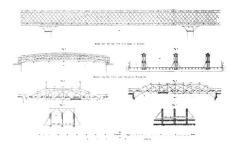

Lattice and wooden bridges of North America (1850)

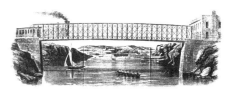

Rider's Bridge, advertisement (patented 1845)

Busseau d'Ahun Viaduct, Creuse, France, Wilhelm Nordling (1863-65)

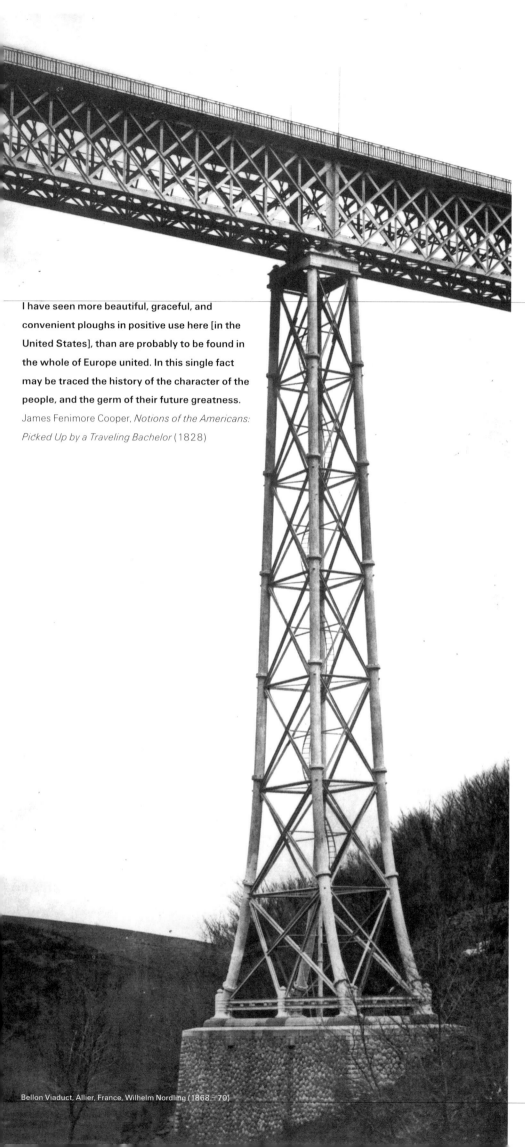

I have seen more beautiful, graceful, and convenient ploughs in positive use here [in the United States], than are probably to be found in the whole of Europe united. In this single fact may be traced the history of the character of the people, and the germ of their future greatness.

James Fenimore Cooper, *Notions of the Americans: Picked Up by a Traveling Bachelor* (1828)

Bellon Viaduct, Allier, France, Wilhelm Nordling (1868–70)

bridge and presented it to an international audience in professional books and journals. By the late 1830s, engineers had begun to build lattice bridges in France, England, Russia, Austria-Hungary, Prussia, Holland, and Ireland.[28]

As the United States and the states of Western Europe transformed themselves into industrial powers, the exchange of ideas allowed a scale of technological development that would not have occurred in one country alone. Building technologies flourished within a reciprocal relationship: exchange of information in these fields was essential for their development, and their development helped exchange to occur. The networks of roads and bridges essential for transportation, communications, defense, and trade were central to the physical and conceptual construction of nationhood. Despite – or because of – the transnational character of technological development, nations erected national identities along with their bridges.

Many historians who have examined building have transmitted nationalistic views with little interference. They used the technology transfer concept to characterize imperialistic activity as well as exchange between technological colleagues in America and Europe. 'Transfer' is based on the idea of technological firsts that acquire great significance within an evolutionary, nationalistic scheme. As a condition for transfer, the 'first iron bridge' existed in a particularly inventive culture, and bears the mark of that culture's 'character' or 'style.' Where the 'first' occurred, however, is often a matter of chance; for example the 'first iron bridge,' built in England, was preceded by others, including one over the Rhone in Lyon, a project that was aborted after the erection of the first arch because of cost.[29] When Condit wrote that 'the practical iron truss was initially a creation of American builders rather than European,' he was trying to claim iron as a first for the United States.[30] Iron bridges, however, weren't commonly built there until a few decades after such practice became common in several European countries. The development of the 'iron truss' was an endeavor that involved many countries – where the so-called 'first' all-iron truss bridge was constructed is just as unimportant for the overall history of structures as the fact that it was 'all-iron.'

The transfer concept reinforces the supposed separateness of cultures, nations, and materials. It works with the evolutionary scheme to support claims of national superiority. Strengthened by

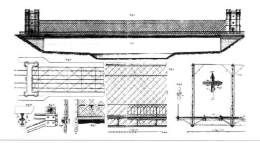

Kinzig Bridge, Offenburg, Germany, Karl Ruppert (1852–53)

One of the greats of France said: the style is the man. Isn't it just as appropriate to say: the works are the nation?

Engineer Berthault-Ducreux (1845)

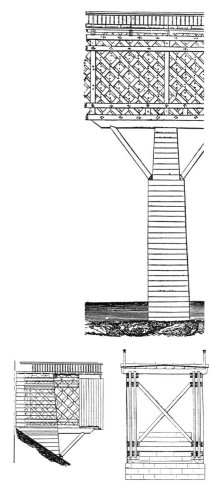

Peacock Bridge, near Reading, Pennsylvania, Moncure Robinson (1839-40)

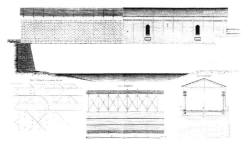

Lattice bridge, Philadelphia-Wilmington Railroad, South Carolina (c.1839)

evolutionary theory, nationalism during the nineteenth century was a tool for the dominance and denigration of non-Western colonial populations.[31] Labels such as 'French' or 'wooden' were used in ways similar to racial classifications – ideology or politics were as important to labeling as any particular physical make-up. When races were considered by some to represent different stages of evolution, 'Anglo-Saxons' claimed to be at the high end of the evolutionary ladder and they touted their iron and steel as the highest achievements of civilized man.[32] Ideas of metal superiority and racial ideology became mixed: industrialists shipped iron bridges and buildings from Britain to India, the Bahamas and other colonies. These were areas which otherwise would have built with wood or other local materials.[33]

Is there an alternative to nationalistic evolutionary accounts of building history and the resulting view of structural design as an inevitable, heroic endeavor? One option is to regard the development of building as a process of exchange. Investigate the reasons why engineers choose or reject ideas and objects. Look at how ideas are interpreted and employed, and

why. As obvious as they may seem, these strategies have often been ignored by structural designers and historians caught in a competitive and nationalistic environment.

Examining building as an exchange process would place engineering more firmly within the sphere from which it is often excluded – that is, 'culture' – because it would reconnect it to the 'non-technical' domains from which it sprang. It might broaden designers' options by encouraging them to reconsider notions of progress and categorization that serve to keep habits in place.

Mythical divides, intended to make reality graspable, result in narratives that do not accurately reflect design activity. Smashing the divides will help demystify design as it defuses nationalist explanation. A structure is a product of culture. It is the result of an intercultural exchange of things, techniques, and ideas. It is not individuals, however, but the relations between them that define design. If you want to understand a culture, look at its bridges.

1 The term 'Great Divides' is used by Bruno Latour, who cites Jack Goody's expression: 'great dichotomy.' See Bruno Latour, "Drawing Things Together," in *Representation in Scientific Practice*, ed. Michael Lynch and Steve Woolgar (Cambridge, MIT Press, 1990), 19-20.

2 The fact that the authors rarely explicitly state their theoretical foundation makes their histories no less theoretically based than those of authors who do. Some examples: Charles Davis Jameson, "The Evolution of the Modern Railway Bridge," *Popular Science Monthly* 36 (Feb. 1890): 461-481; J.E. Greiner, "The American Railroad Viaduct: Its Origin and Evolution," *Transactions of American Society of Civil Engineers* 25 (1891): 349-372; Charles C. Schneider, "The Evolution of the Practice of American Bridge Building," *Transactions of American Society of Civil Engineers* 54 (1905): 213-234; James K.Finch, "Wind Failures of Suspension Bridges or Evolution and Decay of the Stiffening Truss," *Engineering News Record* (27 March 1941); Llewellyn Nathaniel Edwards, *A Record of History and Evolution of Early American Bridges* (Orono, Maine: University Press,1959); Carl Condit, "The Two Centuries of Technical Evolution Underlying the Skyscraper," in *The Second Century of the Skyscraper*, ed. Lynn S. Beedle (N.Y.: Van Nostrand Reinhold, 1988), 11-24.

J. G. James acted as a Linnaeus of bridges; he received information from correspondents all over the world, just as Linnaeus received seeds and plants. James gave three of his bridge articles explicitly evolutionary titles: "The Evolution of Wooden Bridge Trusses to 1850," *Journal of Institute of Wood Science* 9 (1982): 116-135, 168-193; "The Evolution of Iron Bridge Trusses to 1850," *Transactions of the Newcomen Society* 52 (1980-81): 67-101; "Some Steps in the Evolution of Early Iron Arched Bridge Design," *Transactions of the Newcomen Society* 59 (1987-88): 153-87. James occasionally used evolutionary phraseology, e.g., he wrote of 'trusses reach[ing] a much higher state of perfection' ("Evolution of Iron," 84). He was trying to classify and link together all bridges in an evolutionary manner, but he did not explain why he was doing what he was doing.

Stewart Brand's idea of 'vernacular' architecture as evolutionary and 'visionary' architecture as non-evolutionary would seem to ignore the vision and failure behind vernacular architecture. It also seems to dismiss the 'vernacular' experience that is the foundation for 'vision.' Brand, after Darwin, substitutes 'vernacular' for the role of nature and 'visionary' for man. Brand, *How Buildings Learn* (N.Y.: Viking, 1994), 132-55; 188-89; see also Cornell, 332-333 (citation in note 10).

Among general evolutionary theorists of technology, S.C. Gilfillan, in *The Sociology of Invention* (Chicago: Follet, 1935; reprint, Cambridge: MIT, 1970), had a profoundly biological/anthropological view of technology. His aversion to the unthinking use of labels distinguishes his work. George Basalla in *The Evolution of Technology* (Cambridge: Cambridge University Press, 1988) begins his book, with its starkly philosophical title, by stating: 'This study is primarily historical, not an exercise in the philosophy or sociology of technology' (vii). A recent discussion of evolution as an explanation for technological development can be found in Joel Mokyos, *The Lever of Riches* (N.Y.: Oxford University Press, 1990).

3 Theodore Cooper, "American Railroad Bridges," *Transactions of American Society of Civil Engineers* (1889): 50.

4 Re Spencer, see Richard Hofstadter, *Social Darwinism in American Thought* (1944, rev. ed. Boston: Beacon Press, 1955), 31-50.

5 For example, Maximillian II in 1858 chose a Pauli bridge because it was cheapest and its creator was Bavarian. 'Konstruktion Eisenbahnbrücken und das von Pauli'sche Brückensystem,' Verkersarchiv Nürnberg #6823. Thanks to Helmut Hilz for this item.

6 'Sous la main de l'homme, les choses semblent s'animer, s'associer à ses aspirations et, comme lui, lutter pour l'existence': Jules Gaudard, *De l'évolution dans la construction des grands ponts* (Lausanne: Ch.Viret-Genton, 1892); George Michael Danko, "The Evolution of the Simple Truss Bridge 1790 to 1850: From Empiricism to Scientific Construction" (Ph.D. Dissertation, University of Pennsylvania, 1979), 72; Henry Petroski, *Engineers of Dreams* (N.Y.: Vintage Books, 1995), 36, and Petroski, *Invention by Design* (Cambridge: Harvard University Press, 1996), 204-05.

7 See Chris de Bresson, "The Evolutionary Paradigm and the Economics of Technological Change," *Journal of Economic Issues* 21 (1987): 754-57. In addition to revival of the dead and interbreeding, de Bresson points out that technological evolutionists have trouble accounting for speed of innovative change and use of abandoned techniques.

8 A second lattice patent was issued in 1835. Re Ithiel Town and the lattice bridge, see Gregory K. Dreicer, "The Long Span. Intercultural Exchange in Building Technology: Development and Industrialization of the Framed Beam in Western Europe and the United States, 1820–1870" (Ph.D. Dissertation, Cornell University, 1993) and forthcoming book. See also Richard Sanders Allen, *Covered Bridges of the Northeast* (Lexington, Mass.: S. Greene Press, 1957; rev. ed. 1983), and other books in this series.

9 'It is...extremely difficult even to conjecture by what gradations many structures have been perfected, more especially amongst broken and failing groups...which have suffered much extinction; but we see so many strange gradations...that we ought to be extremely cautious in saying that any...structure could not have arrived at its present state by many graduated steps.' Charles Darwin, *The Origin of the Species by Means of Natural Selection, or the Preservation of Favored Races in the Struggle for Life*, 6th ed. (London: John Murray, 1892 [1st ed: 1859]), 380.

10 Darwin, *Origin*, 31. Darwin did not thoroughly examine his own technological analogy. See John F. Cornell, "Analogy and Technology in Darwin's vision of Nature," *Journal of History of Biology* 17 (1984): 317, n.46 and passim. It is very probable that Darwin (1809–1882) was aware of highly publicized civil engineering developments during his lifetime. One journal which he read, *Edinburgh Philosophical Journal* (see Peter J. Vorzimmer, "The Darwin Reading Notebooks (1838–1860)," *Journal of History of Biology* 10 (1971): 107–153) contained early reports of American bridges: e.g. Robert Stevenson, "Description of Bridges of Suspension." *Edinburgh Philosophical Journal* 5 (1821): 237–256, pl.8.

11 Bernard, cited in Georges Canguilhem, "The Role of Analogies and Models in Biological Discovery," in *Scientific Change*, ed. A.C. Crombie (N.Y.: Basic Books, 1963), 509. Evolution has often been characterized as mechanical; for example, J. Walter Wilson, "Biology Attains Maturity in the Nineteenth Century," in *Critical Problems in the History of Science*, ed. Marshall Clagett, (Madison: University of Wisconsin Press, 1959), 407 ff.

12 Siegfried Giedion, *Mechanization Takes Command* (Oxford University Press, 1948, reprint, N.Y.: Norton, 1969), 31. Petroski tries to extract progress from technological evolutionism.

13 If this goal is not defined, it cannot be determined if evolution is taking place. R. Puligandla, "The Concept of Evolution and Revolution" in *Evolution-Revolution: Patterns of Development in Nature, Society, Man and Knowledge*, ed. Rubin Gotesky and Ervin Laszli (N.Y.: Gordon & Breach, 1971), 42. Linear genealogies allow evolutionists to trace technologies to a "unique form." See Franz Boas, *Race, Language and Culture* (N.Y.: Macmillan, 1940), 290–94.

14 'The problem of the house has not yet been stated.' Le Corbusier, *Towards a New Architecture*, trans. Frederick Etchells (London: Architectural Press, 1927), 102.

15 Carl Condit, *American Building: Materials and Techniques from the First Colonial Settlements to the Present* (Chicago: University of Chicago Press, 1968), 94.

16 Years later, virtually all of the sixty-three bridges of the first British railway were stone arches. Henry Booth, "Chemin de fer de Liverpool à Manchester: Notice Historique," *Annales des ponts et chaussées* 1/1 (1831): 86-89. See James, "Some Steps," 154-56, regarding the small effect of the Coalbrookdale Bridge on bridge building. Re doorknobs, see Steven Lubar, "New, Useful, and Nonobvious," *American Heritage of Invention and Technology* (Spring/Summer 1990): 14.

17 Stephen P. Timoshenko, *History of Strength of Materials* (N.Y.: McGraw-Hill, 1953, reprint, N.Y. Dover, 1983), 156.

18 Timoshenko, *History*, 184-86.

19 Nathaniel Rider (1790-1848) patented one of the earliest cast and wrought iron framed bridge systems; Victor C. Darnell, "The Pioneering Iron Trusses of Nathaniel Rider," *Construction History* 7 (1991): 69-81.

20 Georges Ribeill, "Vie et mort des ouvrages d'art: l'exemple des ponts de chemins de fer," (Manuscript, 1992), 7. In the Asnières bridge, the wood rotted and the bolts that held the arch planks together had become 'Wasserleiter' (water pipes). "Ueber die Dauer hölzerner Brücken," *Allgemeine Bauzeitung* 27 (1862): 81-82. Re the wood versus stone debate, see Forest G. Hill, *Roads, Rails and Waterways: The Army Engineers and Early Transportation* (Norman, OK:U. of Oklahoma Press, 1957), 104; James D. Dilts, *The Great Road: The Building of the Baltimore and Ohio, The Nation's First Railroad, 1823–1853* (Stanford, CA: Stanford U. Press, 1993), 70, 73–79. For a recent chapter in the wood vs. metal story, see Eric Schatzberg, *Wings of Wood, Wings of Metal: Culture and Technical Choice in American Airplane Materials, 1914–1945* (Princeton:Princeton U. Press, 19980.

21 C. Couche, "Travaux d'art des chemins de fer d'Allemagne" *Annales des mines* 5/5 (1854): 311-12; Robert Crawford, "The Railway System of Germany," *Transactions of Institution of Civil Engineers* 22 (1862-63): 13.

22 J.G. James, "Overseas Railways and the Spread of Iron Bridges, c. 1850-70," (Published by author, 1987), 27.

23 Re wood construction, see Milton S. Graton, *The Last of the Covered Bridge Builders* (Plymouth, NH: Clifford-Nichol, Inc., 1978), 1–5,9. The different knowledge required for wood and iron bridges, respectively, can be seen in an engineer's advice: "Neither is it safe to entrust light iron bridges wholly to the care of workmen not technically educated; the timber parts of wooden ones maybe;" J.P. Snow, "Wooden Bridge Construction on the Boston and Maine Railroad," *Association of Engineering Societies Journal* 15 (1895): 39.

24 Robert Thorne, "Introduction," in Robert Thorne, ed., *The Iron Revolution: Architects, Engineers and Structural Innovation, 1780-1880* (London: RIBA Heinz Gallery, 1990), 7.

25 "Mit der übergang vom Holz zum Eisen wurden doch ganz neue Perspektiven für die Organisation des Produktionsprozesses eröffnet, die die menschlichen Fertigkeiten im Bewußtsein der Techniker an den Rand rückten." Joachim Radkau, *Technik in Deutschland: vom 18. Jahrhundert bis zur Gegenwart* (Frankfurt: Suhrkamp, 1989), 63.

26 Thorne, "Introduction," 8.

27 Condit, "Building and Building Construction," 1: 373 and Condit, *American Building Art*, 16.

28 Major-General Howard Douglas, *Essay on the Principles and Construction of Military Bridges*, 2d ed. (London, 1832); Guillaume-Tell Poussin, *Travaux d'améliorations intérieures projetés ou exécutés par le gouvernement général des Etats Unis d'Amérique de 1824 à 1831* (Paris, 1834-36); David Stevenson, *Sketch of the Civil Engineering of North America* (London, 1838); Michel Chevalier, *Histoire et description des voies de communication aux Etats-Unis* (Paris, 1840-41); Franz Anton Ritter von Gerstner, *Die innern Communicationen der vereinigten Staaten von Nordamerika* (Vienna, 1842); Karl Culmann,"Der Bau der hölzeren Brücken in den Vereinigten Staaten von Nordamerika . . . in den Jahren 1849 und 1850," *Allgemeine Bauzeitung* 16 (1851): 69-129; pls. 387-97 and "Der Bau der eisernen Brücken in England und Amerika," *Allgemeine Bauzeitung* 17 (1852): 163-222; 478-487.

29 Bernard Marrey, *Les ponts modernes: 18e-19e siècles* (Paris: Picard, 1990), 105, reports that it was in 1755; Georg Christoph Mehrtens, *Vorlesungen über Ingenieur-Wissenschaften 2, Eisenbrückenbau* (Leipzig: Wilhelm Engelmann, 1908), 268, gives the year 1719 and the engineer's name Garrin.

30 Condit, *American Building*, 94. Earlier, in *American Building Art: Nineteenth Century* (N.Y.: Oxford University Press, 1960), 4-5 Condit stated: 'Most of the fundamental inventions in nineteenth century construction, such as the iron frame, bridge truss, and arch, were European accomplishments. American work, with some important exceptions, consisted of adaptations of the original forms rather than innovations.' Daniel L. Schodek, 'clarifies' the issue in Landmarks in American Civil Engineering (Cambridge: MIT Press, 1987), 73: 'The development of the all-iron truss is fundamentally an American accomplishment, although the truss form itself has European precedents and all-iron forms have their European counterparts.'

31 Michael Adas, *Machines as the Measure of Man: Science, Technology, and Ideologies of Western Dominance* (Ithaca: Cornell U. Press, 1989), 307–318.

32 Thomas F. Gossett, *Race: The History of an Idea in America* (Dallas: Southern Methodist University Press, 1963), 144.

33 James, "Overseas Railways"; Gilbert Herbert, *Pioneers of Prefabrication: The British Contribution in the Nineteenth Century* (Baltimore: Johns Hopkins University Press, 1978); Charles E.Peterson, "Early American Prefabrication," *Gazette des Beaux-Arts* [NY] 33 (1948): 37–46.

I am grateful to Cornell University (Ithaca), Deutscher Akademischer Austauschdienst (Bonn), Deutsches Museum (Munich), Bourse Chateuaubriand, Ministère de la Culture (Paris), and Lemelson Center for the Study of Invention and Innovation, Smithsonian Institution (Washington, D.C.) for their generous support. Special thanks to Carolyn Foug and Sharon Joyce for their comments.

on BUILDING MYTHS
Steven Lubar

Bridges are the most metaphorical and political of technologies. Bill Clinton wanted a bridge to the twenty-first century. Robert Moses built parkway bridges designed to keep buses away from the Long Island beaches. Bridges tell stories as well as span spaces. They shape cultures.

Gregory Dreicer argues that bridges not only shape culture, they are culture. They have real histories. But the history that bridge builders and engineers and historians of engineering have told us are more metaphors than reality. Technology does not evolve, iron is not necessarily more advanced than wood, there are no national styles. What has passed for bridge history has been little more than 'anecdotes leavened by a belief in natural selection.'

Dreicer demands that bridge history be incorporated back into human history. He wants us to ask: What were the choices? What were the politics? Look for reasons, not for apparently obvious connections. Don't assume evolution. Look beyond materials, beyond nation, beyond engineering theory. Look to culture. Bridges may be structurally elegant, but they are as historically complex as any other structure. Bridge history, like all history, is messy. It is people, not equations and engineering elegance; and politics, not natural selection and evolution.

Bridges have politics not only in what they span, and why they span, but also in how they span. They are culture as well as technology. Bridges are intercultural both metaphorically and structurally. Smash the divides, demystify design, defuse nationalism. Find bridges across time as well as bridges across space.

Steven Lubar is a curator in the Division of the History of Technology at the National Museum of American History, Smithsonian Institution. He writes on the history of technology and material culture, and is the author of *InfoCulture: The Smithsonian Book of Information Age Inventions.*

on BUILDING MYTHS
Mark Jarzombek

In the past two decades, historians in many fields have given themselves the task of critically reflecting on the epistemological underpinnings of their discourse. But the project is not yet widely practiced among historians of technology. Gregory Dreicer is one of the exceptions. Already known for his path-breaking exhibitions at the National Building Museum, Dreicer, in this article, deals head on with the historiographic problem of how to write a 'history of technology.' The device that Dreicer uses to generate his critique is the Lattice Bridge, a bridge form which was particularly common in the mid nineteenth-century in both the United States and Europe. Dreicer demonstrates how this bridge, when viewed on its own, forces us to rethink basic premises. Neither the conventional notion of 'evolution' nor the oft accepted idea of a 'natural progression' from wood to metal explain the rise and fall of this bridge type. Dreicer's goal is not to throw out the normalized abstractions of earlier historiographic approaches, but rather to demonstrate that one has to view technology not as something that is first produced and then historicized, but as something which, from its inception, codifies its history around self-serving historical mythologies. In other words, technology, like architecture for that matter, is never disinterested from its history, and this means that today's historians, struggling to define technology as a cultural product, have the burden of re-evaluating the legitimacy of some of these historical mythologies.

Mark Jarzombek is Professor of Architectural History in the History, Theory, Criticism Section of the MIT School of Architecture. His most recent book is *The Psychologizing of Modernity: Art, Architecture, History.*

on TECHNOLOGICAL THOUGHT IS DESIGN'S OPERATIVE METHOD
Subrata Dasgupta

In his interesting article, Tom Peters attempts to characterize ways in which technological thought is distinguishable from other thought modes. In particular, he is interested in the contrast between 'hard,' analytical thinking which he associates with 'science,' and the 'soft,' intuitive, contextually situated form of thought which he relates to technology. In this brief review, I will only address a few of his points in order to present slightly different viewpoints.

Peters believes that an important distinction between engineers and architects is that the former think in the 'abstract and analytical language and notation of mathematics,' while the latter draw on 'visual language and graphical notation.' However, the long history of engineering drawing seems to belie this as a *general* characterization of the engineer; and as Eugene Ferguson has shown in *Engineering and the Mind's Eye* (1991), despite the development of analytical theory, engineers of even the most recent past have continued to rely heavily on visualization and graphical imagery for both communication and understanding.

Peters remarks that analytical thinkers tend to regard 'small' matters as of minor consequence, whereas in technological thinking, 'small' means 'small-scale' and is of no less importance than the 'large.' He correctly notes that significant engineering failures may originate because of small-scale flaws. However, historically, even 'normal' (à la Thomas Kuhn) science, has been often concerned with clarifying small details. Think of the ever-increasing accuracy in measurement techniques in physics and chemistry, and the continuing endeavor to determine, ever-more accurately, the universal constants of nature.

Peters makes the further point that technologists focus on 'objects' while scientists deal with 'abstractions' such as concepts and hypotheses. True, the technologists' *ultimate* concerns are objects or artifacts. However, they also frame hypotheses and form concepts. Technologists do not necessarily *talk* about hypotheses. But, as I have attempted to show in *Technology and Creativity* (1996), engineers and inventors implicitly create and test hypotheses and theories in the course of their work.

The point is that technological, scientific, and architectural thinking are, in some important ways, disconcertingly similar, especially at the highest level of creativity. Yet, like Peters, I believe there is something cognitively distinct about the nature of people's thinking when they are 'doing' technology. For Peters, this essence is its hybrid, fluid character, and its free borrowing from other domains of thought. Technological thinking is *pragmatic* in this sense. In *Technology and Creativity,* I expressed a similar view using different terms. Following Michael Polanyi's notion, I suggested that the distinctive feature of technological thinking is the use of 'operational principles' – rules, hypotheses, procedures, heuristics, strategies, mental models – which are not *necessarily* grounded in sound theory, but which are considered valid so long as they work. Operational principles, thus, constitute the most distinguishable form of technological *knowledge.*

Finally, a comment on Peters' conclusion that 'technological thought [is] the premier thought mode of our age.' My first reaction was to emphatically disagree. My later, more tempered, response is to take this as a provocative, interesting hypothesis that deserves to be examined seriously.

Subrata Dasgupta holds the Eminent Scholar Chair in Computer Science, and is Co-Director of the Institute of Cognitive Science, University of Louisiana at Lafayette, where he is also Professor of History. He is the author of *Technology and Creativity.*

You believe in the Palace of Crystal, eternally inviolable, that is in something at which one couldn't furtively put out one's tongue or make concealed gestures of derision. But perhaps I fear this edifice just because it is made of crystal and eternally inviolable, and it will not be possible even to put out one's tongue at it in secret. It's like this, you see: if instead of a palace it was a hen-house, and it began to rain, I might creep into the hen-house so as not to get wet, but I shouldn't take the hen-house for a palace out of gratitude because it had protected me from the rain. You laugh; you even say that in that case it doesn't matter whether it's a hen-house or a mansion. No, I answer, if not getting wet was all one had to live for.

But what if I have taken it into my head that that isn't the sole object of living, and if I have to live, let it be in a mansion? That is my will and my desire. Well, change it then; attract me by something else, give me a different ideal. Meanwhile, I still refuse to take a hen-house for a palace. Let us grant that a building of crystal is a castle in the air, that by the laws of nature it is a sheer impossibility, and that I have invented it out of nothing but my own stupidity and certain antiquated irrational habits of my generation. But what does it matter to me if it is an impossibility? What difference does it make to me, so long as it exists in my desires, or rather, exists while my desires last? Perhaps you are laughing again. Laugh if you like: I will accept all your ridicule, but all the same I won't say I've had enough to eat when I'm hungry, I won't be satisfied with compromise, with the constantly recurring decimal, merely because it exists by the laws of nature and exists *in reality*. I will not accept as my crowning wish a block of flats for poor tenants on thousand-year leases and, in any case, with 'Wagenheim, Dental Surgeon' as the signboard. Destroy my desire, blot out my ideals, show me something better, and I will follow you. Perhaps you will say it is not worth while to get involved; but in that case I can make the same answer to you. We are discussing seriously; and if you don't choose to honour me with your attention, I'm not going to plead with you.

Meanwhile, I am still living and still wanting – and may my hand wither if I bring one brick to the building of that block of flats! Don't pay any attention to the fact that just now I rejected the palace of crystal for the sole reason that one won't be able to stick one's tongue out at it… I didn't say that because I am so given to sticking out my tongue. Perhaps I was angry simply because no edifice at which it is impossible to stick out one's tongue is yet to be found among all your constructions. On the other hand, I would let my tongue be cut right out in mere gratitude if only things were so arranged that I never wanted to put it out again. What does it matter to me that that kind of building is impossible, and that one must content oneself with blocks of flats? Why was I made with such desires? Can I have been made for only one thing, to come at last to the conclusion that my whole make-up is nothing but a cheat? Is that the whole aim? I don't believe it.

Do you know one thing, though? I am certain that underground people like me must be kept in check. Though we may be capable of sitting underground for forty years without saying a word, if we do come out into the world and burst out, we will talk and talk and talk…

Fyodor Dostoyevsky *Notes from Underground*

For [the Russian radical critic Nikolai] Chernyshevsky, the Crystal Palace symbolizes a death sentence against 'your St. Petersburgs, Londons, Parises'; these cities will be, at best, museums of backwardness in the brave new world.

This vision should help us locate the terms of Dostoyevsky's quarrel with Chernyshevsky. The Underground Man says he is afraid of this edifice, because 'one would not be able to stick one's tongue out, or to thumb one's nose, even on the sly.' He is wrong, of course, about Paxton's Crystal Palace, at which thousands of genteel and cultivated tongues were stuck out, but right about Chernyshevsky's; wrong, in other words, about the Western reality of modernization, which is full of dissonance and conflict, but right about the Russian fantasy of modernization as an end to dissonance and conflict. This point should clarify one of the primary sources of Dostoyevsky's love for the modern city, and especially for Petersburg, *his* city: this is the ideal environment for the sticking out of tongues — that is, for the acting out and working out of personal and social conflict. Again, if the Crystal Palace is a denial of 'suffering, doubt and negation,' the streets and squares and bridges and embankments of Petersburg are precisely where these experiences and impulses find themselves most at home.

Marshall Berman   *All That Is Solid Melts Into Air*

On [the Empire State Building's] opening day a carnival atmosphere reigned in the area. Clusters of people craned their necks to study the new structure as far away as Bryant Park on 42nd Street. People jostled for a chance to inspect the marble lobby and buy a ticket to the observation platform on the 86th floor. They crammed into the elevators and shot up to the observation deck, to emerge from the relative darkness of the car into another world. The sudden break with the ordinary cityscape known at ground level could hardly be more dramatic.

One man is quoted as saying 'Central Park looked like a small pasture dotted with tiny puddles of rainwater,' another as remarking that 'the Chrysler Building, its spire gilded by the sun, appeared small and like a toy.' Official visitors…saw men and motor cars crossing like insects through the streets; they saw elevated trains that looked like toys. The *New Yorker* noted 'Bryant Park is a pancake and the Statue of Liberty something to throw at a cat.' People standing on the observation point felt how enormous the building was, and, by extension, felt themselves suddenly enlarged in relation to the rest of the world. They were particularly impressed to see that 'the shadow of the building stretched across the East River and into Brooklyn.' The sun projected their own shadows just as far. Even in bad weather the building attracted visitors. One reporter for the *New York Sun* found himself unable to see more than twenty stories below. 'Street noises came up to him, but his sensation was that of having been wrapped in cotton batting and suspended between earth and sky.' The intimation that one has moved into closer contact with heaven was an important aspect of the skyscraper, expressed in its very name.

Europeans neither invented nor embraced the vertical city of the skyscraper. Europeans banned or restricted electric signs, and rightly saw the landscape of Times Square as peculiarly American. Europeans did not see atomic explosions as tourist sites. Europeans seldom journeyed to see rockets go into space, but Americans went by the millions. There is a persistent American attraction to the technological sublime.

Not only is the sublime a recurrent figure in American thought; potential sublimity has also justified the creation of new technologies in the first place. This was not merely a matter of the rationalization of new projects, or a simple form of class domination in which an overawed populace acceded to new displays of technological power. There is an American penchant for thinking of the subject as a consciousness that can stand apart from the world and project its will upon it. In this mode of thought, the subject elides Kantian transcendental reason with technological reason and sees new structure and inventions as continuations of nature. Those operating within this logic embrace the reconstruction of the life-world by machinery, experience the dislocations and perceptual disorientations caused by the reconstruction in terms of awe and wonder, and, in their excitement, feel insulated from immediate danger. New technologies become self-justifying parts of a national destiny, just as the natural sublime once undergirded the rhetoric of manifest destiny. Fundamental changes in the landscape paradoxically seem part of an inevitable process in harmony with nature.

both passages by David E. Nye *The American Technological Sublime*

A SPIDER'S WAY OF STRUCTURE

Open-ended research leads to the most exciting results and stimulus. The spider and the structural engineer share similar requirements and constraints when designing a new structure. The key to the structure of the spider's web lies in its shape and stress distribution. By allowing large elongation of the threads, the maximum proportion of kinetic energy from a flying insect is absorbed as strain energy. The multiple redundancy of the radial threads ensures that the web will function even if many radials break.

A distinct structural hierarchy in the web is defined by the large difference in prestress. Radial threads are highly tensioned compared to the spirals. If a bee hits and sticks to a few strands of spiral thread they break the impact. The load travels from the spirals to the radials, where much of the kinetic energy is absorbed, and then continues straight out to the supports. Meanwhile, the whole web gently vibrates, dissipating energy through air resistance.

The spider is using the techniques of the late twentieth century engineer, but with much more elegance and precision.

Peter Rice *An Engineer Imagines*

This image is from the 'Mended Spiderwebs' series which came about during a six-week period in June and July of 1998 which I spent on Pörtö, a Swedish-speaking island in the Finnish archipelago. In the forest and around the house where I was living, I searched for broken spiderwebs which I repaired using red sewing thread. All of the patches were made by inserting thread segments one at a time directly into the web. Sometimes the threads were held in place by the stickiness of the spiderweb itself; longer threads were reinforced by dipping the tips into white glue. I fixed

MENDED SPIDERWEBS

EMPATHY

After all that has been said, there can be no doubt that form is not wrapped around matter as something extraneous but works its way out of matter as an immanent will. Matter and form are inseparable. In all matter there lives a will that aspires toward form, but it cannot always fulfill itself. Nor must we imagine that matter is the enemy; rather, form without matter is inconceivable. Everywhere the image of our own physical existence presents itself as a type by which we judge every other phenomenon. Matter is the evil principle only insofar as we experience it as a life negating gravity.

The effects of gravity are always associated with a decrease of vital energy. The blood runs more slowly; the breath becomes irregular and wheezing; the body has no support and collapses. . . . Everything living tries to escape from this and to achieve the natural posture of regularity and balance. The relation of form to matter is conveyed in this effort of organic will to penetrate the body.

Physical forms possess a character only because we ourselves possess a body. If we were purely visual beings, we would always be denied an aesthetic judgement of the physical world. But as human beings with a body that teaches us the nature of gravity, contraction, strength, and so on, we gather the experience that enables us to identify with the conditions of other forms. Why is no one surprised that the stone falls toward the earth? Why does that seem so very natural to us? We cannot account for it rationally; the explanation lies in our personal experience alone. We have carried loads and experienced pressure and counterpressure, we have collapsed to the ground when we no longer had the strength to resist the downward pull of our own bodies, and that is why we can appreciate the noble serenity of a column and understand the tendency of all matter to spread out formlessly on the ground.

both passages by Heinrich Wölfflin,
Psychology of Architecture

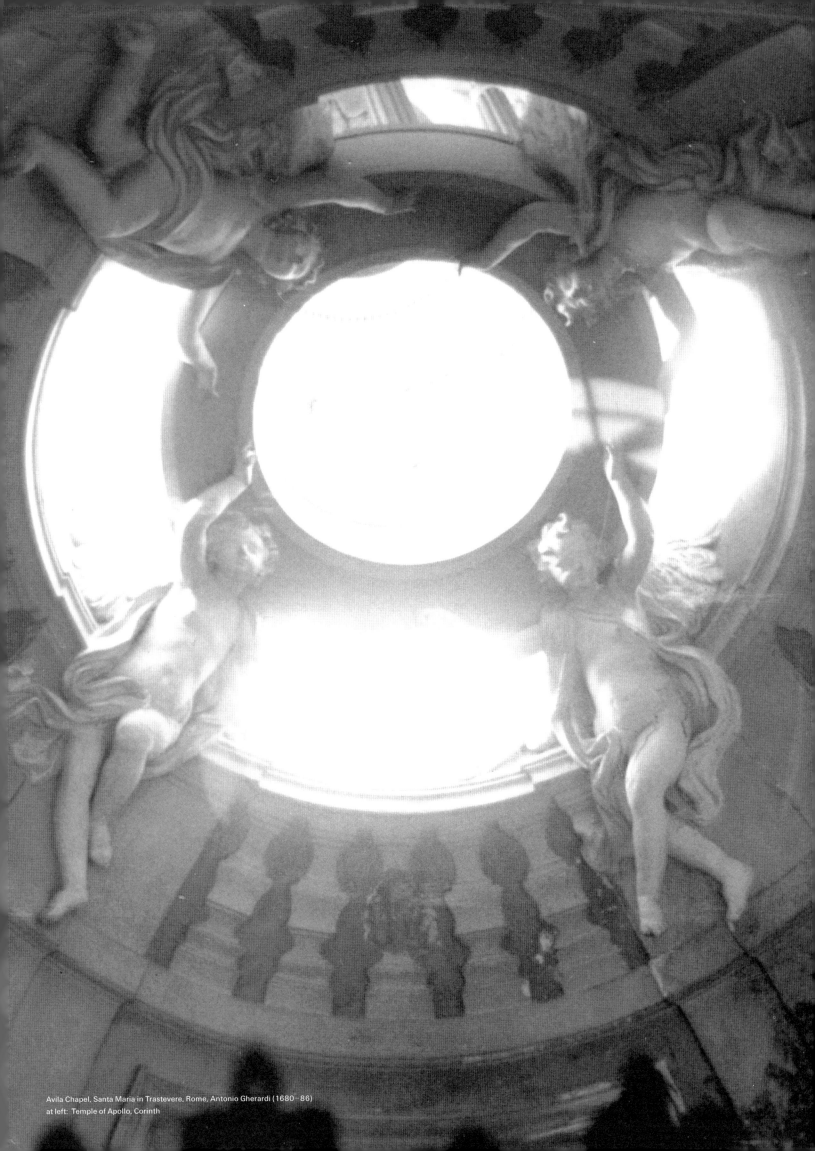

Avila Chapel, Santa Maria in Trastevere, Rome, Antonio Gherardi (1680–86)
at left: Temple of Apollo, Corinth

FORCE

The idea of 'force' has changed drastically since its ancient inception. As early inventions of the human mind, forces were thought to animate the material world and were used to explain natural motions like tidal rhythms, planetary orbits, and falling objects. The regularity of such movements fascinated the early Greeks, who sought the cause of forces in a divine agency or in the idea that all matter was somehow alive. The eventual removal of such metaphysical explanations led to a more scientific and mechanistic notion of force, evident in Galileo's study of beam theory and Newton's Laws of Motion. Now distilled into formulaes and precisely drawn in free body diagrams, force is still a mental abstraction used to describe motion, but it shows little traces of its ancient roots.

DEFINITIONS

The *Encyclopedia of Philosophy* offers a detailed history of the concept of force. A brief tour through this article takes us through a series of hypotheses as to its nature. The author, Max Jammer, begins with this definition:

In the most general sense, force denotes the faculty of action or the power to overcome a resistance. In the physical sciences, it is that entity which changes, or tends to change, the state of rest or of motion of a body. Consequently, it may also be defined as the cause of motion, or more precisely – assuming the validity of the principle of inertia – as the cause of acceleration.

After presenting the units of measurement of force, the *Encyclopedia* notes that force in natural philosophy referred to action and energy; this broader definition tended to blur the boundary between living, thinking beings and the world of matter.

Apart from being used in a figurative sense, such as 'force of habit,' 'police force,' or 'economic forces,' the word 'force,' especially in the natural philosophy of the eighteenth and nineteenth centuries and in the early writings on the principle of conservation of energy (R. Mayer, H. von Helmholtz) signified action and energy. This homonymic use caused considerable confusion at the time. Originally taken as an analogy to human will power, muscular effort, and spiritual influence, the concept early became projected into inanimate objects and played an important role in ancient thaumaturgy, occultism, and medieval sorcery.

ANCIENT GREECE

Greek philosophers pondered over the phenomena of motion, and their various schools of thought shaped early ideas of force that returned in different forms through the centuries. Pre-Socratic thought attributed qualities of living beings to the material world. Jammer explains their model, and links to this notion of animate matter Plato's idea of a world soul:

The early Greek hylozoism of the Milesian school (Thales, Anaximander, Anaximenes) conceived nature as a living, animated, and self-moving being, and consequently did not see a problem in the origin of motion. The concept of force gained prominence only with Heraclitus' doctrine of opposing tensions, according to which force is a primary constituent of physical reality and a regulative element in the universe. In Empedocles' philosophy of love (philia) and strife (neikos), forces, although still conceived in analogy to human affections, became efficient causes of change and motion. In spite of the fact that Plato's natural philosophy relegates the principle of motion ultimately to the existence of a world soul and corresponds in this respect to early hylozeism rather than to the dynamistic teachings of Empedocles and Anaxagoras, the term dynamic, signifying not only transitive activity but also passive susceptibility or receptibility, plays an important role in his doctrine.

ARISTOTLE

Aristotle's revision of Plato led to a more mechanical and dynamic model. But like Plato Aristotle saw force as occurring through material contact. To explain falling and rising objects, he classified objects as naturally grave (heavy) or levitas (light) and as having a natural place:

Although Aristotle, in his conception of nature as physic, still recognized the Platonic notion of force as something inherent in matter, in De Caelo he also approached the formulation of a more mechanical conception of force as a physical emanation from one substance to another: through push and pull bodies affect each other and generate motion in extraneous objects. This Aristotelian notion of emanating kinematic effects, although restricted to contiguous modes of action, is the first instance of the modern dynamical conception of force.

STOICS

The next model of force comes from the Stoics, who conceived of an 'all-pervading substratum called the pneuma.' Its function was the 'generation of the cohesion of matter and generally of the contact between all parts of the cosmos.' The Stoics rejected any possibility of a void within the cosmos. Pneuma had dynamic qualities and also composed the collective breath and soul of all organisms. According to Jammer, Stoic ideas influenced the physical idea of force by providing the model of the force field:

With Posidonius' investigations at Gades of the connection between the tides and the movements of the sun and the moon and his doctrine of a universal tension, the concept of force was generalized as something able to pervade all space. Stoic philosophy thus abandoned the Aristotelian restriction of an immediate linkage between the mover and the moved, and conceived force as a mutual correspondence of action between objects, even when the objects were separated in space. In fact, the Stoics were probably the first to formulate the idea of a field of forces and to regard the universe as a vast system ruled by the interaction of forces.

BURIDAN

Medieval philosophy largely adhered to the Aristotel[ian] model of force. A few thinkers were moved by Neo-plato[nic] ideas, and saw forces as entities that could detach fr[om] objects and be propagated through space. The *Encyclope[dia]* tells us that one medieval Arabic treatise, al-Kindi's *On [the] Tides* held that force could be 'propagated by means of o[pti]cal rays, a theory conducive to astrological exploitati[on.] Early in the fourteenth century, the Stoic notion of a fiel[d of] forces was revived by one John Buridan, who attributed [the] original cause of force to the spin imparted to all bodies [by] their original creator, as Jammer notes:

John Buridan postulates a celestial force which per[me]ates all space and exerts its influence on physical bod[ies.] However, the revolutions of celestial bodies, according [to] Buridan, are not the result of a constant activity of spe[cial] intelligence, but rather of an original rotational impe[tus] communicated to these bodies by the Creator at the be[gin]ning of time.

KEPLER

Kepler reconfigured the solar system by discarding [the] model of circular orbits and constant speeds for a mode[l of] elliptical orbits with equal areas swept out over equal tim[e.] The resulting orbits were constantly changing speed and c[ur]vature, and such variations 'seemed to demand the introd[uc]tion of a force in the heavens, a force acting continually [to] alter the planets' motion at each point in its orbit.' He saw [the] sun as the first mover, and thought it emanated a force called the anima motrix which pushed the planets aroun[d] their orbits. He reintroduced dynamic forces into the celes[tial] sphere, and conceived of forces both of propulsion a[nd] attraction. In the *Encyclopedia*, Jammer praises his meth[od] of observation and downplays the references to anim[ate] celestial bodies:

A decisive stage in the development of the concep[t of] force was reached in Johannes Kepler's search for a qua[nti]tative determination of dynamic activity. In his early writin[gs,] such as the Mysterium Cosmographicum *(1596), Kepler s[till] refers to force as a soul animating the celestial bodies. [His] correspondence, however, and particularly his letter[s] show clearly that his use of the term anima (soul) in his w[rit]ings was merely a metaphor to express the immateriality [of] the principle that governs the mutual movements of ce[les]tial bodies. In 1605, Kepler was already convinced that [the] force of attraction could be subjected to a mathematical [for]malism.*

NEWTON

After Kepler, the clear formulation of the law of inertia by Descartes did away with the need for a force to propel the planets. Instead, it became necessary to explain what force kept the planets in their elliptical orbits rather than travelling off on a straight line. Robert Hooke saw the need to combine inertia with an intrinsic mutual attraction between the sun and its orbiting planets. He understood that the same set of laws governed both the falling of a stone and the movement of heavenly bodies toward each other, as did Newton. In the late seventeenth century, Newton determined the gravitational formulas that underlay both the celestial motions described by Kepler's laws and the terrestrial motions of falling objects. Gravity had the appearance of an innate attractive force in matter, but Newton not only refrained from metaphysical speculation on its nature, he insisted that a mechanical explanation for gravity would eventually be found.

Jammer's *Encyclopedia* account of force summarizes Newton's three interrelated laws of motion.

Newton's definition of force led to a unified treatment of terrestrial and celestial mechanics, and the notion of force became a fundamental concept of physics. Whereas Newton's First Law of Motion or Law of Inertia, according to which every body, unaffected by a force, persists in a state of rest or of uniform motion, may be regarded as a qualitative definition of force (namely, as change of state of motion), the Second Law quantified the concept and provided a meaning for the notion of mass. The Newtonian characterization of force is completed with the Third Law, which states, in essence, that every force manifests itself invariably in a dual aspect: it has a mirror-image twin. For it claims that if A acts on B, then B acts on A with equal magnitude in the opposite direction; or in other words, to every action there is always opposed an equal reaction. Forces, consequently, arise only as the result of a combined interaction of at least two entities. In a universe composed of only one body, no forces are conceivable.

Having thus explored the quantitative aspects of force, and of gravitational force in particular, Newton does not specify the metaphysical nature of force; as far as physical science is concerned, force is an ultimately irreducible notion. Newton's contribution may thus be regarded as the culmination of a conceptual development in a search for a quantitative determination of an otherwise obscure and indiscernible, yet necessary, notion.

Newton and other scientists were reluctant to subscribe to the idea that force of gravity could act over a distance with no intermediary material. Yet others considered this sort of explanation, reliant upon actions over a distance, to be their ultimate objective. Phenomena such as magnetism, electricity, and even capillary action were all theorized as being subject to forces acting over distances.

BERKELEY AND HUME

Elegant as Newton's concept was, it was subject to critique by eighteenth century philosophers who objected to the treatment of force as a real entity when it was, they said, only a mental construct. These pure empiricists denied any existence of force as the cause behind events by claiming that there was no such thing as cause and effect at all, but merely a succession of events in time. They doubted the reality of causal constructions and the so-called 'laws of nature.' Our source continues:

The main criticism of the Newtonian conception of force from the philosophical point of view, however, was directed against the hypostatization of force as a metaphysical entity of an autonomous ontological status. Berkeley, in his De Motu *(On Motion, 1721) opposed this approach and viewed the notion of force as a convenient auxiliary fiction with which to work; for the notion had the same status in science as the concept of epicycle has in astronomy. Terms like force, gravity, and attraction, he admitted, are convenient for purposes of reasoning or computation; for an understanding of the nature of motion itself, however, Berkeley regards them as wholly irrelevant. They should not lead us to the fallacy that they could throw any light on the real efficient causes of motion, for the only objective of physical science is the establishment of the regularities and uniformities of natural phenomena; to account for particular phenomena means 'reducing them under, and strewing their conformity to, such general rules' (Siris, 1744). Hume, Pierre de Maupertuis, and especially the early proponents of modern positivism . . . followed Berkeley in asserting that force is merely a construct in the conceptual scheme of physics and that it should not be confounded with metaphysical causality. Most radical in this respect was Mach's antimetaphysical attitude, in accordance with which he tried to divest mechanics of all conceptions of cause and force and to adopt a purely functional point of view. . . . Ernst Mach identified force with the product of mass and acceleration and thus reduced it to a purely mathematical expression relating certain measurements of space and time.*

But even after this process of purification and divestment of all causal or teleological implications, the concept of force was not eliminated from the conceptual scheme of physics. Its methodological justification lies in the fact that it enables us to discuss the general laws of motion irrespective of the particular physical situation with which these motions are associated. In contemporary physics the concept plays somewhat the same role as does the middle term in the traditional syllogism; it is a methodological intermediate in terms of which we can study the kinematical behavior of a physical body independent of the particular configuration in which it is found.

REID AND JAMES

That critical attitude toward force, initiated by Berkeley and Hume and continued by the positivist thinkers, removed any trace of causal or teleological explanations. Yet they opened up new explorations; since forces were no longer seen as a real agents of cause and effect, the only place they could still be investigated was the same place they originated, within human consciousness. Philosophy turned toward mental and bodily perceptions in the early twentieth century. Our source concludes this history of force with an account of its retreat into the physiological and psychological realm:

The first to deal at length with this problem was Thomas Reid, Hume's immediate successor and founder of the Scottish school. He derived the concept of force from the consciousness we have of operations of our own mind, and especially from the consciousness of our voluntary exertions in producing effects. Reid concluded that if we were not conscious of such exertions, we would not have formed any conception of force and consequently would not have projected its notion into nature and the changes in it which we observe. Kant's younger contemporary, Maine de Biran... considered our own will as the source of the notion of force; in his view, the resistance to muscular effort felt in the case of voluntary activity makes us aware that certain actions are not involuntary acts, but the results of our ego as a source of force. From the twofold nature of the ego as an individual source of action and as inseparably united to a resisting organism, we acquire the universal and necessary notion of force. While the Berkeley-Hume criticism led almost to the exclusion of the concept of force from science and natural philosophy, at the same time it supplied to the more psychologically and physiologically oriented philosophy important arguments to oppose such elimination. For it was claimed that the concept of force stands in the same relation to the sensation of muscular effort as the concept of motion to visual perception, and science without the concept of motion is inconceivable.

Moreover, if one kind of sensation is to be preferred to the others, it should certainly be muscular sensation, the nearest to the psychological experience of volition. Even William James, who, in 'The Feeling of Effort,' in Collected Essays and Reviews *(1920), rejected the so-called feeling of innervation and opposed the view that the resistance to our muscular effort is the only sense that brings us into close contact with reality, contended that reality reveals itself in the form of force like the force of effort which we exert ourselves. The concept of force, according to James, thus remains one of those universal ideas which belong of necessity to the intellectual furniture of every human mind.'*

FORCE AND EMPATHY

This brings us finally back to architecture for as observers and inhabitants of structures, we are aware of the forces acting on them. Heinrich Wolfflin's theory of empathy, which claims we share with the architectural column a physical understanding of heavy loads, is perfectly suited to the twentieth century's reduction of force to a psychological phenomenon.

Sharon L. Joyce

Jammer, Max. 'Force.' *The Encyclopedia of Philosophy.* 1967, III, p. 209-212.

Sambursky, S., 'The Dynamic Continuum,' *Physics of the Stoics* (Princeton: Princeton University Press, 1959), pp. 1-2.

Kuhn, Thomas S., 'The New Universe,' *The Copernican Revolution* (Cambridge: Harvard University Press, 1957), p. 245-9.

6

1965

SIX REQUIRED SEMESTERS OF STRUCTURES

IT IS DIFFICULT TO BELIEVE THAT GRADUATE ARCHITECTURE STUDENTS AT YALE WERE ONCE REQUIRED TO TAKE SIX SEMESTERS OF STRUCTURES COURSES. THE IMPLICATION IS THAT STRUCTURES WAS THE MOST IMPORTANT TOPIC OF STUDY OUTSIDE OF STUDIO — A PRIORITY THAT IS NOW UNIMAGINABLE. THE EVIDENCE WAS FOUND; COURSE BULLETINS SHOW THAT THE EDUCATION OF ARCHITECTS AT YALE HAS BEEN RECONFIGURED SO THAT STRUCTURES IS A MINIMAL OBLIGATION INSTEAD OF A FUNDAMENTAL CONCERN.

PLAN OF STUDY: ARCHITECTURE

Year	Course	Subject	Credit Hours 1st Term	2d Term
I	Arch. 111	First-Year Design	6	6
	Arch. 112	Mechanics and Strength of Materials	3	3
	Arch. 113	Means of Architectural Expression	3	3
	Arch. 116	Materials and Methods	3	3
		Elective	3	3
			18	18
II	Arch. 121	Second-Year Design	6	6
	Arch. 122	Structural Engineering	3	3
	Arch. 123b	Techniques of Presentation		3
	Arch. 126	Mechanical and Electrical Engineering	3	3
	Plan. 10a	Introduction to Urbanism	3	–
	Hist. of Art 53a	American Architecture	3	–
	Hist. of Art 53b	Modern Architecture	–	3
			18	18
III	Arch. 131	Third-Year Design	9	9
	Arch. 132	Advanced Structural Engineering	3	3
	Arch. 145a	Architectural Practice	3	
		Elective	3	3
		Elective-Planning	–	3
			18	18
IV	Arch. 141	Fourth-Year Design or Thesis	12	12
	Arch. 144b	Special Technical and Aesthetic Problems	–	3
	Arch. 146a	Architectural Philosophies	3	–
		Elective	3	–
		Elective (For Thesis students on leave Term 1)	–	3
			18	18

26

3

1970

THREE REQUIRED SEMESTERS OF STRUCTURES

PLAN OF STUDY: ARCHITECTURE

Term	Course	Subject	Units
I	*Arch. A1	First-Year Design	9
	*Arch. A11	Structures	3
	*Arch. A21	Materials and Methods	
	†Elective		3
II	*Arch. A2	Design	9
	*Arch. A12	Structures	3
	*Arch. A22	Graphics	
	†Elective		3
III	*Arch. A3	Second-Year Design	9
	*Arch. A13	Structural Engineering	3
	*Arch. A23	Environmental Controls	
	†Elective		3
IV		Advanced Studio (Design, Housing, or Context)	9
V		‡Optional Course	3
VI		‡Optional Course	3
VII		†Elective	3

*Required courses. Arch. A1, A2, and A3 are to be taken in sequence; Arch. A11, A12, and A13 are also to be taken in sequence.

†Elective courses are normally taken in other departments of the University.

‡Optional Courses which are given in the Faculties of Design and Planning may be offered as fractions of the 3-unit courses indicated on the plan of study.

§Each of the terms requires the four courses and 18 units listed.

20

2

1999

TWO REQUIRED SEMESTERS OF STRUCTURES

NAAB ACCREDITATION

In the United States, most state registration boards require a degree from an accredited professional degree program as a prerequisite for licensure. The National Architectural Accrediting Board (NAAB), which is the sole agency authorized to accredit U.S. professional degree programs in architecture, recognizes two types of degrees: the Bachelor of Architecture and the Master of Architecture. A program may be granted a five-year, three-year, or two-year term of accreditation, depending on its degree of conformance with established educational standards.

Master's degree programs may consist of a preprofessional undergraduate degree and a professional graduate degree, which, when earned sequentially, comprise an accredited professional education. However, the preprofessional degree is not, by itself, recognized as an accredited degree.

The four-year, preprofessional degree, where offered, is not accredited by the NAAB. The preprofessional degree is useful for those wishing a foundation in the field of architecture, as preparation for either continued education in a professional degree program or for employment options in fields related to architecture.

Yale's three-year M.Arch. I degree program is fully accredited by the NAAB.

COURSE OF STUDY*

M.Arch. I: Total Requirement: 108 credits

First Term (Fall)

Required:	Credits:
501a Architectural Design	6
601a Structures I	3
661a 3-D Form and Materials	3
701a Modern Architecture	3
801a Intro to Visual Studies	3
	18

Second Term (Spring)

Required:	Credits:
502b Architectural Design	6
506b Building Project	3
602b Structures II	3
802b Freehand Drawing	3
902b Intro to Urban Design	3
	18

Third Term (Fall)

Required:	Credits:
503a Architectural Design	6
633a Environmental Systems in Buildings	3
851a Intro to Digital Media	3
903a Intro to Planning and Development	3
Elective†	3
	18

Fourth Term (Spring)

Required:	Credits:
504b Architecture Studio	6
508b Systems Integration	3
704b Literature of Architecture	3
Elective†	3
Elective†	3
	—
	18

* In course titles, a designates fall term, b designates spring term, and c designates summer term.
† Two of the electives must be in Architectural History/Theory; and one in Planning, Design, and Development of the Urban Landscape. These designated electives may be taken in any term(s), and may be selected from listings.

NEW REFLECTIONS

THE EDITORS SURVEYED A GROUP
OF EXPERIENCED ARCHITECTS TO
GET A PICTURE OF HOW STRUCTURE
IS ADDRESSED IN CURRENT PRAC-
TICE. WHAT FOLLOWS ARE FIVE OF
THE RESPONSES WE RECEIVED.

1 'THE FUSION OF STRUCTURAL FUNCTION AND ABSTRACT
FORM CREATES A KIND OF BUILDING THAT IS SO FUN-
DAMENTALLY RIGHT THAT MOST OTHER ARCHITECTURE
SEEMS SUPERFICIAL BESIDE IT.' ADA LOUISE HUXTABLE
IN *PIER LUIGI NERVI*, 1960. DO YOU AGREE? ELABO-
RATE. IF YOU DO NOT AGREE, DID YOU EVER AGREE?
AND WHY HAS YOUR VIEW CHANGED?

2 AT WHAT STAGE IN THE DESIGN PROCESS DO YOU
CONSIDER STRUCTURE? DOES IT SHOW UP IN NAPKIN
SKETCHES? HOW DOES THINKING ABOUT STRUCTURE
CONTRIBUTE TO THE DESIGN PROCESS?

3 AS YOUR KNOWLEDGE OF CONSTRUCTION INCREASES,
DO YOUR IDEAS ABOUT STRUCTURE BEGIN TO COME
FROM DIFFERENT PLACES? HOW ARE YOUR SKETCHES
OF STRUCTURAL SYSTEMS DIFFERENT FROM THOSE
YOU MADE AS A LESS EXPERIENCED BUILDER?

4 WHEN DOES THE STRUCTURAL SYSTEM HELP TO
SHAPE YOUR ARCHITECTURE? DOES THE STRUCTURAL
CONCEPT EVER INSPIRE OR DICTATE SPATIAL CONFIG-
URATIONS, RATHER THAN CONFORM TO THEM?

5 DOES THE WEIGHT AND MASSIVENESS OF A STRUC-
TURAL SYSTEM, OR THE LACK OF IT, PLAY A ROLE IN
YOUR DESIGN PROCESS?

6 WHEN DO YOU TRANSFORM WHAT IS CONVENTION-
ALLY SUPPLIED BY STRUCTURAL TRADES
(E.G., A HOLLOW CORE SLAB USED AS A PLENUM)?

7 HOW CONCERNED ARE YOU ABOUT TECTONIC
LEGIBILITY — EITHER THROUGH ORNAMENT OR
EXPOSED CONSTRUCTION? IF YOU VALUE THE EXPRES-
SION OF ASSEMBLY (WHETHER ACTUAL, FICTIONAL,
OR REPRESENTATIONAL) PLEASE ELABORATE.

8 DO YOU HAVE AN ONGOING RELATIONSHIP WITH
A STRUCTURAL ENGINEER? HAVE YOU EXPERIENCED
A PARTICULARLY RICH COLLABORATION?

9 AT WHAT AGE DID YOU DECIDE TO BECOME AN
ARCHITECT? LIST THE TOYS YOU LIKED AS A CHILD.

DEBORAH BERKE

RICHARD GLUCKMAN

1 I agree with Ada Louise, but think that description can apply to many works of architecture and the work of many architects – even the ones that one might not immediately think of as being structurally driven.

2 I consider structure pretty early on; I also consider material pretty early on. I believe they are closely linked. It is part of the design process because I don't sketch things I think are unbuildable. Recently our work is pushing this a little but building is our ultimate goal in every project.

3 My knowledge of construction has increased but the size and complexity of the projects we are doing has also increased, so it is hard to distinguish what is directly linked to experience other than experience makes one an all around 'better at thinking holistically about the project' architect.

4 Structural systems are coordinated with spatial configurations from the beginning – although space comes first, it's usually not by much.

5 The weight of structure is of great interest to me although I haven't had much opportunity to play with it in my work. As the buildings get bigger, I'm hoping to work with that potential.

6 We transform whenever we can that which is conventionally done – but usually to make it more profoundly conventional, more extreme.

7 I am interested in tectonic legibility although it does not have to be literal to be legible. It is a motivating design criteria. I value the expression of real assembly or connections. In my early work I argued that was instead of ornament – I don't know how successful I was. Visible connectors may be what separates our recent work from the more minimal minimalists like Pawson.

8 I have an ongoing relationship with two engineers. Ross Dalland on small residential projects and Robert Silman on larger projects. I don't know that I'd call it rich collaboration as I don't think we push their creative limits at all – but, yes, I have learned from both of them, and respect them immensely.

9 I decided to become an architect at age fourteen or so. My childhood toys had nothing to do with it, walking around New York City and in particular my neighborhood in Queens did.

1 The terms 'Structural Function' and 'Abstract Form' seem obsolete today. In the simplest terms, it's impossible not to agree with this statement. However, in light of the enormous changes that have taken place in the past few years with regard to the making of form, the idea that there is a direct connection between conceptual form and material reality must be questioned. Conceptually, on paper, on the computer screen, new and totally wonderful forms can be visualized, drawn, even computed and calculated. However, until the general construction industry is able to make the same step that architects and engineers have, the making of these forms will be restricted to only the most generous budgets. While the chemical and physical properties of new materials are known in the lab, it may be a while before these materials can be utilized for their structural properties in the field. In the meantime, the construction and structural resolution of non-orthogonal shapes will have to be done on an armature using small modular components.

2 In the middle of the scheme design, as the idea of the building evolves in to a volume. With a small building, the structural idea may come earlier as an expression of the limits of the dimension of the space. Structure is as integral to the design process as thinking about skin or proportion.

3 Yes. The means of defining space become less schematic and assume characteristics of structural or material ideas at an earlier phase.

4 Applying the appropriate structural solution to a specific spatial problem is integral to the proper design of the space.

5 Oppositional characteristics: weight and lightness, solid and void, light and shadow, ad infinitum, are a part of our architectural vocabulary which, we hope, gets expressed in a rational way. This rational expression of oppositions may contribute to a representational ambiguity. That is, structure or skin does not necessarily demarcate space, but can allow for an ambiguous definition based on layered readings of transparency and depth.

6 Using compressive material in tension or tensile materials in compression. Eg. Glass shingles.

7 Very, but not as an end in itself. Tectonic clarity is simply the result of structural clarity. This clarity can lead to an economy of form and, in turn, to an economy of means.

8 Yes, yes. We engage our engineering consultants, whether they are structural or mechanical, at an early stage in the design process. The nature of designing buildings is too complex to separate or sequence the disciplines involved.

9 9 or 10, when my father described to me what an architect did. Wood blocks, Erector set, Electric trains.

THOM MAYNE

CESAR PELLI

1. 'Fundamentally right,' in that architecture for Pier Luigi Nervi *was* structure, in the sense that there is very little distance between structural logic and the demands of a logic of an abstraction. I would suggest a strategy that places a greater distance between the initiating concept (abstract?) and the system of construction that accommodates and supports it. An architecture emerges as an expression of a dialectic between these two realities

2. Subsequent to an elaboration of an organizational idea and the emergence of a language that is integral to an idea – structure is at the 'service of' the broader intentions of the work (a means to an end).

3. The changes taking place in our studio recently have to do with the increase in complexity and scale which puts new demands on construction methodologies.

4. The development of an architecture at some point is completely integral to its materialization, its methods of making – seamless. Certain problem types (a bridge, a concert hall, a dormitory) place demands on a work which require an early involvement of a structural or constructional logic. In most cases, economies of repetition effect organizational or spatial qualities. But in most circumstances, it's the other way around – structure accommodating the spatial qualities of our work.

5. The desired 'effect' of weight – the resolve of gravity, etc., is specific to the interpretive demands of the work, and not limited to the engineer's submission to economy and calculation.

6. Often.

7. Between 1980 and 1990, the expression of material and assembly was equated to an attempt at an authenticity. After, an elaboration (maybe, sometimes, not always) of construction was idiosyncratic to a particular condition.

8. For fifteen years we have worked with Ove Arup & Partners on large projects and Joseph Perazzelli on smaller scale work. This collaborative environment (an understanding of intentions) is as essential to our studio as would be a cinematographer to a director in cinema.

9. When I was eighteen years old. Vacuum cleaners, lawn mower engines, small tractors, most things that either moved or made loud noises.

1. Ada Louise Huxtable was exaggerating to honor Nervi. There are many great works of architecture where 'the fusion of structural function and abstract form' is far from obvious or non-existent. Just think of the buildings of Antonio Gaudí. She was also expressing, in the 1960s, a still rather wide spread hope of a brave new world to be built based on science and reason. Of course, her sentence is ambiguous enough that it can be made to apply to any building we admire.

2. I start thinking about the constructibility of my designs from the very first moment. Structure is a component, sometimes a key component, of constructibility. I avoid napkin sketches. I consider them misleading and, therefore, harmful to the design process. We tend to be seduced by our own sketches and become attached to them while they may end up having little to do with the problem at hand.

3. Thinking about structure is just as important as thinking about function, or suitability to the site, or budget limits. They are all essential aspects of a project that need to be addressed and well resolved to have a good building.

4. Sometimes the structural system has to adjust to the forms required by a complex functional problem, for example, in a theater. And sometimes the structure plays a leading role in the project, as in an airport. In such cases, the structure may suggest spatial configurations. It can never lead them because spaces are built firstly to satisfy the physical and spiritual needs of people. If we make the needs of people secondary to the dictates of the structure, something is wrong with our view of the world.

5. Yes, weight and massiveness sometimes are necessary for purely technical reasons. Sometimes they are desirable as part of our architectural intention.

6. We transform what is supplied by structural trades whenever our design requires it. But if it does not, we prefer to leave them alone because it is cheaper if we do not alter them much.

7. Structural legibility is not always important. I don't need to see the bones in a body to understand its physical integrity. If the structure does become apparent, then I like it to be clear, straightforward, and not prettified.

8. We have worked very well with several structural engineers. Perhaps my longest association is with Charlie Thornton of Thornton Tomasetti in New York with whom we have designed several key structures that include the Petronas Towers in Malaysia, which have a very elegant and sophisticated structural system. Charlie is very inventive and clearheaded. He also understands well my architectural intentions.

9. I entered the school of architecture when I was seventeen years old, but I did not decide to become an architect until I was eighteen. As a child, my favorite toys were books.

TOD WILLIAMS

1   I question the need to use the word 'abstract,' unless
she is referring to his Olympic projects in Rome.
Nervi's forms achieve a higher degree of abstraction
when the requirements are principally for cover
and containment.

2   Structure is both implicit and occasionally explicit in
the earliest sketches. When it is implicit, we make an
effort to recognize its presence.

3   I increasingly believe that a structural sensibility
emerges from forms found in nature, and I increasingly trust my intuition.

4   The structural system shapes our work very early on.
Thus the (structural) concept can both inspire spatial
configurations and configure to them. For example,
concrete block may be simply understood as a bearing wall. Then too a single block and its multiple
might act principally as a space maker. As work
develops, they should have a dialogue. One might
have a louder voice, that needn't be pedantic.

5   I often ask myself whether or not the building should
be heavy (in fact, they are always heavy). Once I know
where and how it is heavy, then I can understand
where and how it might be light.

6   It is always transformed, rarely properly. Your example, one I learned in school, seems too simplistic.
What the plenum is for and how it is transformed (so
that it makes sense structurally and as an air delivery
system) is crucial. In your example we must recognize both structure and air are systems and not
objects. Perhaps the plenum might be considered as
part of a system of structure independent of any
capacity for weight bearing.

7   Tectonic legibility is not an end. It is one aspect of
making remarkable buildings, buildings which live
through their use.

8   Yes, I have admiration and respect for him, and always
enjoy meeting with him.

9   I thought about life in the arts at an early age. I realized architecture could provide an endlessly rich and
rewarding life in college. Growing up in the first
house in a suburb, the surrounding sites were my
playground where I enjoyed toys, cars as well as
dolls, that I imagined to be real.

CREDITS

TEXT SOURCES

Past Polemics

Heyer, Paul, *Architects on Architecture*, Walker Publishing, New York, 1966.

Eero Saarinen on his Work Edited by Aline B. Saarinen, Yale University Press, New Haven, 1962.

Conceptual vs. Actual

The extensive quotation from the essay "Mies van der Rohe's Paradoxical Symmetries" by Robin Evans is reproduced with kind permission of The Architectural Association. This essay was first published in AA Files no. 19, Spring 1990, and subsequently was reproduced in *Translations from Drawing to Building*, co-published by The Architectural Association, London and The MIT Press, Cambridge, MA, 1997.

Skin/Skeleton

Ford, Edward, *Details of Modern Architecture, Volume 1*, MIT Press, Cambridge, 1990, p.422.

Hugo, Victor, *Notre Dame de Paris*, Little, Brown and Co., Boston, 1894.

Dieste, Eladio, "Some Reflections on Architecture and Construction," *Perspecta 27*, Rizzoli International Publications, New York, 1992, p.193-4.

Fontein, Lucie, "Reading Structure Through Frame," *Perspecta 31*, MIT Press, Cambridge, 2000.

Rowe, Colin, "Chicago Frame" first published in *Architectural Review*, London, 1956, subsequently published in *Mathematics of the Ideal Villa and Other Essays*, MIT Press, Cambridge, 1976, p.90.

Elliott, Cecil D., *Technics in Architecture: the Development of Materials and Systems for Buildings*, MIT Press, Cambridge, 1992, p.105

Venturi, Robert, *Complexity and Contradiction in Architecture*, Second Edition, The Museum of Modern Art, New York, 1977, p.35.

Appearance of Solidity

Ruskin, John, *The Seven Lamps of Architecture*, Noonday Press, New York, 1961.

Ford, Edward, *Details of Modern Architecture, Volume 1*, MIT Press, Cambridge, 1990, p.427.

Evans, Robin, *The Projective Cast: Architecture and Its Three Geometries*, MIT Press, Cambridge, 1995.

Cultural Reverberations

Dostoevsky, Fyodor, *Notes from Underground*, first published 1864, trans. Jessie Coulson, Penguin, New York, 1972, p.42.

Berman, Marshall *All That is Solid Melts Into Air*, Simon and Schuster, New York, 1982, p.245.

Nye, David, *American Technological Sublime*, MIT Press, Cambridge, 1994, p.103-4, 282.

Force

ed. Edwards, Paul, *The Encyclopedia of Philosophy*, Macmillan Publishing, New York, 1972.

Empathy:

Wölfflin, Heinrich, "Psychology of Architecture," from Vischer, Robert, *Empathy, Form and Space: Problems in German Aesthetics*. 1873-1893, Getty Center, Santa Monica, 1994

Mended Spider Webs/A Spider's Way of Structure

Rice, Peter, *An Engineer Imagines*, Ellipsis, London, 1994.

Katchadourian, Nina, *Mended Spiderwebs and Other Natural Misunderstandings*, Exhibit Catalog, Debs + Co., 1999.

IMAGE SOURCES

Cover From *International Kongress für Brückenbau und Hochbau*, Zurich, 1926, courtesy of Professor David Billington and the Maillart Archives at Princeton University. Camera-ready art by J. Wayman Williams.

Past Polemics Photograph by Ezra Stoller, courtesy of ESTO.

Thomas H. Beeby All drawings by Thomas H. Beeby. All photographs by Hedrich-Blessing from Ludwig Hilberseimer, *Mies van der Rohe*, Theobald, Chicago, 1956.

Carles Vallhonrat 1. Drawings by Louis I. Kahn courtesy Louis I. Kahn Collection, University of Pennsylvania and Pennsylvania Historical and Museum Commission – All drawings are copyrighted 1977; 2. From Euclid, Elements, Book Thirteen, Page 447 (1533), courtesy of the Department of Rare Books and Special Collections of the Princeton University Library. 3. Photograph by George Pohl from Jules D. Prown, *The Architecture of the Yale Center for British Art*, Yale University Press, New Haven, 1986; Drawings by Pellecchia & Myers Architects, 1977; 4-6. from Vierendeel, *Cours de Stabilite*; 7-10. Reproduced from Max Bill, Robert Maillart: *Bridges and Constructions 3rd Edition*, Praeger, New York, 1969; 11. Photograph by Howard Smagula from Heinz Ronner, *Louis I. Kahn: The Complete Work, 1935-1974*, Birkhauser Verlag, Boston, 1987; 12. Photograph by Robert Wharton from Neil E. Johnson, *Light is the Theme: Louis I. Kahn and the Kimbell Art Museum*, Kimbell Art Foundation, Fort Worth, 1975; 13. Photograph by Frank den Oudsten/Lenneke Buller, Amsterdam, reproduced from Carsten-Peter Warncke, *The Ideal as Art: De Stijl, 1917-1931*, Taschen, New York, 1991; 14. Reproduced from Carsten-peter Warncke, *The Ideal as Art: De Stijl, 1917-1931*, Taschen, New York, 1991, courtesy of Friedman Galleries, New York; 15 & 16. Reproduced from Euclid, *Elements*, Courtesy of the Department of Rare Books and Special Collections of Princeton University Library; 17-20. Reproduced from *What is Mathematics?: An Elementary Approach to Ideas and Methods, Second Edition* by Richard Courant and Herbert Robbins, edited by Ian Stewart. Copyright 1941 by the late Richard Courant, Herbert Robbins and revised by Ian Stewart. Used by permission of Oxford University Press, Inc.; 21. Reproduced from Cyril Stanley Smith, *Metal Interfaces*, American Society for Metals, Cleveland, 1952; 22-24. All photographs reproduced from *VIA*, Publication of the Graduate School of Fine Art University; 25. Drawings by Kohlmaier and von Sartory (hereafter K&S) after DBZ, 1876, vol. 10, no. 87, 26 & 27. Reproduced from *Zeitschrift fur Bauwesen* published by Konigliche Technische Bau- Deputation and Architekten Verein, Berlin, 1916; 28. Courtesy K&S Archives, Berlin; 29 K&S Archives, Berlin; 30 Photograph by Herman D.J. Spiegel; 31 Photograph by Jaimini Mehta Umschlagbild, reproduced from Romaldo Giurgola, *Louis I. Kahn*, Westview Press, 1975.32. Toutes les photographies reproduites dans ce numero sont de Pahl et Alikakos from *L'Architecture d'Aujourd'Hui?*

Guy Nordenson p.37, p.38 photo, p.39 (bottom), p.40 (lower right), p.41 (bottom), p.42 photo: Photographs by Hisao Suzuki, reproduced from *El Croquis: Steven Holl 1996-99* I, Issue #93, 1999, courtesy of Steven Holl Architects and El Croquis; All other photographs provided by and courtesy of Guy Nordenson and Associates; All drawings for Kiasma and Cranbrook by and courtesy of Steven Holl Architects; Drawings for CALA and computer models of MIT by and courtesy of Guy Nordenson and Associates.

Conceptual vs. Actual p.46: Photograph by Carolyn Foug; p.48: Photograph by Ezra Stoller, courtesy of ESTO.

Lucie Fontein p.50, p.51, p.54, p.57 (top, bottom), p.58: Photographs by D. Lepage; p.55, p.56 (top, bottom), p.59: Photographs by Lucie Fontein.

Hugh Dutton p.60 (top): Reproduced from John Hix, *The Glasshouse*, Phaidon, 1996; p.60 (bottom), p.62 (top): Photographs by Hugh Dutton p.62 (bottom), p.63 (second and third image): Computer modeling images produced by and courtesy of the office of Ove Arup & Partners; p.63 (top): Photograph by Adam Vaughan, courtesy of the office of HDA; p.63 (bottom two images), p.64 (background), p.65 (top): Computer modeling images produced by and courtesy of the office of HDA; p.64 (inset): Photograph provided by the office of Bernard Tschumi Architects; p.65 (bottom three): Photographs by Hugh Dutton, courtesy of the office of HDA; p.66 (inset), p.67 (bottom two): Computer rendering by Paul Andreu, courtesy of the office of HDA; p.68 (background): Photograph by Martin Francis, courtesy of the office of RFR; p.68 (inset), p.69 (all): Photographs by Anna Maksumik, courtesy of the office of RFR; p.66 (background), p.67 (top two images): Photographs by Peter MacInven, courtesy of the office of HDA.

Antonio Juarez All images that are credited to "LIKC" bear a Copyright of 1977, and have been provided by and permission granted courtesy of the Louis I. Kahn Collection, University of Pennsylvania and Pennsylvania Historical and Museum Commission. 1. Photograph by Robert Damora, courtesy of LIKC; 2-10, 16, 18-21. LIKC; 11, 13, 15, 17. Anne Griswold Tyng Collection; 12. Photograph by John Abstel; 14. Photograph by Antonio Juarez

Skin/Skeleton p.82-3: (left, center) Photographs by Carolyn Foug, (right) Photograph by Frederick Tang; p.84-5: Photograph by Ezra Stoller, courtesy of ESTO.

Herman D.J. Spiegel All photographs by Herman D.J. Spiegel. All drawings by Spiegel Zamecnik & Shah Inc.

Alan Organschi All photographs courtesy of Gray Organschi Architects. p.96, p.97 (inset, top): Photographs by Guido Organschi; p.99 (inset, bottom), p.103 (bottom): Photograph by Mark Sofield; p.102, p.103 (top) Photographs by Paul McGuirk, courtesy of Paul McGuirk Photography; All other photographs by Alan Organschi.

Peter D. Waldman 1. Reproduced from "Five Points of Architecture," *Ouevre Complete 1910-29, Volume 1*, Le Corbusier; 2. Photograph by Peter D. Waldman, 3. & 4. Collection of Peter D. Waldman, 5. Reproduced from *Ouevre Complete, 1952-57, Volume 6*, Le Corbusier, Edited by W. Boesinger, Les Editions L'Architecture, Zurich, 1957; 6. Reproduced from *Vers Une Architecture*, Le Corbusier, 1920; 7. Collection of Peter D. Waldman; 10-12 Reproduced from *Oevre Complete*, Le Courbusier. 19. Photograph by Celia Liu (skylight); All other photographs by Maxwell Mackenzie; All drawings by Robert Corser

Appearance of Solidity p.115: Photograph by Ariel Apte; p.118: Photograph by Carolyn Foug.

Tom F. Peters p.119: Drawing by John Smeaton 1791; p.120: Photograph by Douglas Hague 1972; p.122 (top, bottom) Photographs by Clotilde Peters; p.123 (top): from *Cresy*, 1847: p.123 (top right), p.124 (bottom right), p.125 (2nd from bottom); p.126 (left), p.127 (bottom two), p.128 (all): Photographs by Tom F. Peters; p.123 (middle right): Photograph by Sue Bucholz; p.123 (bottom): CAD drawings by Steven Roethke, Lehigh University; p.124 (top two): From *Illustrated Exhibitor*, 1851; p.124 (2nd from bottom): Drawing from *Allgemeine Bauzeitung*, 1852; p.125 (top) Diagrams by Tom F. Peters; p.125 (bottom): M. Ros; Maillart obituary, 1940; p.126 (right), p.127 (top), p.129: CAD Drawing by Zarli Sein, Lehigh University.

Gregory K. Dreicer p.130, p.132 , p.135: National Museum of American History (NMAH) Smithsonian Institution; p.133 (left): From Luigi Castiglioni, *Viaggio negli Stati Uniti dell'America settentrionale*, 1787; p.133 (top right): Patent drawing from National Archives; p.133 (bottom right): from John Fincham, *History of Naval Architecture* (1851) p.134 (top): From A.R. Emy, *Traite de l'art de la charpenterie*, 1837, 1841; p.134 (bottom left): reproduced from *Building the Nineteenth Century*, by Tom. F. Peters, MIT Press, 1996 – original source of image is Taylor, Charles. *A supplement to Nicholson's Operative Mechanic, and British Machinist*, translated and arranged from Baron Charles Dupin, "On the commercial power of Great Britian," etc. by C.T. London: printed for Robert Thurston, 1829. (2), 785-792, xi-xxviii, 20 pls.; p.134 (bottom right): From George Vose, *Manual for Railroad Engineer and Engineering Students*, 1874; p.137 (top 3): From *Memoires et comptes rendus des travaux de la societe des ingenieurs civils*, 1848; p.137 (4th down): From *Allgemeine Bauzeitung*, 1851; p.137 (2nd from bottom): From *American Railroad Journal*, 1848; p.137 (bottom), p.138: From E. Collignon, *Les travaux publics de la France*, 1883, NMAH, Smithsonian; p.139 (top): From *Organ fur die Fortschritte des Eisenbahnwesens*, 1854; p.139 (middle): From Illustration, 1844; p.139 (bottom): From Franz Anton von Gerstner. *Die innern Communicationen der vereingten Staaten von Nordamerika*, 1842.

Cultural Reverberations p.142-3: Photograph reproduced from *Crystal Palace: London 1851, Sir Joseph Paxton*, by John McKean, Phaidon- courtesy of the Board of Trustees of Victoria and Albert Museum, London; p.144-5: Photograph by Carolyn Foug.

Mended Spider Webs / A Spider's Way of Structure Photograph by Nina Katchadourian, courtesy of the artist and Debs & Co gallery.

Empathy p.148: Photograph by Beth Neville; p.149: Photograph by Carolyn Foug.

The editors have attempted to trace and acknowledge all sources for images used in this journal and we apologize for any errors or omissions.

ACKNOWLEDGEMENTS

We are deeply grateful to the Graham Foundation for Advanced Studies in the Fine Arts, led by Richard Solomon, for awarding a grant to *Perspecta 31: Reading Structures* in October of 1997. Without this timely support the project would not have been completed.

Significant donations toward the cost of printing this issue were made by:
Cesar Pelli & Diana Balmori
Gordon H. Smith.
The editors and the Yale School of Architecture community thank Mr. Pelli & Ms. Balmori and Mr. Smith for their generosity and support of *Perspecta*.

We thank the *Perspecta* Board of Directors, of the Yale School of Architecture, for selecting our proposal to edit an issue of this distinguished journal and ensuring its publication. The current board members are:
Peggy Deamer
Sheila Levrant de Bretteville
Michael R. Haverland
Gavin MacRae-Gibson
Cesar Pelli
Alan J. Plattus
Alexander Purves
Harold Roth
Robert A.M. Stern, Chair and Dean
of the School of Architecture

Thanks also go to Diane Michonski, Julie Konwerski, and Jean Sielaff at the School of Architecture for their administrative help

As students at Yale our questions were welcomed and encouraged by our structures professors:
James W. Axley, Martin D. Gehner, John D. Jacobson, and Herman D.J. Spiegel.

We owe many thanks to the contributors to this journal, each of whom added a fascinating, thoughtful voice to the conversation about structure and so graciously encouraged our endeavor. In particular, early crucial support and inspiration was provided by Thomas H. Beeby, Guy Nordenson, and Herman D.J. Spiegel.

While the editors bear the responsibility for any deficiencies in the journal, we gratefully acknowledge the positive contribution of those who advised us. The following people provided their valuable time and insight:
Kent C. Bloomer
Steve Bodow
Laura Ciolkowski
Diane Foug
Chris Luebkeman
Granger Moorhead
Naomi Neville
Thomas O'Brien
Alberto Perez-Gomez
Patrick L. Pinnell
Robert A.M. Stern

Many thanks go to our copy editor Grace Farrell for her professionalism and flexibility.

We thank the offices of Robert A.M. Stern Architects, Aero Studios Limited, Gluckman Mayner Architects, Gray Organschi Architects, and Melanie Taylor for supporting our after hours efforts. The designers wish to thank the offices of Doyle Partners, and General and Specific.

Our managing editor Frederick Tang has helped tremendously with obtaining original images, credits and permissions, conducting the survey of architects, and acquiring responses to articles. We thank him for his excellent work.

In the process of obtaining original images and reprint permissions, the following people wisely advised us:
David Billington
Tom Mellins
Pamela Quick of MIT Press
Erica Stoller of ESTO
J. Wayman Williams of JWW Associates
William Whitaker and Matthew E. Pisarski of the Architectural Archives of The University of Pennsylvania.

We thank Sheila Levrant de Bretteville for perceptively recommending that we work with our graphic designers Ariel Apte and Sarah Gephart. Their enthusiasm and talent often carried the project, as they continually refined our thinking, clarified our ideas, and contributed fresh ones. Witnessing the realization of these ideas into graphic form was the most rewarding part of finishing the journal. We are deeply grateful to them.